Social Work
Practice
with African
American Men

SAGE SOURCEBOOKS FOR THE HUMAN SERVICES SERIES

Series Editors: ARMAND LAUFFER and CHARLES GARVIN

Social Work Practice with African American Men

The Invisible Presence

Sage Sourcebooks for
the Human Services
39

Foreword by Jewelle Taylor Gibbs

Janice M. Rasheed
Mikal N. Rasheed

SAGE Publications, Inc.
International Educational and Professional Publisher
Thousand Oaks London New Delhi

For information:

 SAGE Publications, Inc.
2455 Teller Road
Thousand Oaks, California 91320
E-mail: order@sagepub.com

SAGE Publications Ltd.
6 Bonhill Street
London EC2A 4PU
United Kingdom

SAGE Publications India Pvt. Ltd.
M-32 Market
Greater Kailash I
New Delhi 110 048 India

Printed in the United States of America

Library of Congress Cataloging-in-Publication Data

Rasheed, Janice M. (Janice Matthews)
    Social work practice with African American men: The invisible
presence / by Janice M. Rasheed and Mikal M. Rasheed.
        p.   cm.—(Sage sourcebooks for the human services series; v. 39)
    Includes bibliographical references and index.
    ISBN 0-7619-1116-2 (cloth: alk. paper)
    ISBN 0-7619-1117-0 (pbk.: alk. paper)
    1. Social work with Afro-Americans.   2. Afro-American men—
Services for.   3. Afro-American families—Services for.   I. Rasheed,
Mikal N. (Mikal Nazir).   II. Title.   III. Series.
    HV3181 .R37   1999
    362.84'96073—dc21   98-40211

This book is printed on acid-free paper.

99   00   01   02   03   04   05   7   6   5   4   3   2   1

Acquisition Editor:	Jim Nageotte
Editorial Assistant:	Heidi Van Middlesworth
Production Editor:	Astrid Virding
Editorial Assistant:	Patricia Zeman
Indexer:	Linda Dudycha
Cover Designer:	Candice Harman

CONTENTS

IN MEMORY

In memory of my wonderful professors at
Columbia University
School of Social Work, New York City

Dr. Carol H. Meyer

Dr. Samuel O. Miller

Dr. James Jones

DEDICATION

This book is dedicated to the memory of my (deceased) parents,
Mr. and Mrs. Johnnie Matthews, Sr., who spent the better part of
their lives working to provide a quality education for their five children
to enable them to fight the forces of poverty and racism.

FOREWORD

The coauthors of this book, have produced a well-written and informative work that offers a comprehensive, holistic approach to practice with African American men and their families. By developing a multidisciplinary conceptual framework that integrates ecological, Africentric, and critical constructionist theoretical perspectives, these authors provide a broader and more complex context for the assessment and treatment of African American men. Their multilayered analysis of the historical, socioeconomic, and cultural factors impacting the lives of these men and their families in American society offers fresh insights and sensitive appraisals of the realistic barriers and difficult challenges created by pervasive racism, systematic discrimination, and persistent poverty.

This book is particularly useful to social work educators and practitioners because it proposes a variety of innovative and practical strategies to address relevant issues for African American men in micro practice approaches (individual, couple, family, and group treatment) and macro practice approaches (policy formulation, program development, and community practice). One of the major strengths of the book is its final section, *Creating Linkages Between Practice, Policy, and Research,* which provides a critical discussion of conceptual and methodological issues in conducting research on African American men and the implications of such research for practice and policy.

Rasheed and Rasheed have written a well-documented book, including excellent clinical case studies, to illustrate the application of their multidimensional model of assessment and treatment. This book is a significant contribution to the expanding literature on multicultural practice and fills an important gap in the literature by addressing the unique needs and problems of the "invisible" and "endangered" African American males. It provides useful information, thoughtful analysis, and helpful intervention strategies for social work educators, policy and program planners, and practitioners who address the multiple psychological, social, and economic issues confronted by African American men and their families.

Jewelle Taylor Gibbs, MSW, Ph.D.
Zellerbach Family Fund Professor in
Social Policy, Community Change and Practice at
the School of Social Welfare,
University of California at Berkeley

PREFACE

It has been more than 10 years since the publication of Jewelle Taylor Gibbs' (1988) critically acclaimed book that updated the social, political, and economic status of African American males and more than 17 years since the publication of Lawrence Gary's (1981) groundbreaking book on Black men. Although these comprehensive and widely read books served to spark important scholarship on African American men, there has continued to be a dearth of work extending the implications of these pivotal pieces to micro practice interventions (e.g., counseling, psychotherapy, and case management) or to macro practice interventions (e.g., community development and organization, advocacy and program development). Research and policy issues pertaining to adult African American men have also received an uneven treatment and have been relegated a "back seat" in the literature to the recent focus on adolescent Black males and Black teen fathers.

As social work practitioners and other social scientists struggle with the crises facing African American males and African American families, it has become apparent that a more holistic approach, one that more aggressively involves Black men in family practice efforts, needs to be articulated.

This book is aimed at filling a gap in the social work practice and the wider social science literature on Black men. Specifically, this book will take an Africentric and ecosystemic approach to articulating a theory of human behavior about African American men and develop sorely needed (micro and macro) practice approaches.

WHY THIS BOOK WAS WRITTEN

This book has, as its central focus, the development of human behavior theory and (micro and macro) practice approaches with (adult) African American men. Other published works on Black men have focused primarily on sociological status issues and have largely limited the scope of their implications to policy and research activities. These works have not made the critical conceptual leap into a theory of individual, personality, and family development about African American men.

We have three ultimate goals for this book. First, we want to meet the current keen interest in continuing to understand the social, historical, political, and economic contexts of Black men. We also want the individual chapters of this book to move the literature forward in understanding the practice implications of the current policy and research literature on African American men. Our second goal in writing this book is to articulate a theory of human behavior about Black men (Black men as fathers, husbands, sons, etc.). Furthermore, we ground our thinking in ecosystemic theory and aim to provide practice strategies that use a critical constructionist perspective for an integrating and unifying conceptual and theoretical framework. Finally, we want to facilitate the close of the disconcerting schism (the separation and fragmentation of important tasks and functions) that exists among research, practice, and policy activities. This schism is particularly problematic and deleterious to the plight of scholarship on African American men; thus, we consider it imperative to offer models of integration and *interlocking feedback loops* for professionals.

AUDIENCE

This book is appropriate for all those who want to better understand the practice implications of current research and policy issues of African American men. To this end, this book is aimed not only at scholars and educators but also at human service and social service practitioners and administrators who are interested in further refining their micro and macro practice and programming efforts with Black men. Finally, this book is intended to expand thinking on research and policy issues about African American men.

OVERVIEW OF THE BOOK

Using existing social science literature, and our original ethnographic research on Black men, we examine and develop clinical theory. We then present (micro and macro) practice strategies with African American men using an Africentric perspective to complete the conceptual frameworks or lenses used in this book.

This book is composed of four parts, with 11 chapters that develop the topics in each part. In the first part, Chapter 1 presents a brief overview of the social, political, and economic issues that have an impact on the role functioning and experiences of African American men and implications for the field. Chapter 2 outlines theoretical and conceptual frameworks or perspectives that can be used in the theory in understanding African American men. These frameworks can provide for a much more culturally balanced and culturally appropriate approach in working with Black men. Chapter 3 examines clinical theories and issues of human behavior of African American men with regard to these men's individual, personality, and family development issues and tasks.

Part II focuses on micro practice issues and strategies. Chapter 4 presents individual counseling and therapy issues and strategies with African American men that offer new insights on practice approaches. Chapter 5 provides an overview of issues in therapy with African American men and the women in their lives and presents counseling approaches with Black couples. Chapter 6 explores therapy issues in the father-child dyad and the larger extended family system, and it offers new insights in clinical practice with Black fathers, their children, and their extended families. Chapter 7 presents issues in working with Black men in groups and explores various group types, formats, and purposes.

In Part III, we discuss macro practice issues and strategies. Chapter 8 is an overview of policy issues that have an impact on the lives of low-income African American men and low-income African American fathers. Chapter 9 explores obstacles that exist for African American men in receiving social services and obstacles that exist in key governmental agencies. In this chapter, we also suggest other issues that should be addressed in developing, designing, implementing, and evaluating social service programs for African American men. This chapter also provides an overview of case management issues and offers new directions in providing case management and casework services to low-income African American men. Chapter 10 provides an overview of issues in community organization and community development that are relevant in work with Black men and provides community practice strategies and advocacy approaches.

We conclude the book with a single chapter that provides a conceptual and theoretical framework for research that will facilitate the development of theory and practice with African American men. Methodological issues in research on African American men are also examined. This chapter also describes how research activities can inform theory and practice about African American men (thus creating an interlocking feedback loop) through proactive ideographic and nomothetic research activities using postpositivistic, postmodernist, Africentric, and bicultural research paradigms. Specific examples of research methodology that can be facilitative of African American male research are also presented.

CONCLUDING REMARKS

Inappropriate and negligent micro and macro practice efforts with African American men are no doubt fueled by research and policy activities that homogenize and marginalize African American men and their experiences. In light of this state of practice and scholarship, we wrote this book with the primary goal of bringing African American men out of the shadows and margins of practice activities. To this end, we have titled this book *Social Work Practice With African American Men: The Invisible Presence* to embody our central notion that African American men have an ***invisible presence*** in theory, practice, research, and policy.

ACKNOWLEDGMENTS

First, we give honor to God, who is the head and the center of our lives–We thank the Lord, Jesus Christ, for "you are the source of our strength and the strength of our lives!"

We thank Mr. Jim Nageotte, editor at Sage Publications, and Drs. Armand Lauffer and Charles D. Garvin (both of the University of Michigan at Ann Arbor) for their tremendous encouragement, enthusiasm, and support from the initial book prospectus throughout completion of this book project. We also acknowledge the special contribution of Dr. Charles D. Garvin for his thoughtful guidance throughout the writing of this book.

Dr. Janice Rasheed acknowledges the support that she received from Dr. Joseph Walsh, Dean of the School of Social Work at Loyola University Chicago, School of Social Work, who provided a reduced workload during the writing of this book, that greatly facilitated its completion. A special thanks goes to Dr. Yolande Wersching, social work bibliographer and librarian at Loyola University Chicago, for her patience and assistance in the literature search. A very special thanks goes to my mentor and friend/mother/sister, Dr. Letha A. (Lee) See of the University of Georgia, for her endless encouragement, guidance, and love. (God bless you Lee, for the mentoring that you so generously give to so many young African American women in the "academy.") Finally, I acknowledge the ongoing mentorship, support, and encouragement of Drs. Lawrence Gary, Bogart Leashore, Paula Allen-Meares, Ann Hartman, Jewelle Taylor Gibbs, Stephen J. Wernet, Samuel D. Johnson, and Edith Freeman.

Dr. Mikal Rasheed acknowledges the ongoing support and encouragement from Dr. Sandra Alcorn, Dean of the George Williams College of Social Work at Aurora University. I also thank my mother, Mrs. Leone Little, for her unwavering support and belief in my potential as a scholar. (I thank you, mother, for encouraging me to be a lifelong learner.) Finally, I express my appreciation for the ongoing support and mentorship of Dr. Jean Kantambu Latting of the University of Houston, School of Social Work.

Part I

CONCEPTUAL AND
THEORETICAL ISSUES

Chapter 1

INTRODUCTION
Social Work Practice and African American Men

The following passage is an excerpt from an interview held by one of the authors with a 32-year-old African American man; he was responding to the interviewer's questioning about his (prior) lifestyle choices:

> I let myself get involved in such a dangerous life style 'cause I felt like dead was better than playing with death ... on my 18th birthday when most young men begin to seriously think about their future and [life] choices I looked around at the other [Black] men in my neighborhood, at the [Black] men in my family and it was then, that I realized that I was more afraid of living than I was of dying!

This disturbing quote exemplifies and affirms the prior social science literature that describes a bleak picture of the current status and socio- and politicoeconomic issues facing African American men in the United States. As embodied in the previous passage, it is not difficult to feel the sense of anguish, despair, and hopelessness experienced at one time or another by many Black men, despite their current socioeconomic status. (Many African American men, even those who have become upwardly mobile and aspirant, have roots in a poverty-stricken background.)

A review of the literature on African American men in the past 30 years (1968-1998) reveals a downward spiraling of the status and conditions of Black men. The following is a selected summary of social statistics:

The average life expectancy for Black men is 64.6 years (vs. 72.9 years for White men).

The HIV infection mortality rate is 72.9% (vs. 52% for White males); the HIV mortality rate for African American males has more than doubled in the past 10 years.

Homicide (especially gang-related violence in poor, urban areas) is the leading cause of death for Black males 15 to 34 years old and the second leading cause of death for Black men 25 to 44 years old (eight times higher than the homicide rate for White males).

Alcohol abuse, substance abuse, and depression have been recognized as the most significant mental health problems facing Black men.

Suicide is the third leading cause of death for young Black men.

It is estimated that 44% of Black men are functionally illiterate.

There is a 40% to 70% high school drop-out rate for Black men, which is the highest drop-out or "push-out" rate of all racial and gender group classifications in the United States.

In the past 20 years, the number of Black men receiving college degrees has not increased (< 3% of all students who obtain 4-year college degrees are Black men).

Fifty percent of the prisoners throughout the United States and in federal prisons are African American, although Black men comprise only 6% of the total U.S. population (they are incarcerated at six times the rate of White males).

Ninety-five percent of all African American men are not in prison, but by the time Black males reach the age of 19 one in six will have been arrested.

Twenty-nine percent of all African American men live in poverty (vs. 9.8% of White men); this percentage increases to 45% for minor Black males.

Twenty-three percent of Black men ages 20 to 24 and 12% of Black men ages 25 to 44 are unemployed—twice the rate of unemployment for White men.

Working-, middle-, and upper-class Black men are more likely to experience somatic stress reactions or ailments that include headaches, low back pain, diabetes, heart trouble and high blood pressure (Austin, 1996; Federal Bureau of Investigation, 1986; Gibbs, 1988; Majors & Gordon, 1994; Parham & McDavis, 1987; Taylor, 1977).

Even more alarming and disconcerting than the previous overwhelming statistics is the fact that African American men are worse off today than they were 20 years ago (Gibbs, 1988; Taylor, 1987). In fact, African American men are the only racial or gender classification group that has experienced such a "downward spiraling" of social conditions as evidenced by the previous social status indicators.

Researchers, social scientists, academicians, practitioners, politicians, and other public service figures have pondered these staggering figures relative to the plight of African American men. Their analysis as to why these conditions continue to exist for Black men are likely to depend on their "professional worldview"—that is, from what arena do they draw on (i.e., political, cultural, economic, historical, psychological, social, as urban planners, and as community or economic developers) and which of the available theoretical frameworks are utilized in the analysis of this phenomenon. All these professionals tend to agree that there are a myriad of factors operating within this contemporary scenario, and that racism, poverty, and a unique form of (Black male) gender oppression all play prominent roles.

Despite the alarming statistics enumerated previously, however, there are a growing number of middle-class and professional African American men (Bowman, 1989). The following quote, excerpted from an ethnographic interview held by one of the authors with an African American man (a 43-year-old professional), depicts a different but equally painful scenario that typically faces middle class or professional Black men, despite their occupational and economic success:

> It has been my experience here and in other organizations that, we as Black men, are assumed to have an inferior education, and I have had to spend a lot of my time insuring White executives, that I can do it ... My experience in growing up has been all about the Black male image. Even though the image I grew up with, in my close-knit family is different from what is out there [in society] ... I guess I've been trying to disclaim that image. This is why a lot of times I have tried to overcompensate to counter those images [of Black men] ... Being the only Black male (in a senior management position), I know that I can't let my guard down, because if I do, they are going to... (Note: the interviewee never finished this sentence.)

The previous narrative poignantly illustrates the deleterious impact of the sociohistorical-politico baggage that haunts African American men, even those who have defied enumerable obstacles throughout their developmental life span.

Social work and other professions (e.g., psychology and counseling) and the academic disciplines (e.g., sociology and political science) have produced an underwhelming response to the crises facing African American men and thus their families. Social work professor, Paula Allen-Meares made an impassioned "appeal for social work action" to the (social work) profession in her commentary piece in the professional organization's journal (Allen-Meares & Burman, 1995). She points out the "discomforting silence from the social work profession" and the fact that "our interventions must refocus off antisocial activities and individual pathology ... to [societal] inequities based on race, gender, and socioeconomic status" (p. 271).

The remainder of this chapter provides an overview of the implications that the previously outlined current status and issues of African American men pose for the field relative to theory development, practice approaches, programming, policy, and research activities. In addition, we critique the field's prior response(s) to the needs of African American men along these same lines.

THEORY DEVELOPMENT

Theories about African American men have, for the most part, failed to capture the complexity and diversity of their social status and unique experiences. As a result, practitioners and academicians are given a distorted, homogenized version of Black men that has also tended to pathologize the behavior and development of African American men. For instance, the field has failed to conceptualize the behavior of African American men within the larger contexts of their families or to view them as a viable and important subsystem of the larger family gestalt.

Recent theorists have begun to incorporate the Africentric perspective in theory development regarding African American men (Harris, 1995). Earlier reliance on the use of a Eurocentric perspective, however, no doubt operated to conceal the strengths of Black men and further a deficit view of their behaviors.

Theories have also failed to acknowledge the uniqueness of developmental experiences (especially in light of unique sociohistorical and politicoeconomic forces). Also, theories or frameworks have not begun to explore the variation of these experiences or capture the variability of how each person experiences similar circumstances. It is no wonder that we are ill equipped to provide adequate direction in policy, practice, and programming when the various social science fields have been given such an inadequate map (or just one map) for all Black men. This book uses existing and emerging theoretical and conceptual frameworks that can provide a more accurate basis from which practitioners can develop more effective assessments and interventions with African American men.

PRACTICE STRATEGIES

Social work and other practice approaches have been slow to translate the societal concerns of African American men into strategies for counseling, psychotherapy, and the provision of social services. In fact, the field has reinforced a **negative invisibility** and further marginalized Black men in previous practice efforts. This implies that the field is cognizant of the plight of Black men but has wittingly or unwittingly operated to persistently nudge African American men into the margins of practice efforts, attempting to teach their families how to survive without them.

Unequivocally, practice approaches that empower Black men and uncover new ways of helping these men are needed. These practice strategies must be contextualized, shaped, and contoured by the unique sociohistorical experiences and politicoeconomic forces that face these men. In essence, what is needed is a wider set of lenses for practice strategies that use schema that encompass the realities of African American men. These new lenses also need to be able to search for the strengths and positive attributes of Black men.

PROGRAMMING

Social service and human service organizations have woefully neglected and compartmentalized the programming needs of African American men. The field has not made an effort to conceptualize programs with Black men as central figures; some programs, however, are designed specifically to target Black men, but these often have the impact of further fragmenting social services to the Black family. Family-based programs that embrace the centrality of Black men in their families are sorely needed. In addition, social workers and other related professionals and academic disciplines need to critically evaluate the unique gendered obstacles that exist for Black men attempting to use social service and human service agencies.

Programs that support the cultural strengths and acknowledge the "cultural vulnerabilities" of these men are scarce (Rasheed & Johnson, 1995), as are programs that target unique developmental stress points and unique developmental vulnerabilities. Social service programs need to articulate or reframe their program objectives so that they can facilitate adaptive, functional, Africentric behavioral alternatives. This book addresses these concerns and conceptualizes programming approaches that meet the needs of Black men in light of current social status indicators.

POLICY

The combined forces of racism, poverty, and adolescent or teen fathering significantly impact the lives of many African American males. Social policies have failed to aggressively address these issues; rather, policymakers have continued in the vein of the "culture of poverty" framework, which does not focus on or seek to strengthen the functional and adaptive familial behaviors of this population (Rasheed, 1998a). In essence, policymakers have shown a limited understanding of the cultural and ecological contexts in which African American male development occurs.

Rather, social policies in the United States have historically created obstacles to the role functioning of African American men as husbands and fathers. These obstacles are especially apparent in the "mother-only" or "mother-focused" social policies that decrease (rather than increase) possibilities for coparenting and father involvement. Many policies assume irresponsibility and are often conceptualized from a paternalistic, negativistic, and antagonistic perspective. What is needed are "sex-neutral" policies that encourage the centrality of African American men in their families and policies that support and strengthen the role functioning of Black men.

RESEARCH

Research activities are central to theory-building processes; thus, theory development lays the foundation for and gives guidance to practice, programming, and policy activities. It is therefore critical that the field continue to better understand the unique methodological issues in studying Black men and continue to embrace newer and emergent conceptual and theoretical frameworks for research that do not pathologize the behaviors of African American men. It has been well documented that former lines of research created and reinforced negative stereotypes of Black men that were often based on skewed, decontextualized data (Bowman, 1989).

Future lines of research need to focus on better understanding the impact of racism, sexism, and discrimination on the intrapsychic-functioning and role-functioning behaviors of Black men. That is, research must be based on the life-span development of African American males, which will increase understanding of the developmental shifts and changes that are catalyzed by Black men's unique situations and stressors.

Overarching all the previous issues and concerns is the need for future research to be more holistic in examining the dilemmas of the African American male and not to continue to isolate the study of potentially interrelated issues, such as education, employment, crime, violence, gang behavior, and family relationships. A strengths-oriented approach can possibly provide a better understanding of the interplay of these factors. Practitioners, program architects, urban planners, and policymakers are in dire need of research that employ a wider spectrum of research approaches that pose some new questions—questions that are grounded in the real-life experiences of African American men.

CONCLUDING REMARKS

Social work and other related professions and academic disciplines have moved research and the resulting practice literature about African American men (for the most part) out of the days of *cultural imperialism;* that is, the days when research, theory, and practice regarding Black men were characterized by a monolithic, paternalistic, pejorative, "looking glass" quality. Previous research and theory development tended to perpetuate the notion that the key to understanding Black men should be (or could be) based primarily on the perception of others (hence, the looking glass approach) or on Black men's relationships with others—that is, their relationships with the dominant or oppressive Eurocentric core culture.

Racism and discrimination are important conceptual frameworks in developing theory, research, practice, programming, and policies, and it is important that we do not give superficial attention to these frameworks as we address issues concerning African American men. Furthermore, we must be careful not to allow scholarship and resulting practice activities to digress in new, deleterious directions. That is, we need to continue to seek to reverse current trends in research, theory development, practice, programming, and policy that appear to be moving in the direction(s) of fragmentation, decontextualization, and the marginalization of Black men in social work practice activities.

Chapter 2

THEORETICAL AND CONCEPTUAL FRAMEWORKS FOR UNDERSTANDING AFRICAN AMERICAN MEN

The basic experience reported by many African American males is one of invisibility. This theme is poignantly explored by the noted African American male author Ralph Ellison in his book *The Invisible Man* (1952/1989). Another noted African American male author, James Baldwin, writes about a related theme, the marginality of African American men, in his critically acclaimed book *Nobody Knows My Name* (1963/1993). In a similar vein, much of the professional (academic) literature about African American men supports these portrayals of their experiences—that African American men exist on the margins of society's social consciousness. Not only is the Black man invisible on the social landscape but also the troubling social status indicators, as presented in the previous chapter, indicate that African American males are in trouble.

The challenge for social and behavioral scientists is to illuminate those historical, sociopolitical, and economic factors that have exiled the African American male to the periphery of social and economic life. Traditionally, the image that has emerged as the prototypical African American male is one of a man who is socially and economically paralyzed. If we adjust our lens (or employ a different set of lenses), however, we would scan the social landscape of African American life and another image would emerge. This image is a profile of an African American man who is not crippled by the ravages of racism. We see in his face determination, perseverance, and resiliency. This is the picture of an African American man who has defied the odds. This man, although perhaps wounded and weary from his confrontations with racism, exhibits a strength of character. This is the image of a man who demonstrates an ability to carry out the tasks of daily living without totally succumbing to the potentially debilitating effects of racism.

9

More significantly, this man does not stand alone. He is a part of a larger collective of African American men that includes lower-class, working-class, and middle-class Black men. Within this larger collective of African American men, however, are men whose behaviors, lifestyles, values, and belief systems do not conform to prevailing social mores and values and thus do not meet the approval of many. Within their sphere of influence, however, these men represent strength and resiliency.

In 1995, this "collective" converged on Washington, D.C., for the *Million Man March*. In this historical moment, these African American men publicly ripped away the shroud that conceals their "invisible presence." This event paints a new image, a portrait demonstrating the diversity represented by African American men throughout the United States. Although representing different segments of the African American community, these men bonded together through a common vision of African American male solidarity.

Although a significant historical event in African American and American history, the *Million Man March* symbolically presents a challenge to those who theorize about the African American male. Theories on African American men can no longer cast them as invisible or ignore their diversity. Future attempts at understanding the Black male must use theoretical and conceptual frameworks that capture the complexities of African American men's lived experience. Furthermore, these theories must address the diversity of perspectives among African American males while recognizing the commonality of their experiences and vision.

The authors contend that theories about African American men must acknowledge the strength and resiliency of those African American men who, on a daily basis, valiantly struggle against difficult odds. Additionally, applicable theories on African American men must be culturally sensitive by giving recognition to the unique culturally based expressions of their behaviors. Finally, theories on the African American male experience must also speak to issues of liberation and empowerment while recognizing the constraining impact of oppressive environments.

Because theories inevitably guide practice decisions, program planning, policy making, and research efforts, it becomes imperative to ensure a solid foundation for these decisions. To facilitate the previously outlined theoretical requirements in this area, we have chosen three conceptual and theoretical perspectives that can be employed to guide theory building: the *ecological* perspective, the *Africentric* perspective, and the *critical constructionist* perspective. These perspectives are presented and explored here as organizing conceptual frameworks that can guide our understanding of the unique historical and sociocultural realities of Black men and thus more effectively guide social work practice and research activities.

These perspectives or frameworks possess two important features. First, they possess the ability to inform decision making about the use of specific explanatory theories, practice models, and interventions. (These perspectives or frameworks, however, do not prescribe any specific personality theories, explanatory theories, or social work practice models.) Second, within the assumptive framework of each of these perspectives is an ideological commitment to a "strengths orientation." Thus, as decisions are made regarding explanatory theories, practice models, and research approaches, these perspectives draw deliberate attention to indications of strength and resiliency. These perspectives suggest strategies for challenging debilitating and depotentiating narratives that may exist as a result of experiences with oppression and racism.

Each of these perspectives or frameworks offer an important theoretical and conceptual piece to the overall gestalt of theory building of African American men. For instance, the ecological perspective provides a conceptual lens to examine the transactions between the African American male and his biopsychosocial environment. The Africentric perspective provides a framework in which to incorporate the unique cultural worldview as emergent from the African American experience. Finally, the critical constructionist perspective allows us to explore the unique and individual impact of societal factors on the construction of African American male identities through their language and personal narratives.

EXISTING THEORETICAL PERSPECTIVES IN THE STUDY OF AFRICAN AMERICAN MEN

Overview of Perspectives

This section presents an overview of existing theoretical perspectives used to understand African American males and their experiences. We present this overview of theoretical perspectives using classification schemes developed from the works of Bowman (1989) and Oliver (1989).

There are many theories that attempt to understand and explain the socio- and politicoeconomic status of African American males. Many of these theories have been used as the theoretical underpinnings for research efforts, policy making, and social service interventions. In reviewing these theories, we find that there are common themes and assumptions shared between the various theoretical formulations. Thus, we are able to classify specific theories into broader categories or schemes according to their "shared assumptions" about African American men. Using Bowman's (1989) and Oliver's (1989) classification schemes, the following theoretical perspectives emerge: the *deficit/pathology* perspective, the *oppression* perspective, the *coping* perspective, and the *ethnocultural* perspective.

The deficit/pathology perspective focuses on maladaptive behaviors. It supports the hypothesis that cultural, psychological, genetic, or all three deficits are the primary cause(s) of these maladaptive behaviors (Garrett, 1961; Jensen, 1973). (This perspective dominated the earlier studies on Black males [Evans & Whitfield, 1988; Gary, 1981].) A variation of the deficit perspective is the "culture of poverty" orientation (Banfield, 1970; Moynihan, 1965). Proponents of this orientation argue that the cause of social problems can be found in the distinctive cultural values and traditions within lower-class communities.

The oppression perspective also focuses on maladaptive rather than adaptive behaviors. Unlike the deficit/pathology perspective, external societal barriers are considered as the fundamental causes of maladaptive behaviors (Clark, 1965; Glasgow, 1980; Kunjufu, 1982; Wilkinson & Taylor, 1977). The emphasis in this perspective is on the victimization of African American males by existing race and class barriers. In this perspective, institutional racism, internal colonialism, underclass entrapment, urban poverty, and the technological transformation of the economy causing joblessness are considered as primary causes of the African American male's marginal status (Wilson, 1987).

The coping perspective focuses on those African American males who manage effective responses to stressful obstacles. Although oppressive environments are acknowledged, the coping perspective focuses on understanding adaptive rather than maladaptive behaviors (Bowman, 1985, Cazenave, 1981; McAdoo, 1981). Further attention is given to understanding the processes that enable many "at-risk" African American males to struggle against adversity and to excel despite the odds.

Studies grounded in the ethnocultural perspective similarly focus on adaptive modes of cultural expression rather than on maladaptive behaviors. This perspective emphasizes the cultural foundations of proactive responses to institutional barriers. Attention is given to the subjective aspects of culture and looks at the psychological, attitudinal, and expressive behavioral patterns unique to any given culture. Within this perspective are two orientations. One supports the proposition that African American ethnic patterns are reactions to America's racial oppression (Sudarkasa, 1981); and the other views the unique ethnic patterns of African American males as *African adaptations* rather than as cultural residues of oppression (Akbar, 1991; Asante, 1981; Baldwin, 1981; Myers, 1985; Oliver, 1989).

Bowman (1989) suggests that each of the previously discussed perspectives merely illuminates disparate aspects of the African American male experience. For example, the deficit/pathology perspective, although identifying the maladaptive behaviors of at-risk African American males, tends to reinforce a "victim-blaming" ideology. The oppression perspective, by giving attention to the destructive aspects of race and class barriers, tends to depict African American males as "helpless victims." The coping perspective, by emphasizing adaptive responses to societal barriers, may minimize the underclass entrapment of African American males. Finally, the ethnocultural perspective, although having the ability to identify indigenous cultural resources available to Black males, may operate to underemphasize the adaptive responses that the coping perspective could potentially serve to illuminate.

Both Bowman (1989) and Oliver (1989) call for an integrative theoretical perspective that incorporates the unique features of each perspective into a comprehensive, balanced, and culturally sensitive conceptual framework. Bowman views this integrative perspective as the *role strain and adaptation model*. This model examines the objective difficulties and subjective reactions to obstacles faced by African American men as they engage in valued social roles. These difficulties are a result of barriers that exist in the social environment, personal limitations, conflicts at the environment-person interface, or all three.

Oliver (1989) proposes a *structural-cultural* perspective that suggests that the high rate of social problems among African American men is the result of structural societal pressures and dysfunctional cultural adaptations to these pressures. He theorizes that African American men have failed to adequately respond to White racism, and this has resulted in specific styles of behaviors that these men have developed in response to structurally induced social pressures. Oliver believes that even the most problematic dysfunctional adaptation involves two factors: the failure of African American men to develop an Africentric cultural ideology and the tendency of African Americans, especially lower-class Blacks, to tolerate the "tough guy" and the "player of women" images as acceptable alternatives to traditional definitions of manhood.

Critique of Existing Perspectives

We contend that there are conceptual limitations within the existing perspectives outlined previously, especially in the integrative models proposed by both Bowman (1989) and Oliver (1989). Bowman, for example, does not consider how socially constructed images and representations of Black males potentially have an impact on how African American men are perceived by society. By neglecting this factor, Bowman does not address "the ontological assumption that Black masculinities are not biological, they are socially constructed within a framework of power relations or dynamics often dominated by powerful White men and subordinated minority males" (Franklin, 1994, p. 279). Oliver, however, does address the impact of negative male representations but seems to imply that the source of these images stems from a maladaptive response to structural conditions. Oliver does not appear to acknowledge that these representations are often "given" to African American males and are not "constructed" by them.

We note that "theoretical conservatism" is a principle that serves to guide our conceptualizations throughout this book in that we strive to retain and build on those theoretical elements that have well served this area of concern. To this end, it is important to point out that existing frameworks, as outlined previously, are incorporated within our proposed perspectives. Specifically, we contend that the oppression, coping, and role strain perspectives are major elements of an ecological orientation. Additionally, the ethnocultural and structural-cultural perspectives are also embodied within the Africentric orientation as advanced in this book.

We believe the major point of divergence from both Bowman (1989) and Oliver (1989) is in how we view the use of theory. Both Bowman and Oliver seek to formulate an integrated theory primarily as a heuristic for sociological research purposes. Our task and objective for this book is to present frameworks that are appropriate for social work theory, practice, and research. With this task in mind, we present the following overview and discussion of our proposed perspectives.

UNDERSTANDING THE AFRICAN AMERICAN MALE:
SOCIAL WORK PERSPECTIVES

Previously, we discussed the difficulty of any single theory, framework, or perspective to adequately conceptualize the complexities of the African American male experience. We propose that an approach to theory building is needed in this area of concern that frees the theorist from the limitations of a specific explanatory model while allowing the selection of theories that can illuminate salient aspects of the African American male experience. We attempt to accomplish this task by using three broad theoretical perspectives rather than specific theories. Each of these perspectives (the ecological framework, the Africentric orientation, and the critical constructionist perspective) provides a broad conceptual foundation for selecting specific personality theories, explanatory theories, and practice models. These perspectives also allow for greater flexibility in developing strategies for assessment and intervention.

In the remainder of this chapter, we present these perspectives as the organizing conceptual frameworks for this book. We present an overview of each perspective and briefly examine how these perspectives address the African American male experience. Following this overview, we discuss how these perspectives can be integrated to guide our understanding of the complexities of the African American male experience.

The Ecological Systems Perspective: Some Basic Assumptions

Bronfenbrenner (1979) defines the ecological approach as the "scientific study of the progressive, mutual accommodation throughout the life course, between an active, growing human being and his or her environment" (p. 188). Key to the ecological perspective is understanding the dynamic and complex transactions between persons and their environment. These transactions connect the person and environment in a unitary system in which both shape and influence each other through a process of continuous and reciprocal exchanges. In this relationship of mutual influence, the person not only adapts to his or her environment but also participates in creating the conditions in which he or she must adapt (Hartmann, 1958).

The ecological framework draws from a rich variety of theories to form its conceptual framework. Grounded in biology and systems theory, the ecological perspective has incorporated concepts from ethnology, ego psychology, stress theory, role theory, symbolic interaction theory, developmental theory, and the dynamics of power relationships (Green & Ephross, 1991). Given this broad conceptual base, the ecological perspective allow us to take a multisystemic view of a person's experience.

As a model of social work intervention with individuals, families, and groups, this perspective is not defined by traditional methodological distinctions. Rather, this perspective requires the use of differential individual, family, group, community, or all these approaches in response to client needs. Clients and environments are viewed from a fieldwide perspective that broadens the assessment lens to incorporate the multiple systems, resources, institutions, events, and social contexts in which the client transacts.

A summary of the basic assumptions of the ecological perspective is offered by Green and Ephross (1991, p. 271). The following are the basic assumptions:

The capacity to interact with the environment and to relate to others is innate

Genetic and other biological factors are expressed in a variety of ways as a result of transactions with the environment

The person-environment forms a unitary system in which humans and environment mutually influence each other

Goodness of fit is a reciprocal person-environment process achieved through transactions between an adaptive individual and his or her nurturing environment

People are goal directed and purposeful, humans strive for competence, and the individual's subjective meaning of the environment is key to development

People need to be understood in their natural environment and settings

Personality is a product of the historical development of the transactions between persons and environment over time

Positive changes can result from life experience

Problems of living need to be understood within the totality of life space

These assumptions articulate that the ecological perspective is a broad and comprehensive conceptual framework. Within this perspective, there are several concepts that are particularly relevant to our discussion of African American men: life course, adaptation, stress, coping, habitat, niche, power, and oppression.

Life Course

Instead of viewing the human being as moving through fixed, sequential, developmental stages from childhood to adulthood, the ecological perspective examines the unique pathways of development that each human takes through the course of his or her life (Germain & Gitterman, 1996). The ecological perspective views human development as following nonuniform, unpredictable pathways of biopsychological development within the context of diverse cultures and environments. One's life course is shaped by one's adaptation to specific transactions and coping with life stressors over time.

According to Germain and Gitterman (1996), life course theorists place human development within the context of historical time, individual time, and social time. Historical time refers to the effects of social change on birth cohorts. Individual time refers to the experiences, meanings, and outcomes of personal and environmental factors during the life course. Social time is the collective temporal experience as reflected in the unexpected transitions and traumatic events experienced within a family, group, or community. Viewing human development along this multidimensional view of time is key to the ecological perspective.

Adaptation, Stress, and Coping

From an ecological perspective, there is recognition that both the self and the environment, at every level (biological, psychological, social, and cultural), are constantly changing. Adaptation is defined as the capacity to adjust to change. Adaptation is not a static or a reactive state. It is a dynamic process that calls for an ongoing effort to fit the ever-changing condition of environmental demands with a person's needs and aspirations.

Changing conditions can also produce stress. Change can bring about an imbalance between the demands placed on a person and his or her capacity to meet those demands. This imbalance or perceived imbalance can be the precondition for stress. Stress can arise in three domains in a person's life: (a) life transitions involving developmental changes, status role change, and crisis events; (b) the unresponsiveness of social and physical environments; and (c) communication and relationship difficulties in families and other primary groups.

Although stress may be debilitating, these stressors may call forth hidden capabilities that can be mobilized to ameliorate the impact of the stressors—that is, the capacity to cope with stress. Coping responses can reduce, eliminate, or accelerate stress. Successful coping draws on particular personality attributes and untapped resources within the environment. Furthermore, successful coping can enhance self-esteem, competence, autonomy, and problem-solving capacities.

Habitat and Niche

In an ecological framework, people are understood in terms of their location within their environment. The ecological concept that refers to a person's setting or location within their environment is *habitat*. As the concept of environment is described within an ecological framework it becomes much broader than one's habitat. The environment includes not only one's physical or geographical location or habitat but also the sociopolitical, cultural, and economic context that surrounds one's lived space. It is the broader context of culture, economics, and politics that determines if one's habitat is supportive of the mental, physical, and social functioning of the individual.

The sustaining and nurturing resources within one's habitat are further determined by one's *niche*—that is, one's social position, class location, and economic status within the overall social structure. A good or *enabling niche* is one that avails the occupant the rights of equal opportunity to educational and economic resources (Kilpatrick & Holland, 1995; Taylor, 1997). There are, however, individuals with devalued personal or cultural characteristics, such as color, ethnicity, gender, sexual orientation, age, poverty, or other types of oppression, who are entrapped in niches that are incongruent with fulfilling their human need and their well-being (Germain, 1985; Kilpatrick & Holland, 1995; Taylor, 1997).

Power and Oppression

Within an enabling niche are supports that can affirm one's sense of personal power, competence, and self-esteem. Furthermore, an enabling niche can represent a position from which one can express and affirm one's social power. An entrapping niche, however, contains elements that rob one of that self-affirming power. An entrapping niche further blocks one from those resources needed to acquire that power. Thus, persons in an entrapping niche are people with a vulnerable status—a status of powerlessness.

The concept of oppression denotes relationships that are unequivocally negative and that create a differential power imbalance. These relationships impair human growth and on a systemic level are destructive to both the physical and the social environment (Germain, 1985).

Power withheld and abused by dominant groups becomes oppressive power. This form of power shapes and gives meaning to the experiences of those held captive within entrapping niches. The experience of powerlessness and oppression becomes the primary theme in their transactions with the environment. This experience becomes one of the major themes in their life narrative.

Ecological Perspective and the African American Male

The social vitality and the physical resources of African American communities are frequently not examined or linked in a systematic manner to explore the synchrony between the socioeconomic structure and life expectations and opportunities of African American males. Using an ecological framework allows us to consider the primacy of sociohistorical and cultural forces and the interplay of various subsystems (intrapsychic, familial, friendship, and other informal networks as well as formal institutions, such as governmental agencies) in the influence of the overall role, function, and life cycle of African American men.

A key to understanding the African American male is recognizing how his family, community, and the prevailing sociopolitical and economic structure are intricately linked to his sense of self, life expectancy, and life opportunities. How the African American male adapts to the complex networks of these multiple systems is critical. These multiple contexts provide the physical, social, cultural, economic, and spiritual resources that impact the social and spiritual vitality of the African American male.

Within the ecological systems perspective, there is a focus on life course issues. As we approach the African American male from a life course or life cycle orientation, we can inquire into how the African American man's experience of self and others changes as he grows and matures. A life course orientation enables us to understand how race and gender impact different life cycle issues and life tasks.

For example, for African American men there are salient role performance goals, pressing role barriers, and critical role conflicts that are present across the life cycle and at each stage of adulthood (Bowen, 1989). The critical life cycle task for many African American men is to overcome discouraging barriers to personal achievement in salient life roles. The struggle to overcome these barriers becomes the precondition for stress, a condition that particularly affects the physiological condition of African American males.

How African American men adapt to and cope with life issues and environmental demands is addressed by an ecological orientation. The experience of being in an entrapping niche because of one's race and gender is an appropriate concern from an ecological perspective. The state of powerlessness and the striving for recognition are acknowledged within this framework. The interdependent relationship between the African American male and his multiple environments is a valid justification for an ecological systems perspective.

The Africentric Perspective: A Cultural Orientation

The Africentric perspective directs us to the worldview, the cultural values, and ethos of people of African descent. This perspective represents a set of beliefs, philosophical orientation, and assumptions that reflect basic African values as expressed within an American sociocultural and political context. As an "emerging paradigm in social work practice" (Schiele, 1996), the Africentric perspective provides a culturally sensitive framework for understanding the African American male experience. In addition, an Africentric perspective can guide us in developing intervention approaches that reflect the unique lived experiences, values, and worldview of African American men.

The Africentric Worldview

Africentrism is a perspective that reflects a distinct worldview from an African-based, but American frame of reference. An Africentric orientation combines the elements, science, mythology, and philosophy of the African cultural system, juxtaposes the African and American ways, and integrates the values derived from the historic experience of African Americans to provide the clearest perspective on the unique group of people called African Americans (Asante, 1988). In essence, Africentrism reflects one's philosophical and spiritual acceptance, the intellectual acknowledgment, and celebrations of the unique hybrid and historical development of the African American ethnocultural heritage.

Within an Africentric cosmology are basic assumptions about the human domain (Schiele, 1994; 1996; Swigonski, 1996);

Human identity is a collective identity rather than an individual identity (i.e.,"I am because we are")

The spiritual or nonmaterial component of human beings is just as important and valid as the material components

The "affective" approach to knowledge is epistemologically valid

All things are interconnected; there is a oneness of mind, body, and spirit

There is an appreciation of "analog" thinking rather than dualistic thinking

There is a phenomenological time (i.e., present oriented) tied to events

There is a pervasive, experiential, and participatory spirituality

These assumptions undergird a worldview and a value system that is believed to reflect, in an archetypal manner, the African American's existential mode of "being in the world."

Africentrism and the Social and Behavioral Sciences

The challenge for many "Africentric-oriented" social and behavioral scientists is to correct the (mis)application of theories of human behavior that are based on a positivistic and Eurocentric worldview that are inappropriate for explaining the behaviors of African Americans (Akbar, 1979, 1984; Baldwin & Hopkins, 1990; Bell, Bouie, & Baldwin, 1990; Kambon, 1992). As a perspective for social work theory, practice, and research, Schiele (1996) views the Africentric perspective as making the following contributions: (a) It promotes an alternative social science paradigm that is reflective of the cultural and political reality of African Americans; (b) it dispels the negative distortions about people of African ancestry by legitimizing and disseminating a worldview that dates back thousands of years and resides in the collective memories of people of African decent; and (c) it seeks to promote a worldview that facilitates human and societal transformation toward spiritual, moral, and humanistic ends.

The human service implications of the Africentric perspective have been enormous. Africentrism counters the deficit model that focuses on the dysfunction of people of color by acknowledging the resiliency that resides within African remnants in African American culture. This perspective can be seen as an intervention paradigm that promotes transformation of Blacks from a state of dependence to independence and self-reliance (Asante, 1980; 1988; M. Karenga, 1996). Variations of the Africentric perspective have been used in the design and implementation of prevention programs for African American children and their families (Crawley, 1996). Furthermore, this perspective has provided a framework for theory, program development, and research within Black communities (Long, 1993: Nobles & Goddard, 1992, Randolph & Banks, 1993).

Africentrism as Narrative

The Africentric perspective presents an epistemological challenge to the existing positivistic paradigm that has long dominated the social and behavioral sciences (Schiele, 1996). In this respect, an Africentric perspective can be grouped with those feminist and other postmodern and postpositivistic perspectives that challenge the logical positivistic "scientific" paradigm.

The Africentric perspective, however, is not without some controversy in that it has political and historical implications. The major point of controversy is that this perspective presents a revisionist view of history, highlighting the primacy of African contributions to Western civilization (Lefkowitz, 1996).

The controversy regarding the legitimacy of the Africentric view of history is not the subject of our discussion. Our point is not to sidestep the argument around the historical validity of the claims of Africentric scholars. Our intent is to advocate for this perspective as a theoretical framework for social work. We view this in part as being accomplished by identifying the "narrative truth" of Africentrism.

In the contemporary discussions regarding the distinction between "historical truth" and narrative truth, we can discover the significance of the Africentric perspective. In these discussions, there is recognition that history is not only a chronicling of events but also an expression of the meaning and significance given to events. One can go as far as to say that history is narrative. Brunner (1986) states, "These narratives, once acted out 'make' events and 'make' history. They contribute to the reality of the participants ... Can anyone say, a priori, that history is completely independent of what goes on in the minds of its participants?" (p. 43). The following is the question for social and behavioral scientists: What is the significance of the Africentric perspective being viewed as a narrative?

Africentrism, Narrative, and the African American Male

A critical issue for African American males is the representation of African American men through various forms of the media. Often, these narrative representations, articulated by non-African American men, are valorized as the "truth" about Black men. An Africentric perspective provides an interpretive frame to understand the African American male experience. It provides a cultural space for African American men to speak their voice, to create their own text, and to "make" their own events and history (such as the *Million Man March*). This effort on the part of African American men becomes political when they challenge the dominant *metanarratives* that valorizes non-African American male experiences while marginalizing the African American male's voice. An Africentric perspective is a narrative that brings challenge into the realm of social work practice theory and research.

Baldwin (1985), an "Africentric psychologist," views the African American male as the primary target of a psychocultural war protracted by the dominant social order. Baldwin proposes that the only hope for survival of the Black community and of the African American male is through the allegiance to a cultural framework and social practice that is grounded in an Africentric perspective. In Oliver's (1989) structural-cultural perspective, much of the difficulties encountered by African American males are viewed as failures in developing an Africentric cultural ideology.

The Africentric perspective serves a dual purpose in that it provides a template for understanding the unique cultural frame of reference of African American men. As Bowman (1989) suggests, this perspective can address the unique psychological, attitudinal, and expressive patterns unique to Black men that represent African-based adaptive behaviors. Of equal importance for many Africentric behavioral scientists, Africentrism is a perspective that articulates a value system that should inform theory, practice, and research with African Americans in general and Black men in particular. Finally, an Africentric orientation or worldview can provide a *cultural holding environment* to protect the African American male from further psychocultural assaults.

Critical Constructionism: A Framework for Social Work Intervention

The critical constructionist perspective is a synthesis of several streams of contemporary thought: *postmodern social constructionism* and *narrative theory* (Freeman & Combs, 1996; Laird, 1989), *critical social theory* (Habermas, 1971), and Freire's (1973) concept of *critical consciousness.*

Social Constructionism and Narrative Theory

Briefly stated, in a social constructionist worldview, ideas, beliefs, customs, and all those things that make up our psychological reality are socially construct- ed within the context of human interactions and expressed through the medium of language (Freeman & Combs, 1996). Language is the means for organizing and structuring our life experiences. It is the narrative that we construct about our lives that provides us with a sense of personal identity. Our narratives further reveal the significance of our lived experience within the context of our social world (Polkinghorne, 1988).

Although an increasingly popular approach in social work practice, a purely *narrative* approach to social work practice has the possibility of being apolitical and relativistic. A purely narrative approach could conceivably ignore the broad- er sociopolitical context in which social work practice is conducted. According to Fish (1993), within much of the narrative approach, politics and power are under- stood at the level of the helping relationship. The level of the clients' or social worker's position within the larger social order is not considered, however. Supporting this critique of the narrative metaphor in clinical work, Laird (1989) states,

> In [family] therapy we tend, in general, to be more interested in the par- ticular narratives and stories of individuals and families, rather than the sociocultural narratives that construct the contextual realm of possibility from which individuals and families can select the ingredients and focus for their own narratives. (p. 430)

These criticisms clearly imply that in social work practice, one cannot understand the significance of a client's problem (or narrative) without recognition of the material, power-laden, and affectively charged elements of the prevailing socio- cultural metanarratives and their influence(s) on the client's lived experience.

Critical Social Theory and Critical Consciousness

One of the important contributions of critical social theory is that it contextu- alizes the meaning of our lived experience by locating that experience within a specific historical, economic, and political context. To say that the "personal expe- rience is the political experience" underscores one of the basic assumptions of critical social theory. Any understanding of our personal narrative must include an inquiry into our social, political, and economic position within the social order. We must view our narrative (and our client's narrative) with a critical eye to uncover the extent to which the unique reality of our lived experience is shaped by the dominant social and political ideology.

In critical theory, to understand the meaning of personal narratives is to ana- lyze how the dominant social, political, and economic structure facilitates, con- strains, or oppresses one's sense of identity. Stevens (1989) states,

> Racism, sexism, classism, ageism, and heterosexism are some of the fun- damental dogmatic ideologies that are internalized in social structures and thus operate in unexamined ways. These kinds of ideologies both limit the concrete alternatives open to individuals and maximize the life opportunities of some groups by minimizing those of others. (p. 58)

The critical theorists view liberation (from an oppressive ideology and structure) as an indispensable condition of the quest for human potential and authenticity (Stevens, 1989). Liberation is attained by first developing a state of "critical consciousness", that is, achieving an awareness of how the social, political, and economic ideology constrain our sense of agency and identity (Freire, 1973). Informed by this new awareness, we can then take action against those oppressive structures and articulate in our own "voice" a narrative of self that represents our unique lived experience.

Critical Constructionism and the Black Male

Previously, we suggested that there is a diversity of perspective among African American men in the sense that they do not fit stereotypical and monolithic models of "Black masculinity." As African American men describe their lived experiences, however, they seem to share a common experience of oppression and marginalization. There are those African American men, however, who, by virtue of their social status and economic success, appear to have escaped the virulent impact of racism and oppression. We hear in their personal narratives or stories, however, how they have had to negotiate their Black masculinity in the larger world from an initial position of powerlessness.

Although there is no singular set of conceptual constructs that can capture and render, in a meaningful manner, the experience(s) of Black men, we can with good reason state that African American men, as a group, encounter common social and cultural representations of Black masculinity. These (frequently) negative representations or images give shape and contour to the lived experience of the African American male.

A critical constructionist perspective acknowledges that reality is socially constructed and that the socially constructed representations of the African American male tend to constrain and define him in problematic ways. This perspective enables us to understand the significance and complexities of socially constructed Black male identities. The critical constructionist perspective also provides a framework for developing intervention strategies that can empower African American men.

In using the critical constructionist perspective, we can attend to how African American men construct their narrative identities and acknowledge the diversity in which these identities are expressed. This perspective offers the professional the opportunity to recognize multiple African American male voices as they resound within the "chorus" of a heterogenous African American community. Each African American male voice is liberated to speak its own reality and is not constrained to the *metanarrative* of the entire ethnocultural group. This perspective, however, also gives clear recognition of how the social realities of racism and oppression can influence the language of Black mens' narrative(s).

CONCLUSION: INTEGRATION AND CONVERGENCE

The three metatheories or perspectives outlined and discussed in this chapter share important points of integration and convergence. Namely, the ecological systems perspective sets the stage by addressing how the multiple environments, in which African American men interact and transact, can be supportive or debilitative to their well-being. The ecological systems orientation also emphasizes how the life cycle allows one to focus on how race impacts the Black male's ability to fulfill life roles and developmental tasks across the life span. The Africentric perspective gives attention to an articulation of a culturally sensitive narrative that supports an ethnic and communal-based identity, value, and worldview. Finally, the critical constructionist perspective instructs us how to challenge those dominate narratives that rob the African American male of his psychological, social, and spiritual vitality.

Our task throughout this book is to further articulate these theoretical and conceptual frameworks or perspectives in practice, programming, policy making, and research activities in a way that captures the unique experience(s) of masculinity from an African American male perspective. Although these perspectives represent different lenses, they all revolve and converge around the integrating themes of strength, resiliency, oppression, and empowerment. These metatheories or perspectives that we strategically blend and hence refer to as a **"critical practice"** approach or framework for practice with African American men will enable us to hear and give voice to the "voiceless"—the African American male with the *invisible presence* in our respective professions.

Chapter 3

THE ADULT LIFE CYCLE OF
AFRICAN AMERICAN MEN

> For the Black man attaining any portion of manhood is an active process.
> He must penetrate barriers and overcome opposition in order to assume a
> masculine position. ... Throughout his life, at each critical point of devel-
> opment, the Black boy is told to constrict, to hold back, and camouflage
> his normal masculinity. Male assertiveness becomes a forbidden fruit,
> and if it is attained it must be savored—privately!
> —Grier and Cobbs (1968, p.49)

Much of the current social science literature on African American men tends to
focus on adolescent males, 13 through 18 years of age. As the statistics indicate,
males in this age group are highly vulnerable. Thus, attention has been directed
toward understanding the vicissitudes that teen African American males face as
they cope with the complex developmental demands of adolescence. In recent
social science literature, there has been a dearth of attention given to the life cycle
issues of adult African American men, hence the following question: What are the
major developmental issues and life tasks that adult African American men
encounter? In this chapter, we attempt to answer this question.

The major life cycle concerns for African American men are examined in this
chapter. Such concerns include masculine identity development, individual and
personality development, and family development (i.e., paternal role functioning,
conjugal relationships, and extended family relationship issues). Key to this discussion will be an examination of how the factors of poverty and racism significantly influence the individual, personality, and family life cycle development of
African American men.

In this chapter, an effort will be made to challenge the cultural-deficiency theoretical perspectives previously used in theory development with African
American males. These perspectives have characteristically portrayed African

American men as emasculated, ineffectual, and peripheral members of the Black family. Through the use of the ecological, Africentric, and critical constructionist perspectives, we are better able to identify the cultural strengths and the sociocultural vulnerabilities of African American men, resulting in a more contextualized theory of human behavior. The theoretical and conceptual orientations used in this book and that inform the following discussion of the adult African American male offer a more balanced and realistic portrayal of the life cycle issues of African American men.

THE "DREAM": A METAPHOR FOR
UNDERSTANDING BLACK MALE DEVELOPMENT

A theoretical framework that has informed many studies on adult male development is provided by Levinson (Darrow, Klein, Levinson, and McKee, 1978). In this seminal volume, *The Seasons of a Man's Life,* these authors delineate the developmental tasks of men as they move from childhood to adulthood. On the basis of his qualitative study of adult men, Levinson (1980) proposed that each man's life is shaped and structured around his involvement and investment in significant roles and relationships. Hence, life structures involve

> One's relationships: with self, other persons, groups and institutions, with all aspects of the external world that have significance in one's life ... the life structure stems from the engagement of self with the world. ... Adult development is the story of the evolving process of mutual interpenetration of self and world. (p. 278)

These life structures change and evolve through a man's life and profoundly influence his personality development, patterns of interactions with others, and success in coping with the tasks of living.

A life structure is thus a bridge between the inner psychological world of a man and his outer world of relationships, all within a broader ecological context. It is through life structures that a man projects himself as a man into the world. How a man initially projects himself is explained by Levinson (1980) through the intriguing concept of the *Dream.* In Gooden's (1989) explanation of the Dream, he states;

> While it often includes a particular job and or a family, it transcends those specific achievements to indicate a heroic self-image capable of motivating the young person to the commitment and responsibility that the achieving that Dream demands. In its most developed form, the Dream gives shape and substance to the wishes, longing, and fantasies to be a special person in the world of adults. (p. 65)

The Dream motivates the young male to work on those aspects of himself that are believed to be incongruent with his dreams. This heroic self-image compels him to struggle to become "one's own man." The Dream becomes the organizing passion that shapes identity and a man's life course. For Levinson (1980), a viable adult male life requires the capacity to dream and the ability to sustain the motivation needed to transform the Dream into actuality. This effort cannot be accomplished alone. A man needs a mentor, sponsor, guide, teacher, adviser, or confident who believes in his Dreams so that these Dreams can be actualized.

Dreams also have an ecological significance. Along with a mentor, there must be an enabling niche, an ecological space that contains the vital resources and relationships of family, work, and community that can support and nurture the Dream. What happens, however, if as a result of an impoverished or oppressive niche, the Dream is delayed, deferred, or rendered unattainable?

Dreams and the Impact of Racism and Poverty

A review of the social science literature of the past 30 years yields two variables that profoundly affect Dreams, or the formation of satisfactory life structures, and personality development and life cycle issues of adult African American men: racism and poverty (Gary, 1981; McAdoo, 1988, 1993; Staples, 1995). For many African American men, racism and poverty are intimately intertwined factors that significantly influence their life cycle.

Gibbs's (1988) edited book reflects the grim picture that portrays many African American males today as impoverished. She contributes much of their plight to the interaction of racism and poverty. The downward spiraling of many of these young Black males often begin after the fourth grade, when their minds shut down due to inadequate education in the inner city. These inadequacies lead to high drop-out or "push-out" rates, which in turn lead to menial dead-end jobs (Gibbs, 1988). In desperation, many of these men turn to drugs, crime, gangs, or all three, which further complicate and burden personality development and other developmental tasks that may affect their sense of identity. All these factors inevitably operate to defer or destroy the Dream and create unstable personal and familial relationships.

Any discussion of the developmental experiences of African American men cannot ignore the two critical factors of racism and poverty. In the special case of low-income African American males, the interaction of racism and poverty creates unique life cycle issues. Even those African American males who have escaped the oppressive grip of poverty continue to experience developmental concerns that are profoundly influenced by racism. Throughout this chapter, the factors of racism and poverty will be woven into the discussion of masculine identity development, individual and personality development, and family development.

LIFE CYCLE ISSUES OF ADULT AFRICAN AMERICAN MEN
Masculine Identity Development

Traditionally, men have bestowed manhood on other men. Classical forms of initiation have mostly occurred in an all-male surrounding away from any female influence. Through prescribed forms of rituals, or designated activities, manhood is granted and validated under the watchful eyes of approving elders or mentors. These initiatory experiences help young males to formulate, imitate, and eventually integrate a sense of masculine identity. In the absence of formal cultural initiation rituals, there are often informal male subcultures that provide the context for validation of male identity (Raphael, 1988). Whether formal or informal, these rituals serve to confirm a male as a man and to socialize him to conform to the prevailing images of adult masculinity.

From a critical constructionist perspective, the prevailing images of masculinity are fundamentally grounded in widely shared beliefs about what behaviors constitute male gender roles. Therefore, the scripts for masculine gender roles emerge not from a predetermined biological imperative of "maleness." Rather, masculine identity is "developed through a complex process of interaction with the culture in which we both learn the gender scripts appropriate to our culture and attempt to modify those scripts to make them more palatable" (Kimmel & Messner, 1995, p. 10). The developmental task for many men is the struggle of fitting into a culturally prescribed role for masculine behaviors. According to Pleck (1981), measuring up to culturally prescribed gender role expectations is, in fact, a difficult task. Traversing the gap between the "ideal" masculine image and the existential and behavioral realities of the individual man can be the cause of considerable stress.

Images of Masculinity

What are the dominant contemporary images of masculinity? What are the beliefs about masculinity that infiltrate the dreams of young males and direct the gender role socialization of men. The following are some of the prevailing images of male masculinity: (a) Men must be emotionally stoic and deny vulnerability; (b) Men must be preoccupied with work status, achievement, and success; (c) men are to be forceful and interpersonally aggressive; (d) men should reject what seems feminine; (e) men must have an aggressive need to defend oneself; (f) men are preoccupied with sex and sexuality; (g) men should be economic providers for their families; and (h) men should be protectors of home and family (Goffman, 1963). Goffman provides a description of the male ideal when he states:

> In an important sense there is only one completed unblushing male in
> America: a young, married, white, northern, heterosexual Protestant
> father of college educated, fully employed, of good complexion, weight,
> and height, and recent record in sports. Every American male tends to
> look out at the world from this perspective, the constituting one sense in
> which one can speak of a common value system in America. Any male
> who fails to qualify in any one of these ways is likely to view himself—
> during moments at least—as unworthy, incomplete, and inferior. (p. 128)

Gender Role Strain

Although the previous descriptions are viewed by many as markers of manhood, they do not represent clear and consistent rules that govern the behaviors of all men. Pleck's (1981) gender role strain theory examines the difficulties that men encounter in attempting to live out male gender role expectations. According to Pleck;

1. All gender roles are operationally defined by gender role stereotypes and norms.
2. Gender role norms are contradictory and inconsistent.
3. The proportion of individuals who violate gender role norms is high.
4. Violating gender norms leads to social condemnation.
5. Violating gender role norms leads to negative psychological consequences.
6. Actual or imagined violation of gender norms leads individuals to overconform to them.
7. Violating gender norms has more severe consequences for males than females.
8. Certain characteristic prescribed by gender norm roles are psychologically dysfunctional.
9. Each gender experiences gender role strain in its paid work and family roles.
10. Historical change causes gender role strain.

Implicit in these propositions is that gender role socialization may have tremendous psychological and social cost (Pleck, 1995). The consequences of failing to fulfill male gender role expectations may result in low self-esteem and other negative psychological consequences. For those who fulfill these expectations, there may be long-term and traumatic side effects for the individual male and for others in his life structure. For example, there are gender role expectations that prescribe behaviors that are dysfunctional in a relational or familial context.

An additional factor that may also contribute to gender role strain is the impact of racism and poverty. Racism has profoundly shaped the gender role model and expectations for African American men. These two factors determine the opportunities available to achieve and fulfill specific gender role expectations. Racism and poverty further impact the behavioral expressions of masculinity, resulting in what may appear to be dysfunctional masculine behaviors. These dysfunctional behaviors in turn create other difficulties for African American men.

There are many unanswered questions about the African American male experience. For instance, how do African American males carve out a defined sense of Black masculinity in a society that often denies their existence? Are there clear events or rituals that mark the transition of an African American male from childhood to adulthood? What are the developmental milestones and tasks that represent progression through the life cycle? Finally, the following is a very central question: What are the models of African American male masculinity that propel the developmental thrust? It is with this last question that we shall proceed with our discussion on how African American men develop a sense of masculine identity.

Images of Black Masculinity

What are the sources of Black masculine images? For many, professional athletes and entertainers serve as the most visible model of Black masculinity. The Dreams sustaining the personal growth for young African American men are often translated into the imagery of sports or the stage. These entertainers and athletes serve as heroic images that become the substance of these young men's Dreams. The reliance on such images, however, has potentially disastrous consequences. In discussing the athleticizing of the Black male image, Hoberman (1997) states;

> Black athleticism has complicated the identity problems of Black
> Americans by making athletes the most prominent symbols of African
> American achievement. This has done much to perpetuate the invisibility
> of the Black middle class, by making Black professional achievement a
> seldom-noted sideshow to more dramatic media coverage of celebrities
> and deviates. (pp. 9-10)

This quote speaks to the exploitation of a specific image of Black masculinity that results in a radical constrainment of the possibility of other viable African American male images emerging in the Dreams of African American men.

Other negative influences on the masculine identity development of African American men are society's enduring and pervasive stereotypes of Black male sexuality (Staples, 1995). Black men have been viewed not only as gendered beings but also as "embodied beings"—that is, they are viewed primarily as "physical beings," thus placing emphasis on their physicality. This of course contributes to the athleticizing of the Black male image. The Black male as an embodied being has defined his role in the social order as much as has his gender. Franz Fanon (1967), the Black psychiatrist and philosopher from Martinique, spoke of this "embodiment" of the Black male as symbolizing, in the minds of non-Blacks, sexuality and aggressiveness. Hoberman (1997) writes;

> The Black male style has become incarnated in the fusion of Black ath-
> letes, rappers, and criminals into a single menacing figure who disgust
> and offend many Blacks as well as Whites. The constant, haunting pres-
> ence of this composite masculine type is maintained by news coverage
> and advertising strategies that exploit the suggestive mixture of Black
> anger and physical prowess that suffuses each of these roles. (p. xix)

The Black male body—as athlete, as entertainer, and as criminal—becomes a composite image of African American male masculinity. It is an image that generates fear. Hence, the Black male is seen in a stereotypical manner as a "species" to be caged and tamed. (Could this not be, in part, an explanation for the fact that more than 45% of prison inmates are African American men—a symbolic expression of the caging of this species?)

What is the impact of the previously discussed images on the masculine identity development of African American men? On one level, the African American man encounters models of masculinity that represent stereotypes that exclude him from a viable position within mainstream society. He is surrounded by the masculine images of the dominate culture, such as presented by Goffman (1963). The images offered to him, however, are insidious facsimiles of the dominant culture. These (stereotypical) images leave rather limited options for expressing manhood; becoming a professional athlete or entertainer is a Dream that is outside the skills and talent of the majority of African American males.

The Impact of Black Male Images on Low Income Men. The internalization of prevailing (dominant sociocultural) standards as norms for gender role identities, along with difficulties in actualizing these standards, significantly impacts low-income African American men. This conflict can result in many dysfunctional masculine behaviors. Frustrations may result from low-income African American men comparing themselves with the standards of the dominant culture. These standards tend to dictate male gender roles.

The low-income Black male must develop and manage a masculine identity in the context of economic and social obstacles, grounded in racism and poverty. Given the inequalities in earning potential, employment, and limited access to educational opportunities, he finds it difficult to achieve specific male roles, such as provider and protector.

Cool Pose: A Strategy for Survival. African American men may reconcile the societal dissonance of their existence through the employment of a "ritualized form of masculinity" referred to in the social science literature as *cool pose*. Adopting a cool pose entails behavioral scripts—that is "physical posturing, impression management, and carefully created performances that deliver a single critical message—pride, strength, and control" (Majors & Billson, 1992, p. 4). This form of "being a man" is expressed through handshakes, walking, eye work, body stance, and facial expressions.

Majors and Billson (1992) view cool pose as a coping mechanism par excellence. Cool pose is a means of establishing a sense of presence in a hostile and indifferent world. This behavioral style represents a means by which many African American men proclaim to the world that they are proud, powerful, strong, and in control; it is an affirmation that shouts "we are" in the face of a world that screams "you are not." Cool pose is a functional behavioral response designed to express and embellish manhood, although it may appear on one level to represent dysfunctional behaviors.

"Coolness" comes from African culture. It represents a sense of control, an ability to exhibit grace under pressure, a notable confidence, and a mystic coolness of character. Cool pose is a unique fusion of African heritage with the experience of racism in the United States. To be cool is to stay detached during intense encounters with racism and poverty. An Africentric understanding of cool pose articulates this phenomenon as an attempt by African American men to express themselves, as men, in a culturally oppressive and race-conscious society (Langley, 1994). It is a way of psychologically and emotionally surviving a restrictive society. Coolness brings balance, stability, confidence, a sense of control, and a sense of masculinity to the lives of African American men in an oppressive environment.

Cool pose is an expressive performance that helps African American men counter the stress that can result from racial and social oppression. One wonders, however, if a psychological and physical toll can result from this inhibition of emotions and coolness of expressions. Many contemporary social scientists view cool pose as a coping mechanism with a double-edged sword (Langley, 1994; Lazur & Majors, 1995; Majors & Billson, 1992; Majors and Gordon, 1994;) such that cool pose is a masking strategy that relies on the denial and suppression of deep feelings. Some researchers and social scientists speculate that cool pose helps to explain the fact that African American men, in higher numbers than White men, commit suicide and experience stress-related illnesses (Langley, 1994; Lazur & Majors, 1995; Majors & Billson, 1992; Majors and Gordon, 1994).

Although a potentially adaptive response in dealing with racism and poverty, cool pose can represent a self-destructive stance toward the world. Hence, the denial and suppression of intense emotions can potentially lead to violence, risk-taking behaviors, or other forms of overdetermined or "hypermasculine" behaviors when important human emotions, such as fear, vulnerability, and intimacy, are not acknowledged and openly resolved. In addition, one wonders what is the impact of cool pose on developing successful life structures.

In essence, cool pose is a phenomenon that transcends all social classes of African American males. There are enumerable forms of coolness that can be displayed by all African American males: lower class, working class, and middle class. The behavioral difference of how cool pose can be displayed between the various socioeconomic classes of Black men is likely to be one of subtlety among the more "acculturated" Black males as opposed to a more pronounced display of coolness or cool pose among (less Eurocentric) lower- or working-class Black males. In addition, cool pose may be a more salient behavioral response for lower-income African American males due to their higher level of vulnerability to social stressors. Cool pose, however, can be a reaction of any African American male dealing with the ambivalence and confusion stemming from conflicting norms and standards of masculinity. Because this ambivalence and confusion can transcend class locations; cool pose is a symbolic vehicle to express and validate a sense of self and masculinity regardless of socioeconomic status (Langley, 1994).

Hidden Images of Black Masculinity. There are many positive images of Black masculinities that are a part of the African American experience but are hidden and distorted by society. For instance, images of the hard-working, resilient family man, the spiritual man, the political man, the defender of the community, and the African American man who stands up for self and confronts racism all exist within the African American experience and persist in the collective consciousness of African American men. This collage of African American men has sustained many African American men throughout the diaspora.

In Hunter and Davis's (1992) study, the African American male subjects defined their manhood in terms of self-determination, accountability, pride, perseverance, commitment to family and community, and an existential ideology (spirituality and humanism). There is evidence, however, of the acceptance of many of the traditional stereotypical notions of manhood—that is, physicality, strength, competitiveness, and aggressiveness. These men express a belief that manhood rests on foundations other than the traditional notions of masculinity. Hunter and Davis conclude;

> It is important to note that these findings suggest that the dynamics of race, culture, and class have forged varied constructions of manhood, whose contours and shades are not limited to the hegemony of masculinity or the politicized images of Afro-American men. (p. 477)

Black Masculinity: The Need for Mentors and Rituals. One of the routes to masculine identity is through a mentorship relationship. In Levinson et al.'s (1978) study of masculine psychosocial development, they write, "The mentor relationship is one of the most complex and developmentally important a man can have in early adulthood" (pp. 99-100). Mentors are not father substitutes but are typically older males who provide guidance, counsel, and support to younger males. This relationship, which is often intense, serves a transitional function for the young person by helping him to mature into adulthood with a sense of masculine identity (Osherson, 1986). Furthermore, the presence of mentors is often central to men's career success (Vaillant, 1977).

Although mentors are seen as crucial to the development of masculine identity, African American males experience a low level of mentorship relationships or difficulties in sustaining such relationships during the period of early adulthood (Gooden, 1989; Herbert, 1990). In circumstances in which there is an absence of a positive relationship with a father, the scarcity of successful adult males available for mentoring is likely to more severely impact the development of a positive Black male identity. Furthermore, low-income males tend to show greater dependence on peers for support and approval in their striving for a masculine identity (Harris, 1995).

Exacerbating the previously mentioned problems of a lack of mentors in impoverished neighborhoods is the impact that street gang infestation has had on these men's opportunity to "bond" with other neighborhood males. The literature reports incidents of men being afraid to even speak to other males on the street for fear that they will violate gang affiliations or be pressured into a gang membership (Rasheed, 1998b). This dreadful reality no doubt contributes to these men's sense of alienation and anomie. Their isolation has caused them to feel that no one in their life space cares about them, and that everyone has given up on them (Rasheed, 1998b). As a result, the men have come to rely on emotional insulation.

The African American male's difficulty in developing a cohesive sense of self and ego syntonic definition(s) of manhood is no doubt exacerbated by the lack of developmental milestones in his impoverished life space. To this end, there is a trend among directors of programs for low-income African American men and religious organizations to institute "rites of passage" rituals based on Africentric principles (Rasheed, Fitzgerald, & Howard, 1996). The development of such rites of passage programs along with mentorship programs, based on values grounded in the African American experience, can provide a basis for culturally syntonic African American male images. (Group work strategies are discussed in Chapter 7.)

Individual and Personality Development

Racism and Alienation

Thirty years have passed since Grier and Cobbs (1968), two eminent Black psychiatrists, wrote about theories of Black personality development. In their book *Black Rage,* they chronicled the impact of racism on personality development and mental illness within African American communities. Through their careful analysis, they described how social and cultural oppression is insidiously linked to emotional conflicts. A compelling argument is presented suggesting that many psychiatric "disorders" displayed by African Americans may in fact represent adaptive responses to a racist environment. Hence, Grier and Cobbs posit that the etiology of individual psychopathology among African Americans has socio-historical and sociocultural origins.

Another significant analysis of individual and personality development issues is offered by Franz Fanon in his work, *Black Skin, White Masks* (1967). This work represents a psychoexistential analysis of the Black experience. Although not specifically addressing the African American experience, Fanon recognizes the vulnerability of the African-based psyche, under continued exposure to racism. In analyzing Fanon's work, Bulhan (1985) identifies five aspects of alienation caused by the experience of racism and oppression: (a) alienation from the self, (b) alienation from the significant other, (c) alienation from the general other, (d) alienation from one's culture of origin, and (e) alienation from creative social activities. The first form of alienation involves alienation from one's physical self and personal identity. The second form of alienation speaks to an estrangement from one's family and group. The third form of alienation is best illustrated by the tension and paranoia characterizing the relationships between Whites and Blacks. The fourth form of alienation involves estrangement from one's language and history. The final form of alienation speaks to the denial and abdication of self-determined, socialized, and organized activity. All these forms of alienation occur in the lives of African American men.

African American male authors have explored the concepts of alienation and "invisibility" of African American men (Ellison, 1952/1989; Baldwin, 1963/1993). One of Ellison's protagonists so eloquently states,

> I am an invisible man. I am a man of substance, of flesh and bone, fiber and liquids, and I might even be said to possess a mind. I am invisible, understand, simply because people refuse to see me ... they see only my surroundings, themselves, or figments of their imagination—indeed, everything and anything except me. (p.3)

In many respects, these authors speak from their own painful experience as African American men. Their novels are autobiographical accounts of their personal struggles for social recognition and acceptance as human beings and as African American men.

Other contemporary African American male authors write about the persistent sense of existential alienation argue that America has made the Black male the *universal bogeyman* (Hutchinson, 1994), and depict African American men as bruised, vilified, and mistreated (Cose, 1995, p. 51). Various descriptions of the psychological and emotional experiences of African American males suggest that this group of men must continually negotiate a sense of *"otherness"* and a *negative invisibility* in their struggle throughout the developmental life cycle (Rasheed, 1998b).

Alienation and Low-Income African American Males. Low-income African American men may become emotionally detached from themselves in the face of harsh societal realities. This detachment may cause a lack of "inward" understanding. This point is keenly illustrated in an ethnographic interview with a Black male counselor (Rasheed, 1998b)[1]:

> Many of the [poor, Black] men have no real concept of self. ... They are denied the knowledge of self. ... They want, but do not know what they want ... and are easily led. ... They have limited vision, as their world is often no larger than a 10-block radius from where they were born. (p. 273)

One of the most persistent themes discussed in the social science literature on lower-income African American men is the mens' feelings of powerlessness and helplessness. These feelings can cause a sense of shame, doubt, low self-confidence, and even chronic depression in some men (Crawley & Freeman, 1993; Rasheed, 1998b). These men feel so demoralized by their economic disenfranchisement that their self-esteem has taken a brutal beating in the process.

These psychological characteristics are also likely to emerge in job interviews and in "job-readiness" activities. Prior research revealed that these men are sometimes reluctant to try for the "better" jobs, or do not try as hard to get them, because they lack self-confidence (Rasheed, 1998b).

The overburdened, complex, and complicated early developmental responsibilities and tasks of many low-income men are likely to leave these men feeling angry with themselves, even if in their later adult years they are able to put their lives together. This anger is likely to be internalized by the men, further rendering them at risk for somatic and depressive symptoms.

Alienation and Middle-Class African American Men. The experience of alienation is not limited to lower-class African American men. Middle-class men also encounter a sense of alienation. In his book, *The Rage of the Privileged Class,* Ellis Cose (1993) lists 12 "demons" that professionals of color may encounter as a result of racism. These areas are not gendered and may be experienced by both men and women of color. In a study of African American male human service managers (Rasheed, 1997), the demons enumerated by Cose did in fact structure the experiences of many of these African American professional middle-class men. The following are the 12 manifestations of alienation:

1. **Inability to fit into a white environment:** This reflects difficulties in fitting into an organizational culture that is perceived to prescribe certain behavioral expectations, such as forms of speaking, manners, dress, and educational "pedigree," that the Black man may or may not possess. Professional Black men report having to conform to a particular behavioral profile that is more strenuously applied to Black men than to White men.

2. **Exclusion from the club:** This sense of social isolation may occur even if the African American man has the "right" credentials. In many organizational and corporate settings, there are certain affiliations, associations, and networks among White male colleagues such as private clubs that still may exclude African American men.

3. **Low expectations:** In this instance, the African American male is not expected to perform above minimal standards. He may also be seen as an "affirmative action baby." He hears innuendos that he was hired based on his color rather than his skills. Such low expectations may motivate the African American male to overachieve to prove that he can do more and is in fact better qualified than his White coworker.

4. **Shattered hopes:** A sense of failure that is exacerbated by previous experiences of racism is a psychological consequence that may result if continued striving to be better than one's colleagues does not yield the fulfillment of the Dream—that is, if one never gets the big career-making assignments or the desired promotions.

5. **Faint praise:** When an African American is given the opportunity to demonstrate his abilities and skills, he may be singled out as the "exception." Statements from White colleagues such as "You are different from most Blacks I've worked with" can have profound emotional consequences for the African American man. Such statements indicate that the speaker, in fact, assumes the inferiority of other African Americans.

6. **Presumption of failure:** These demons also emerge when there is a questioning of whether an African American male is truly qualified for a particular specific position. The assumption is that there is a lack of qualifications and prerequisite skills to perform the desired duty. It is not uncommon in clinical or social service settings to hear African American males describe how their qualifications and experiences were ignored or underrated (Rasheed, 1997). Anger, rage, and a sense of hopelessness can result.

7. **Coping fatigue:** Coping with the previous demons requires considerable emotional and psychological energy. This can result in stress, fatigue, and other psychosomatic symptoms.

8. **Pigeonholing:** Professional and working-class African American men report that their occupational or job opportunities are often limited to prescribed areas (Rasheed, 1997). They are typically assigned only African American clients or assigned to the community affairs division or other affirmative

action-related responsibilities or all three. These men perceive these types of assignments as resulting in dead-end careers—the concrete ceiling; hence, the impact on the Dream is obvious.

9. **Identity troubles:** African American males report that they need to be especially attentive to negotiating and managing how they are perceived within an organizational setting (Rasheed, 1997). They have to be especially mindful of being pigeonholed because this could result in a lack of recognition for broader talents and skills. Other image considerations include apprehension if they project a clear sense of Black masculinity; they wonder if they will have to confront some preconceived notions and stereotypes about African American males. If they attempt to project an image that compromises a sense of racial or ethnic identity, however, they threaten to negate a part of their internalized identity. These identity conflicts are common experiences for the middle-class professional African American man.

10. **Self-censorship and silence:** Withholding one's feelings to oneself, enduring affronts, and swallowing disappointments are the common dilemmas that face many working-class and professional African American men in occupational settings. Being cognizant of the consequences of "speaking out" causes many working-class and professional men to constantly struggle with how to portray themselves. The African American man is aware that differential rules apply to how he is viewed when he speaks out. What may be defined as positive and assertive behavior on the part of White males may be seen as aggressive behavior if displayed by an African American male. The specter of the "angry aggressive Black male" is evoked in the consciousness of others.

11. **Mendacity:** The "collusion of silence" regarding racial issues can take on the form of deception, or the acting as if race is not an issue, even when there is evident racialization of interactions and decisions.

12. **Guilt by association:** Many working-class and professional African American men encounter the presumption that they are just like the "other" Black men. Thus, they are not seen as individuals and not assessed based on their unique talents, skills, and other individual characteristics. They are seen as a monolithic part of a larger group of "others."

Microaggression and Alienation. The 12 factors discussed previously profoundly shape the life structure and the Dreams of working-class, middle-class, and professional African American men. Additionally, these experiences are typically compounded with experiences of microaggressions (Pierce, 1970). These microaggressions continue to remind African American men of their devalued sociopolitical status. African American men may unconsciously anticipate these microaggressive acts when interacting with "majority culture" (Langley, 1994).

Pierce (1970) suggests that if one does not respond to these microaggressive assaults and insults resulting from oppression, an individual may (a) internalize his anger and become depressed; (b) convert these angry feelings into psychosomatic symptoms, such as hypertension and ulcers; and/or (c) attempt to reduce his level of frustration through alcohol and drug abuse. Regardless of the outcome, the result is an intensification of a sense of alienation and despair. This form of alienation creates a range of dysfunctional behaviors amplified by the oppressive nature of covert and overt racism, including the following (Bowman, 1989; Jones, 1989; Rasheed, 1998b; Wilson, 1990):

Displacement or compensation (e.g., antisocial disorders and crime)

Denial or emotional insulation (e.g., substance abuse or alcoholism)

Repression or suppression (e.g., psychosomatic illness and disability)

Internalization of negative stereotypes of Black males (e.g., hypermasculinity and compulsive "womanizing")

Displaced aggression or sublimation of anger or rage (e.g., depression or suicide)

Hidden Voices: Coping With the Impact of Racism

Although many studies critically analyze problematic behaviors, there are "hidden voices" of Black men who speak of more adaptive responses to racism and oppression (Hunter & Davis, 1992). These are the men who successfully adapt and cope with the stress of the unique life tasks of African American men. They are the men whose life structures reflect adaptation through ego syntonic responses. Their lives reflect a sense of agency and purpose. Their survival strategies involve developing the following (Crawley & Freeman, 1993; Hunter & Davis, 1992; Langley, 1994):

Flexible family roles

Cohesive family bonds

Consanguineous relationships

Racial consciousness and system blame

Taking leadership roles in religious or community efforts

Religiousness and spirituality

Ethnic achievement orientations

Cool pose or posture as a symbolic expression of masculinity and an attempt to offset the "zero image" of Black males in this society

These men do not frequently appear at the doors of human service agencies. They are also typically ignored in the social science literature. In many respects, these men have achieved a sense of masculinity that affirms their sense of racial and ethnic identity while transcending the debilitating impact of racism on their psyche. Many of these men have been able to reconcile Black masculinity with adaptive and coping behaviors that promote survival in the social mainstream. These men are the potential mentors for young African American males. There is a pressing need for mentors for African American males with behavioral qualities that are "acceptable" as masculine and a need for mentors who have managed to work in the world of work and meet the expectation of mainstream institutions (Harris, 1995).

Family Development

Paternal Role Functioning

Discussion of the parental role functioning of African American men has been unidimensional and has primarily focused on the inadequacies of the African American male as a parent. Perhaps the most misleading information in the social science literature is that all African American fathers fathered children as adolescents. Researchers admit that this phenomenon is difficult to quantify because this population has been elusive and difficult to locate in research efforts (Miller, 1994). Despite our inability as researchers to quantify this social phenomenon, young fatherhood remains a critical developmental issue in the overall life cycle of a significant number of African American males. Hence, failure (early on) in the pivotal developmental task of providing for one's children can only increase a male's sense of vulnerability (Madhubuti, 1990).

Many low-income African American men internalize dominant core values regarding the work ethic and the economic expectations of their paternal role functioning. This ethic is expressed by a low-income, noncustodial father in an ethnographic interview (Rasheed, 1998b) as follows:

> "...I've begun to think of myself, as a person of worth ... for the first time in my life, I have a legitimate job and was able to buy school clothes for my four kids." (p. 273)

This vignette also serves to highlight the issue that money has become the "feeling focus point" and replaced the importance of feelings or the pursuit of self for many low-income African American men who have experienced long-term unemployment.

In the absence of stable, living-wage earning jobs, many poor African American men have found it necessary to assume noninstrumental (i.e., noneconomic) parental and familial roles (McAdoo, 1993). These men develop innovative ways of establishing a role for themselves vis-à-vis their children. For example, prior research revealed that the men perform maintenance tasks and odd jobs around the house of their children's mother as a way of contributing to their children's welfare (Rasheed, 1998a). Other examples in the literature include going over to their children's house to read bedtime stories or acting as escorts for their children through dangerous neighborhoods, thus giving the mother a reprieve and allowing the children more opportunity to participate in evening extracurricular activities (Rasheed, 1998a).

The coparenting efforts of this population of men, however, are often thwarted by residual and unresolved tension in the relationships with their children's mothers (Rasheed, 1998b) in that the relationships are often characterized by tension, resentment, and anger. This is frequently a remnant of earlier inconsistent paternal efforts that typically characterize the teen parenting years. Also clouding and complicating these fragile relationships are situations in which the mother has a new significant other who has assumed paternal responsibility. The fathers often express sadness and disappointment as they realize, sometimes for the first time, that the mothers have gone on with their lives, often not leaving a clearly defined role for these unmarried/noncustodial biological fathers (Rasheed, 1998b).

It is important to note that African American men do assume a significant paternal role. They are not shadowy figures on the periphery of family life as reflected in the earlier social science literature (Moynihan, 1965). Working-class and middle-class African American fathers are seen as "significant others" to their children. Contrary to notions of Black male inaccessibility as fathers, studies reveal that middle-class African American fathers participate more in child care than do White fathers (Danealk, 1975; Gillette, 1960).

The paternal role is significant to the African American male. This role, however, is often thwarted by the consequences of poverty and racism. Attempting to fulfill the gender role expectation of fatherhood without economic support creates a serious challenge for the low-income African American father. Low-income fathers may seek alternative means to meet these expectations, and in doing so they become vulnerable to social criticism and may seek to withdraw into a state of anonymity.

Conjugal Relationships

As African American males grow into early adulthood, conventional gender and family roles make their performance as husbands or mates become especially critical (Erickson, 1980). African American men who envision an uncertain economic future may also anticipate problems in commitment to marriage. There may be a greater sense of hesitation in undertaking a role that cannot be fulfilled in the face of adversarial social and economic factors.

It should be noted that the literature has begun to acknowledge the impact of sociohistorical forces and environmental factors, such as racism and poverty, on Black men's relationships with Black women. Taylor's (1992) research revealed that there is a positive relationship between low socioeconomic status and the level of "internalized racism" (i.e., racial self-hatred) of the husbands; it is especially interesting that low socioeconomic status did not have the same effect on the level of internalized racism of the wives in this study. Furthermore, this research revealed that marital satisfaction is affected by the level of internalized racism in Black couples—that is, couples reporting less internalized racism tend to report more marital satisfaction. One can conclude from this study that poor or low-income African American men are more vulnerable than their spouses in adopting negative self-images and attitudes and, as a result, their marriages are more likely to be less satisfying.

Conjugal role ambiguity and gender role strain, caused largely by oppressive attempts to mimic paternalistic, Eurocentric relationship values and ideals, are probable causes of Black male-female relational conflict. African American men are frequently confronted with gender role strain, such as role expectations to be protector and provider for one's family, in that these roles are given relatively high status in our society. Billingsley (1992) points out that there are African American men who, because of poverty, may feel subservient and relatively powerless in comparison to White men, in part due to a higher economic dependence on Black women. This experience may result in an unconscious search for importance. This experience may also result in womanizing and engaging in hypermasculine behaviors in an effort to enhance self-esteem and to counter feelings of economic impotence (Bowman, 1989; Jones, 1989).

Cazenave's (1979) study of working-class African American men showed that they endorse the role of the provider compared to other roles, such as husband, father, and worker. Therefore, if an African American man perceives his primary role as that of a provider, being unemployed or underemployed cuts into the heart of his identity and feelings of worth.

In their study of middle-class Blacks and Whites, Cazenave and Leon (1978) found that White middle-class men tend to emphasize the more expressive or egalitarian aspects of their male role. African American middle-class men, however, tend to emphasize more of a "traditional" approach to their male role (e.g., work hard and be a good provider). The conclusion drawn from this study is that because White middle-class males occupy a dominant position in society, they do not have to prove their masculinity. Hence, they do not have to keep the status quo and do not have to assert themselves in traditional ways to prove their manhood. Therefore, they can afford to be more expressive and less traditional in their familial role behaviors.

African American men, especially those moving into middle-class/professional positions, may also place a high priority on the provider role rather than the role of husband. Middle-class African American men may feel a need to maintain a "majority status" in performing male roles. This may cause many middle-class Black men to work long hours to attain the highly desired "good life," thus leaving less time for family life and further complicating this arena of their role functioning.

The precariousness of low-income African American men's economic position in the provider role may in turn affect their thinking about their role definition in conjugal relationships. As a result, low-income African American men may experience a lack of definition of masculinity and a lack of a definition regarding relationships with women. As one African American male psychologist poignantly expresses (Rasheed, 1998b),

> "They've allowed other people to define themselves [as men, fathers, and husbands]. ... The courts, the gangs, the welfare system, the mothers of their children, girlfriends, White society ... everyone gets to define who they are ... except them." (p. 273)

Other factors that can negatively impact conjugal relationships include: the sense of emotional isolation, the need to demonstrate sexual prowess, and other aspects of hypermasculine behaviors. These forms of behaviors can have profound implications for intimate couple relationships in that they can impact couple communication, create issues of power and control, and generally cause the African American women in their lives to feel frustrated with their male partners (Boyd-Franklin, 1989). Other issues that result from the interactional dynamics of

African American couples, given Black men's unique socioeconomic and politi-cohistorical experiences in the United States, are discussed in Chapter 5.

Extended Family Relationships

"Burnt bridges" is a persistent relational theme regarding low-income African American men and their extended families (Rasheed, 1998b). As revealed in an interview with a social service provider in a program for Black men (Rasheed, 1998b), one key informant states, "Many of these guys have blown it so bad, in the past, due to their earlier immaturity and early responsibility ... their extended family relationships are often left permanently damaged, they are left without an ear." (p. 276)

Intergenerational issues in the family of origin of low-income African American men are another important theme to be considered. Previous research revealed that these men may hold negative paternal images projected by their families about Black men in general and Black fathers in particular (Rasheed, 1998b). These powerful family processes further inhibit their ability to come to terms with their own feelings of loss, rejection, and abandonment, especially in circum-stances in which their fathers were absent due to early death or separation.

In the case of middle-class professional African American men, the conse-quences of upward mobility may create a sense of pride in the family of origin. Career success, however, could result in an *emotional cutoff* from the family of origin. In their struggle for success, they may encounter rejection and a lack of support from their families. Other men, in their quest for success, may emotion-ally disengage from their families in an attempt to manage a more assimilated identity. Such emotional distancing can result in feelings of alienation, isolation, and anomie from cultural moorings. As these men move to establish families of their own, these unresolved intergenerational issues may reemerge. The **interper-sonal familial dynamics** that emerge in the families of African Americans are dis-cussed in Chapter 6, in which we outline practice strategies for family therapy.

AN AFRICENTRIC PERSPECTIVE ON LIFE CYCLE ISSUES

The journey from childhood to adulthood provides formidable challenges for the African American male. In his journey, he has to master many developmental tasks, some of which are unique to the African American male experience. These factors uniquely impact development and are outlined later. Crawley and Freeman (1993) articulate distinctive developmental issues and tasks that face the African American males that may impact life structures and Dreams. These developmen-tal issues and tasks include, but are not limited to, the need to

refine healthy identity that transforms or transcends societal messages of inferi-ority, pathology, and deviance based on color, race, culture, or all three;

strengthen skill for negotiating bicultural and multiracial environments;

engage in the struggle against social injustice;

manage and transform experiences of social injustices and societal inconsisten-cies based on race or color; and develop and implement parenting skills for instructing children how to survive and negotiate the multiracial, bicultural environment and society.

When Africentrically based cultural values, norms, and behaviors versus Eurocentrically based cultural norms and ideals of adulthood behavior are compared, a vivid contrast emerges between the two ethnocultural worlds. Within the Africentric worldview, role flexibility, an emphasis on the "collective good," interdependence, an emphasis on humanism, spirituality, and "oneness with nature" are the cultural ideals that Black men experience. In stark contrast, within the Eurocentric worldview, role compartmentalization, rugged individualism, independence, competitiveness, materialism, and "mastery over nature" are the cultural ideals that Black men experience as they interact with the dominant culture. These contradictory and inherently incompatible structural and cultural messages no doubt create significant turmoil for African American men in their quest to juxtapose the two cultural worlds. This conflict of worldviews is intensified in light of the gender role rigidity that tends to exist for males versus females. It is incumbent on researchers, practitioners, and program planners to find ways to help Black men mediate their dual existence and develop culturally syntonic ways of becoming men and being masculine.

CONCLUSION

This chapter explores the vicissitudes that impact the life cycle issues (i.e., individual personality, masculine identity development, and family development—paternal, conjugal, and extended family roles) and hence developmental tasks of African American men. To this end, this chapter challenges cultural-deficiency theoretical perspectives previously used as a template to understand the human behavior of African American men. The ecological, Africentric, and critical constructionist perspectives as described in this book are used as a new set of lenses in which to understand the complex and unique life cycle issues and tasks of African American men.

In subsequent chapters, we discuss the task of attempting to facilitate functional, desirable, and culturally syntonic models of masculine identification and development for African American men for *micro practice* activities (e.g., individual, couple, family, and group) and *macro practice* activities (e.g., social policy analysis, community development, program planning, implementation and evaluation, and research).

NOTE

1.   In this book, all quotes from Rasheed (1998b) are used with permission from The Hawthorn Press.

Part II

MICRO PRACTICE ISSUES AND STRATEGIES

Chapter 4

INDIVIDUAL THERAPY WITH
AFRICAN AMERICAN MEN

In Part I, we examined the array of psychological, sociocultural, and economic stressors that face African American men and are intensified by the persistence of racial oppression or poverty or both. Racism and poverty are considered primary contributors to the emotional and psychological maladjustment of African American men. Dr. Martin Luther King (1963) passionately echoes this sentiment; he believes that the forces of racial oppression and poverty are so severe for African Americans as to be "emotionally damaging and psychologically destructive" (p. 118). Emerging from the wake of this devastating tide of racism, many African American men are left with a fractured sense of self, a truncated self-esteem, a sense of alienation, anomie, and hopelessness (Chinula, 1997; Fanon, 1967).

African American men who find it difficult to cope with the stressors inherent in being a Black male, in a social context that also renders them "invisible," are prime candidates for mental health intervention. Despite this apparent need, African American men have often resisted this form of (psychological) problem solving from mental health practitioners. Similarly, the various helping professions have also resisted pursuing an aggressive agenda of mental health programming and practice interventions aimed at ameliorating the psychosocial distress experienced by African American men. Consequently, human service professionals and the clinical practice literature have been slow to develop strategies for culturally sensitive and "oppression-sensitive" counseling with this population.[1] Thus, African America men are often left bereft of the professional psychosocial support needed to cope with their vulnerable, at-risk, and endangered status.

This chapter takes on the challenge of identifying and developing culturally sensitive and oppression-sensitive approaches to individual therapy with African

American men. In Chapters 5-7, we continue with this challenge in examining various clinical approaches to working with African American men in couple, family, and group therapy. Additionally, community practice strategies are outlined in Chapter 10.) Factors impacting the mental health status of African American men and their implications for mental health counseling are presented. An integrative perspective or **"critical practice"** approach, which has special applicability for developing and implementing psychological intervention strategies for African American men, is further articulated (and illustrated through case discussion) in this chapter.

"EMBITTERED AND EMBATTLED": THE PSYCHOLOGICAL DISTRESS OF AFRICAN AMERICAN MEN

The contemporary status of African American males in the United States has been described as vulnerable, at risk, and endangered. The tenuous status of African American males within American society molds the very substance of their lived experiences. As outlined and delineated in Chapter 1, African American men encounter higher rates of unemployment, higher poverty rates, lower income status, lower status occupations, lower social status, residential crowding, and substandard housing. Chapter 3 examined the behavioral and psychological consequences that can result from these cumulative stressors and can potentially impact African American men's ability to perform in key social roles, including husband, father, and economic provider.

African American men live under the constant threat of social and cultural extinction. Gibbs (1988) poignantly and concisely describes African American males as being "miseducated by the educational system, mishandled by the criminal justice system, mislabeled by the mental health system, and mistreated by the social welfare system" (pp. 1-2). In essence, African American males live in a state of constant vulnerability that impacts the very core of African American men's personal identity and self-esteem as well as their ability and potential to cope with the stress of everyday living. Life under the constant threat of social and cultural annihilation can render Black men "embittered" and "embattled" (Gibbs, 1988).

Washington (1987) delineates the following three broad classifications of stressors that exert chronic levels of mental health distress on African American men:

1. **Psychological stressors:** stressors that occur on the intrapsychic and interpersonal levels and are often experienced as alienation, powerlessness, helplessness, inadequacy, lack of self-esteem, cultural estrangement, and social isolation.

2. **Sociocultural stressors:** social and cultural expectations and requirements that can induce anxiety, guilt, conflict, suppressed aggression, and sexual tension if one does not adjust or conform (or overconform) to dominant cultural norms.

3. **Economic stressors:** stressors that are due to unemployment, underemployment, job losses, health catastrophes, loss of personal property, and gross
   indebtedness, which in turn can contribute to or reinforce a sense of powerlessness, helplessness, and inadequacy.

In light of the fact that racism and oppression are the sociocultural conditions
under which African American men exist, these psychological, sociocultural, and
economic stressors have the further potential to profoundly impact the African
American male's sense of masculinity and expression of the "masculine ideology." The acceptance and internalization of these ideological expectations of manhood are typically thwarted by the external forces of racism and greatly intensify
the stress of being an African American man.

This array of chronic stressors can tax the coping and adaptive capacities of
African American men. For example, there are African American men whose coping capacities are taxed beyond their available psychological or social resources
or both. As a result, these African American men may cope with the frustrations
of daily living by (Johnson, 1998)

1. Taking out their frustration on other African Americans as reflected by the
   "Black on Black" murders

2. The excessive use of alcohol and drugs to cope with the "bad feelings"
   resulting from feelings of anger, frustration, and confusion

3. The use of wit and humor to minimize the seriousness of their life situations
   and conditions

4. "Identification with the aggressor" (i.e., joining forces with the source of
   oppression) and thus lashing out at other African Americans as a way of
   being accepted or affirmed by the oppressor

5. Displaying intense and immobilizing anger at White people and manifestations of antiblack racism

6. Staying cool ("cool pose") and denying their situation by trying to remain
   unaffected by their feelings

7. Burying the anger and hurt feelings, which can result in feelings of chronic
   depression and hopelessness

THE EXPERIENCE OF AFRICAN AMERICAN MEN
IN PSYCHOLOGICAL THERAPY

Despite the multiple stressors that African American men encounter, these situations do not necessarily lead them to mental health counseling. Franklin (1992)
notes that African American men do not customarily use counseling or therapy to
handle psychological distress. In fact, despite these stressors, not all African
American men are rendered psychologically, socially, or economically impaired
or incapacitated. Many African American men demonstrate resilience in their ability to draw from their personal wellspring of strength to effectively cope with
these stressors. Other African American men have the resources within their eco-

logical niche to buttress them against the destructive storms of racism and oppression. African American males who do not have such resources, however, are the subject of this chapter (and subsequent chapters).

In the minds of many African American men (and women), to use counseling is, in part, an admission of having a "mental illness," a clear stigma within large sectors of the African American community. Counseling also goes against one of the primary directives of the masculine ideology—that is, "a man should be able to be and stay in control." Seeking help from a person who allegedly has the ability to "get into your head" (i.e., a "shrink") can be perceived as an admission that one cannot "handle one's own business." Counseling thus represents an admission of failure or loss of control or both. The hypersensitivity to a loss of control on the part of many African American men is further exacerbated by the "helping" process. For instance, many African American men may experience or perceive (or both) relatively little control over their destiny. Hence, their resistance to counseling may be an attempt to preserve whatever vestiges of control that they feel they have over themselves and their lives.

Many African American men initially become involved in counseling (or therapy) via a referral from a human service professional or a legal organization. In these instances, the goal of counseling is likely to be intrusive, punitive, adversarial, or corrective rather than collaborative, preventive, and developmental. Counseling in such circumstances is likely to raise serious issues of trust, power, and control. These factors clearly contribute to the unwillingness on the part of African American men to engage in the helping relationship (Franklin, 1992; Gibbs, 1988; Sutton, 1996). As a result, African American men may approach counseling with some intrepidation and apprehension; this apprehension is often interpreted by practitioners as resistance (i.e., an unhealthy and defensive attitude toward the counseling process or the counselor or both).

In light of these factors, questions are often raised as to whether African American men can be engaged in any form of psychotherapeutic intervention. Research has suggested that more directive and less prolonged introspective approaches to therapy and counseling seem more appropriate for African American men. For example, in one study an active counseling style was preferred by African American men (Okonji, Ososkie, & Pulos, 1996). That is, active therapists were seen as those who functioned as teachers or models, and who were willing to "confront" clients about their problematic behaviors.

Other clinicians and researchers have challenged such findings by suggesting that there is an implicit racist bias inherent in such conclusions. These conclusions tend to imply (or explicitly state) that African Americans lack the ego strength, motivation, intelligence, introspective capacity, and the ability to delay gratification to be engaged in a long-term, "insight-oriented" mental health counseling process (Bradshaw, 1978; Edwards, 1988).

The "myths" of the unsuitability of African Americans for intensive treatment may in fact reflect the bias of the mental health profession rather than a sound clinical analysis of the ego capacity of the African American client. This bias is articulated in research conducted on African American male clinical (social work) supervisors (Rasheed, 1997). In this research project, one of the participants was a psychodynamically oriented clinical social work supervisor. He reported that he was discouraged from becoming a clinical social worker as a graduate student. He was told by one of his professors that, African American men lacked the capacity to be empathic and therefore could not make good psychodynamic therapists" (Rasheed, 1997).

The fact remains that few African American men seek or stay in intensive insight-oriented therapy. There is no evidence, however, to conclude that African American men do not have the ego capacity to form a therapeutic relationship or the ability to use insight to understand their emotional difficulties. The resistance to engagement in long-term intensive mental health counseling may not be due to individual character structure but to a sociocultural view about long-term insight-oriented therapy.

Negative views toward long-term psychotherapy may be grounded in a wariness of the metapsychological and Eurocentric concepts of psychological theory; the stigma attached to "going for help" for psychological problems; and the costly, time-consuming structure of intensive, long-term therapy (Edwards, 1988). These factors, rather than the "ego capacity" of African Americans in general and African American men in particular, may mitigate against involvement in insight-oriented psychodynamic treatment. Therefore, consideration of mental health interventions for African American men should be a priority. The issue becomes one of determining what forms of intervention may be sufficiently culturally and oppression sensitive to address the mental health needs of African American men.

ISSUES OF SPECIAL SIGNIFICANCE IN CLINICAL PRACTICE WITH AFRICAN AMERICAN MALES

Although most clinical theories postulate that emotional difficulties arise from unresolved unconscious or conscious conflicts or both, questions that should be raised in clinical practice with African American men are whether racism and oppression impact the intensity of these conflicts and attempts to resolve them and which defenses or protective strategies might be mobilized to cope with these conflicts. These issues beg the question: Does being an African American male influence the dimensions of emotional conflict and impact the resolution of these emotional conflicts?

These questions are answered, in part, by examining the types of clinical issues that are typically presented in psychological treatment by African American men (Jones & Gray, 1983). The clinical issues herein to be explored are (a) problems of self-esteem, (b) problems with aggression, (c) sexual problems, and (d) dependency problems.

Self-Esteem

Self-esteem encompasses issues of identity and self worth—major concerns for African American males. As an African American male attempts to synthesize elements from his experiences to form a cohesive sense of self, the materials from which he draws on often contain negative images, distorted representations, and emotionally laden stereotypes about African American males. Thus, there may be difficulty in incorporating and integrating these images to form a viable, cohesive sense of self. Intrapsychic conflict may result as African American males attempt to reject or deny (or both) those aspects of self that are rooted in these negative representations. This intrapsychic struggle can result in a fragile and/or a fragmented sense of self-esteem, self-worth, and identity.

Aggression

Many African American men have experienced difficulties in managing anger and hostile feelings in reaction to their rejecting and hostile environment. Because African American men are cognizant of their feared and threatening social image of the "aggressive Black male," however, they may display too much control of aggressive impulses (repression) or too little control (immature defenses) as they encounter situations that (should rightfully) provoke anger and rage (Grier & Cobbs, 1968). Unfortunately, African American males who display healthy forms of assertive behaviors may experience that these behaviors are perceived by Whites as aggressive and confrontational. These conflicting and confusing experiences (i.e., assertiveness being viewed as aggression) can result in the inappropriate channeling of aggressive drives and hostile feelings. Thus, difficulties in managing aggressive impulse can result in symptomatology such as substance abuse, criminal activity, depression, and suicide.

Sexuality

Issues regarding sexuality may emerge that concern problems of intimacy, sexual performance, sexual desire, sexual identity, and sexual orientation. Additionally, sexual issues may underlie other psychological problems, such as dependency and aggression (Jones & Gray, 1983). These sexual concerns and the unwillingness to explore these issues may be profoundly influenced by the stereotypes and images of Black male hypersexuality. These images may result in some African American men becoming counterphobic by boasting of sexual adequacy while cloaking intimacy and sexual performance problems (Sutton, 1996).

Dependency

With regard to dependency, the concern regarding the African American male is the extent to which he feels that he has the ability and the capacity to care for self and be autonomous and self-directed—that is, become independent. Independence may be hindered and complicated by social forces that inhibit the development of competency and effectance. The social forces of racism and oppression may in fact create a sense of perpetual social, economic, and subsequent psychological dependency for some African American men. Racism and oppression can thwart the effort toward mature adulthood by reinforcing the infantilization of the African American male. An African American male can

ceptualized as integrative frameworks that are not wedded to any specific or theoretical practice model. Similar to these approaches, the practitioner oriented
toward a critical practice perspective can utilize psychotherapeutic techniques and
methods from different (psychological) theoretical schools and social work practice models. The (integrative) critical practice approach calls for intervention
simultaneously at multiple levels (i.e., micro and macro) that target affective, cognitive, behavioral, and systemic changes.

Adapting and expanding on Comas-Diaz's (1994) principles for clinical practice with women of color and applying them to a critical practice approach with
African American men, the critical practice approach is based on the following
principles:

1. There must be a recognition of the systemic and societal context of racism
    and oppression and social ideologies that are infused with the virulent dis-
    ease of racism. Such recognition allows both practitioner and client to
    become aware of how their lived experience (or personal narrative) has been
    impacted by these forces.

2. Effective mental health intervention must be based on a deliberate effort of
    both the practitioner and the client to be aware of how their location or posi-
    tion within the social political order shapes their identities and the context
    and content of the helping relationship.

3. There must be identification of personal narratives, cognitive distortions,
    and language that reinforce a sense of disempowerment, pejorative classifi-
    cations of difference, or a truncated sense of self-esteem (e.g., identifying
    dichotomous or binary thinking, such as "superior/inferior" or "White males
    are good/African American males are bad").

4. There must be support for self-assertion and reaffirmation of both racial and
    gender identity as well as development of a more integrated identity as an
    African American male.

5. There must be a search for increased self-mastery and achievement of
    autonomous dignity.

6. There must be support for the African American male client in his work
    toward social change, by challenging anti-Black racism and other forms of
    bias encountered within his particular ecological niche. (This principle also
    includes improving the conditions of other men, women, and children of
    color.)

The critical perspective offers the practitioner the opportunity to recognize the
"multiple voices" and "multiple realities" of the heterogeneous population of
African American men. Each voice is liberated to speak its own reality and is not
constrained to a metanarrative of the entire population of African American men.

Generally, these (raced and gendered) metanarratives are developed by non-
African American men to describe African American men. The proposed integrative critical practice approach facilitates a process in which African American men
become aware of being the "creator" and owner of their own destiny. Once
empowered by a new sense of selfhood, Black males can then take action to
change debilitating social structures around them.

become trapped in the vortex of social, economic, and psychological deper and hence become embittered and embattled.

HEARING THE MULTIPLE VOICES OF AFRICAN AMERIC MEN: THE "CRITICAL PRACTICE" APPROACH

The integrative perspective or **critical practice approach** (as develop advanced in this book; see Chapter 2 for additional theoretical and conc background detail) is grounded in the ecological, critical constructionis Africentric perspectives. The critical practice approach is informed t assumption and ongoing analysis of the impact of sociocultural and soci ical factors on the presenting (mental health) problems of African Am males as being an integral component of the clinical process.

We suggest that the critical practice approach is specially suited to ass practitioner in bringing cultural and political realities into their work African American men. This perspective provides clear recognition of the realities of racism and oppression and how they can operate to impact the tal health of Black men. Additionally, the emphasis on identifying and bu on the strengths (individual, cultural, and environmental) of Black men t this approach a particularly vital one.

The critical practice approach is as an optimal framework for understa the social and psychological distresses of African American men (and oppressed, socially devalued, or marginalized persons). This proposed c practice approach has the potential to inform and guide practitioners to African American men to challenge negative (societal) representations of masculinity with an increased sense of self-mastery and dignity. One of tl goals of the critical practice approach is to liberate the African American to become the subject of his own biography rather than to be a victim or b dered invisible in the "narrative" of others.

For mental health interventions to be successful with African American mental health practitioners must move beyond prior corrective, deficit, or pu approaches. A movement toward an empowerment perspective and a cult and oppression-sensitive approach to clinical practice with African Americal is clearly indicated. In counseling African American men, perspective emphasize facilitating normal human development and fostering manhood i ty within an Africentric cultural context should be used (Lee, 1990). Practiti must be attentive to fostering self-mastery, dignity, and an integrated gende racial identity in addressing psychological issues with African American me propose that the critical practice approach addresses many of the previous cerns and gaps in counseling and therapy approaches for African American

The critical practice approach shares many of the elements of the social empowerment practice model (Gutierrez, Parsons, & Cox, 1998; Lee, 1994 Lillian Comas-Diaz's (1994) integrative model for psychotherapeutic work women of color. Both the empowerment model and the integrative model are

The methodology for developing a critical consciousness—a key element of the critical practice approach with African American men—involves a *dialogical approach* to relationship building and engagement, requires *critical reflection* as a part of the assessment process, and promotes *readiness toward action* as part of the intervention planning (Freire, 1973). The phases engagement as "reflective dialogue," assessment as "critical reflection," and intervention as "liberating action" are described and illustrated by a case discussion demonstrating the critical practice approach.

Relationship Building as Reflective Dialogue: The Foundation for Clinical Engagement

Establishing the Helping Relationship: The Issue of Trust

Establishing a therapeutic working alliance is critical to the success of building a helping relationship with African American men or any client. Several conditions must be met to facilitate this working alliance. First, there must be an agreement between the client and the clinician on the desired outcomes or goals of the helping relationship. Second, there must be an agreement on tasks that are to be undertaken by the practitioner and those to be undertaken by the client to accomplish the work of problem solving. Finally, there must exist some relational bond between the practitioner and the client (Bordin, 1979). In counseling with African American men, these are but few of the factors that need to be taken into consideration in establishing a helping relationship.

One element that can impact the working alliance is the obvious presence of race and gender. In the broader social context, race and gender have clear power implications. There are power differentials across both cross-racial and cross-gender relationships. Certain members of social groups, based on race and gender, have more status, privilege, and power than others. Similarly, the clinical relationship has a greater potential for replicating these broader social dynamics. As a result, Black men may be hypervigilant to the power dynamics of the helping relationship and their status within this relationship. These (power and control) dynamics may (negatively) impact the willingness of the African American male to emotionally invest in the helping relationship and thus have a negative impact on the development of trust within the therapeutic relationship. These factors may become particularly salient in cross-racial and cross-gendered helping relationships.

Anderson Franklin (1992) examines these issues as he explores how African American men engage in clinical relationships. One of the key issues he raises is the difficulty African American men may have with trust in the clinical relationship. African American men may exhibit a healthy "cultural paranoia" toward "helping" relationships in light of their prior experiences with racism and oppression (Grier & Cobbs, 1968). This cultural paranoia is especially evident in (helping) relationships that are focused on punitive or rehabilitative issues rather than helping relationships that have a developmental focus. It is in these types of helping relationships that the practitioner clearly represents the social order and may be seen as an agent of social control.

Without a doubt, key to working with African American men is the development of trust. One method suggested in the literature to achieve this sense of trust is to allow the African American male client to express a degree of skepticism without overly interpreting it (Franklin, 1992). Franklin elaborates;

> A common pitfall in work with African American men is engaging the process too quickly and thus undermining the therapeutic bond. ...Trust is a fundamental issue in work with African American men. Respect, genuineness, and integrity must be conveyed and should never be taken for granted, the African American man's openness to therapy and the helping process should be acknowledged and nourished. ... After trust is established, the empowerment process can begin. (p. 354)

Engagement as Reflective Dialogue

In the previous quote from Franklin (1994), respect, genuineness, and integrity are identified as being key to building trust in a clinical relationship with African American men. These factors are the basis for engaging the (African American male) client in the helping relationship. From a critical practice perspective, the first step in the clinical relationship with African American men is to engage them, through the medium of trust, in a reflective dialogical relationship. Here, the practitioner listens to their stories and explores their unique life experiences as they relate to personal problems. The practitioner also inquires about broader ethnocultural factors, such as race, class, culture, and gender, and their (potential) impact on the client's (self) "narrative" as well as their impact on the presenting problem.

The dialogical relationship involves the practitioner taking a ***nonhierarchial position*** in the client-worker relationship and becoming more of a "cultural consultant" to the African American male client. Describing the client as colleague is more suggestive of a mutual, culturally sensitive, and oppression-sensitive approach to counseling African American men (Ivey, 1995). The client becomes a partner with the practitioner in exploring different and more empowering "ways of being" and "ways of being masculine."

As the practitioner assumes this position in the dialogical relationship, he or she must be aware of his or her own social positionality (i.e., race, gender, and class) within the sociocultural and economic milieu. The practitioner's social location shapes the social context of the helping relationship and significantly impacts the dynamics of power. The dynamics of power and control are significant, however, regardless of the race or gender of the practitioner in therapy with the African American male.

Clinical Assessment as Critical Reflection

Understanding and assessing the presenting problems of African American men requires a broad conceptual lens that includes multiple levels of assessment. In this coinvestigation of Black mens' personal, social, and ethnocultural realities, both therapist and client identify in the client's life experiences those meaningful themes related to sociopolitical or relational constraints on the personal experiences of African American males (Korin, 1992). This stage of clinical assessment is followed by the process in which problems and contradictions in experiences are identified, with emphasis on the contextual issues. As the examination and reflection on the contradictions occur, major emotional changes (often anger) may occur (Ivey, 1995).

The problems are redefined and an unfolding "restorying" process is initiated while a new liberating perspective is identified (Laird, 1989). This liberating perspective is not just intrapersonal or interpersonal. It takes on the quality of understanding how the Black male's social, cultural, political, and economic context impacts his sense of personal and social power. This process encourages a reconnection with self and culture. It also allows one to be aware of the ability to reconstruct one's own reality.

Ivey (1995, pp. 68-69) provides the following assessment questions that can be helpful at this stage of critical reflection:

What is common to your stories? What are the patterns (themes)?

How do you think about these stories, and how could you think about them differently?

Which of your behaviors and thoughts are yours? Which of them come from your cultural surrounding and life history?

How do family stories and family history relate to your conception of self? Of your cultural background? How do the two relate?

What parts of you are driven by internal forces and what parts are driven by external forces? How can you tell the difference?

Standing back, what inconsistencies can you identify?

As you look back on all we've talked about and/or done, what stands out for you? How? Why? How do you/we put together all we've talked about?

What rule(s) were you (or the other person or group) operating under? Where did the rule come from? How might someone else describe that situation (another family member, a member of the opposition, or someone from a different cultural background)? How do these rules relate to us now?

How might we describe this from the point of view of some other person, theoretical framework, or language system? How might we put it together using another framework?

What does our family and our educational or work history say about the development and operation of oppression?

What shall we do? How shall we do it together? What is our objective and how can we work together effectively? Or likely, How can the client-colleague manage his or her own affairs and take action as a leader in his or her own right?

Although these questions are not gender or race specific, they can be modified and adapted for use with African American men. These questions have experiential and existential import—that is, they connect the presenting problem with the larger sociopolitical themes of African American men. These questions also allow for a critical inquiry about the specific social context(s) or social location(s) in which an African American male's multiple experiences are embedded. This inquiry allows both the clinician and the client to identify the unique impact of the African American man's experiences with oppression and the inherent contradictions emerging from his position within **multiple** sociopolitical locations. Equally important, this critical reflection also allows for an understanding of whether the African American male client has internalized narratives that are supportive, liberating, and potentiating or narratives that are constrictive or destructive.

Clinical Intervention as Liberating Action

Liberating action gives birth to a state of critical consciousness. Liberating action then becomes the basis and goal of intervention with the African American male as critical reflection and action becomes the basis for personal, interpersonal, and social change. Franz Fanon (1967) gives direction to the need for liberating action; he states,

> When the Negro makes contact with the White world, a certain sensitizing action takes place. If his psychic structure is weak, one observes a collapse of the ego. The Black man stops behaving as an actional person. The goal of his behavior will be The Other (in the guise of a White man). For the Other alone can give his worth ... self esteem. (p. 154)

Freire (1983) echoes these sentiments; he states,

> One of the basic elements of the relationship between the oppressors and oppressed is prescription. Every prescription represents the imposition of one man's choice upon another, transforming the consciousness of the man transcribed to into one that conforms with the prescriber's consciousness. Thus, the behavior of the oppressed is prescribed behavior, following as it does the guidelines of the oppressor. The oppressed having internalized the image of the oppressor and adopted his guidelines are fearful of freedom. Freedom would require them to reject this image and replace it with autonomy and responsibility. Freedom is acquired by conquest, not by gift. It must be pursued constantly and responsibly. Freedom is not an ideal located outside of man. (p. 31)

Hence, Fanon (1967) and Freire (1983) assert that one of the main impacts of racism and oppression is that it fragments the self and robs a person of a sense of "agency" or purpose. Thus, by implication, the goal of clinical intervention with African American men is to restore and strengthen the autonomous functioning of the ego and achieve a sense of autonomy from "The Other" (i.e., the oppressor) and encourage African American men to be "actional persons."

Liberation is achieved through the capacity to understand the internalization of oppression through narratives that prescribe behaviors from the oppressor and to say **"no"** to those prescriptions. This rejection is achieved through the creation of alternate narratives. As Freire (1983) points out, this sense of autonomy may not be easily achieved, it requires inner struggle that leads to outside action.

The nature of this struggle is articulated by Wimberly (1997a) as he describes the process of reauthoring one's narrative. According to Wimberly, the reauthoring process, although possible and necessary, is not easy. Even though life narratives (worldviews) emerge from the lived experiences of the narrator and are given meaning through the process of social interaction, they often seem fixed, immutable, and have a sense of ontological authenticity. These narratives, however, can be challenged by significant life transitions and crisis. Such crisis can shatter the existing narrative and thus precipitate a restorying process that enables one to meet new challenges or to explain a current situation that has great emotional significance.

An example of this process is reflected in the experiences of an African American male college student in his early twenties following the Rodney King incident:

> Jerome, who grew up in an integrated community, went to a predominately White, state university in the southwest and was a member of a predominately White fraternity. He had his worldview shattered following the Rodney King incident. Prior to the event, he adamantly defended a worldview of assimilation. Following the incident, he entered therapy with one of the authors, visibly confused, shattered, and angry. He spoke of his disillusionment with White people, especially his White "friends." This event precipitated a journey toward redefining himself as a African American male rather than a male who happened to be African American. Later in his college career, he placed first in a "Mr. Positive Black Male" event. This pageant involved a presentation and research on key elements of African American history.

Jerome's journey in many ways is an example of the stages within the Minority Identity Development model (Cross, 1995). Jerome moved from an active Preencounter stage (the idealization of Whites and the denigration of "blackness") to an immersion-emersion stage (the idealization of blackness and increasing distance from Whites).

Another consideration is his stage of (psychosocial) development. As a late adolescent, Jerome was still in the process of consolidating his personal identity. This example demonstrates how a contemporary racially charged event propelled this young African American **male** to reauthor his personal narrative regarding his African American male identity. This is but one example of the "racial restorying" process precipitated by crisis and transition.

Reauthoring, restorying, or reediting one's narrative can open up new possibilities that otherwise might be hidden or not allowed to come forth. White and Epston (1990) describe this process as discovering hidden possibilities or "historically unique outcomes" (p. 56). As for Jerome, he discovered new possibilities and sought out new information from his African American heritage that contradicted his preencounter narrative. His new narrative gave his life new meaning and a new (positive) attribution of self.

Challenging Stress Through Liberating Action

In counseling with African American men, practitioners can use narrative and "cognitive" methods that help the client cope with anger, frustration, and stress and interrupt these emotions before they escalate (Johnson, 1998). The therapeutic task is to engage the African American male client to

1. Identify situations in which he becomes highly emotionally reactive and stressed

2. Identify the core beliefs, values, assumptions, and attitudes underlying one's problems with a particular situation or stressor

3. Identify and interrupt habitual ways of looking at the world and examine how inner dialogue and body language can trigger anger, stress, and rage

4. Challenge limiting narratives that habitually cause rage and or stress reactions

5. Develop more effective ways to cope with stress and anger through reauthored narratives and new behaviors

These therapeutic tasks (for coping with stress) are a logical choice for some of the presenting problems of African American men, in large part due to their briefness and directness. Clinicians must be extremely cautious, however, not to convey the belief that the problems facing African American men can always be eradicated quickly and solely through a change of cognition or perceptions. This approach does have empowering implications in its ability to enhance coping by countering negative internalized narratives or self-talk. Of equal importance, this approach can further empower African American men to take action against externalized discriminatory practices. In essence, this approach can enhance self-worth and move African American men toward creating more empowering (personal) narratives and a heightened sense of social and political consciousness and activity.

The last and most crucial step in the process of developing interventions to support liberating action is the mobilizing of African American men to change their context. This task is accomplished by identifying new narratives or **editing** existing narratives that potentiate and empower them as Black men. Here, practitioners facilitate Black men's movement toward transforming their lives and challenging "limiting situations" or personal and social problems that constrain or marginalize their potential.

Liberation as Reconnection

We suggest that liberation in the context of the critical practice approach for African American men is not just a movement toward self-transformation, developing a sense of hyperindividuality, or achieving (ego) autonomy from the social order. Liberating action also involves the client and practitioner codeveloping strategies for the African American male's reconnection to a communal or ecological perspective. The goal of intervention is to facilitate a connection with an Africentric worldview and the existing, latent, and potential strength that resides within the broader African American family and community.

Wimberly (1997a) suggests that the reauthored narratives for the African American male should include the capacity to see the world through the eyes of African American women. This could increase the African American male's empathy for the African American woman. The outcome could be a challenge of the hegemonic and compulsive masculinity (indicative of [an idealized] Eurocentric perspective) in favor of the more communal, egalitarian, and androgynous position that is more representative of an Africentric cultural frame of reference (Wimberly, 1997a). Such narratives can support the effort at understanding issues of male-female relationships in new and more potentiating ways.

Reauthored narratives for African American men should also promote cross-generational connectedness. To view oneself as a integrated part of a family, with heritage across generations, creates a repository of strength and connection for the African American male. In a traditional African sense, it allows men to connect with the "ancestors" and to find their niche in a multigenerational history of struggle, resiliency, and survival.

Practice Application: Case Illustration and Case Discussion

To further illustrate how a critical practice approach informs the engagement, assessment, and interventive planning processes in individual therapy and counseling with African American men, the following case is presented.

Case Illustration

Mr. Samuels (a pseudonym) is a 44-year-old, single African American male who was seen in individual therapy by one of the authors. Mr. Samuels's presenting concerns were recurring crying spells, feelings of sadness, poor concentration, and overall depression. These feelings, which lasted more than 2 months, were beginning to impact his job performance; he was a lead chemical engineer in a local chemical manufacturing company. He described himself as one who had always been in control of his emotions. He was now concerned that he was gradually losing control, and he did not know how to handle his feelings of depression, because this was a completely new experience for him. There were several recent events that he believed were contributing to his current emotional state. One significant event was the recent separation and pending divorce of his parents after 50 years of marriage. Mr. Samuels had also ended a relatively long-term relationship. In addition, his 48-year-old brother was a drug addict and recently lost his job. For the past year, Mr. Samuels attempted to persuade his brother to get substance abuse treatment to no avail. He is also concerned that these losses are propelling him into a "midlife crisis" in that he is now questioning his views about himself, relationships, and his spiritual values.

Case Discussion

Diagnostically, Mr. Samuels is manifesting an adjustment disorder with depressed mood. His difficulties and depression revolve around coping with a series of significant losses in his life. These losses have caused him to reevaluate many aspects of his life, thrusting him into what he has defined as a midlife crisis. The mutual established goal of intervention was to work toward alleviating his depression so that he could return to his previous level of functioning. The specific objectives for intervention were for him to verbalize his disappointments related to his recent losses and to identify internal cognitive messages that supported his depression. During the therapy process, key elements of the (integrative) critical practice approach guide exploration of how his experiences as a Black male contribute to his depression.

In the second session, Mr. Samuels was asked to what extent did being a Black male impact his depression or contribute to the presenting problems. This line of inquiry was appropriate in that Mr. Samuels had requested, through his company's Employee Assistance Program, an African American therapist. Rather than exploring why he wanted to be seen by an African American, engagement in a *reflective dialogue* provided the format for discussing his unique lived experience(s) as a Black male.

As we began to *critically reflect* on his experiences, he began to examine how his sense of personal identity, self-esteem, sense of personal agency, and identity as a Black male changed and shifted as he moved through various roles and situations in his life, including his workplace, his intimate relationships, and his role as son and sibling in his family of origin. It was significant how these multiple and somewhat contradictory experiences contributed to his depression.

In his family of origin, his perception was that his siblings always saw him as "different." He was a serious student and had always been career driven. Since he had achieved a degree of success, he believed that his siblings both admired and envied him. This family dynamic, along with the fact that he was closer to his parents than to his siblings, caused a sense of alienation and disengagement from his siblings. Although he still had a concern for his siblings, it was difficult for him to help his brother with his drug addiction.

From his college experiences, he developed a degree of comfort in interracial relationships to the extent that he felt his family did not quite understand his worldview, which they believed was "White." This worldview, which he describes as somewhat conservative, had impacted other areas of his life. Although he did not date interracially, his experience was that many Black women had questioned his "blackness" due to his other intellectual interests and his comfort in being in a predominately White work environment. Several of the women in his life had failed to acknowledge his "wider self," which he believed transcended stereotypes of what are considered stereotypical to be "Black male interests." Furthermore, he believed he had to continually justify his interests in addition to proving his blackness. The recently broken relationship was especially significant in that this person was one of the few who accepted his complexity. He was beginning to consider marriage for the first time when the relationship began to dissolve. He was not only concerned about the loss of this relationship but also concerned about finding another relationship in which he did not feel he had to prove his blackness.

Finally, being the only Black male in a professional and supervisory position in his company, he encountered several situations in which his authority was challenged. He was not sure whether his subordinates challenged him because he was Black, because he was a supervisor, or both. His work environment was highly competitive. He was uncertain to what extent the competitive environment of the workplace contributed to his difficulty. He was also aware that perhaps race played a critical part in his supervisory interactions. His prime concern was that he had no experiential or cognitive framework in which to decipher and interpret his colleagues' responses and reactions to him.

His depression compounded his problem in that he did not believe that there was anyone in his work environment or social network who he could call on for peer support. He believed he had to maintain the image of self-control on the job and not appear to be weak, vulnerable, or incompetent. He wondered or suspected that as a Black male he was under additional scrutiny by work peers and upper management. Being in such a position, he felt powerless, increasingly unable to maintain the persona of self-control, and fearful that such a persona would shatter and his real vulnerability would be exposed.

The intervention or *liberating action* phase focused on challenging the internalized cognitive and essentialistic representations of blackness and of Black males that caused him to question his own identity and that supported his depression. These images are interpreted as oppressive beliefs generated within the social order and internalized as constraining beliefs about self. Attention was given to multiple but sometimes competing ways of being a Black male and how this contributed to his depression.

We examined how to live with this tension and how to contest the limiting representations or negotiate multiple meanings of Black maleness rather than deny or ignore the fact that there are multiple ways of being a Black male. As we talked about how to contest these limiting representations and affirm liberating representations both internally and externally, we discussed how he could be more assertive on the job and in relationships on issues of Black maleness. In the workplace, the task was to identify and address racism as it impacted his job. In intimate relationships, the task was to affirm representations and expressions of himself that challenged the notion of a singular way of being a Black male.

Also important for him was to reconnect with a Black religious institution. He believed that he needed a spiritual reconnection that included both his spiritual self and a communal self. He wanted that sense of membership in a church.

This case illustrates the meaning of being an African American male and the impact this has on Mr. Samuels's psychological distress. This discussion is followed by a critical reflection of how the experience of being a Black male reflected dimensions of class, gender, and race. Furthermore, these reflections reveal how monolithic views of Black maleness contribute to the presenting problem(s). Without such critical reflections on the impact of sociocultural and sociopolitical realities and by focusing only on loss issues, the therapist would not have attended to the salient impact of these important factors in Mr. Samuels's life.

One of the clinical issues addressed with Mr. Samuels is how to liberate or differentiate a sense of intact self from his family of origin while maintaining a healthier emotional reconnection with his family. Using the authors' integrative critical practice approach, a corresponding clinical objective is to liberate a sense of unique self as a Black male from limiting or essentialistic representations of Black maleness. This liberating action technique freed him to consider more gratifying relationships but could be accomplished only by maintaining an awareness and connectedness with the broader but complex sociocultural experience of blackness.

SUMMARY

Using an integrative critical practice approach in attempting to understand the African American male experience offers the potential for an important shift toward a perspective or framework that supports the expression of multiple and varied worldviews and emphasizes the relativity of gender, race, culture, and ethnicity. This clinical framework also emphasizes the variability of the impact of these multiple worldviews on the individual experiences of African American men. Practitioners need to hear the unique sociocultural voice(s) of their Black male clients and should not have to compare or evaluate their understanding of African American men to other gender or ethnocultural groups. The integrative critical practice approach represents a potentially important cross-cultural assessment and interventive framework that can facilitate the overall provision of individually tailored, culturally sensitive (i.e., culturally appropriate and effective), and oppression-sensitive practice with African American men.

CONCLUSION

We emphasize how critical social theory, critical consciousness, and Africentrism are important elements within the total gestalt of the *integrative critical practice approach.* These theories help to contextualize the (individualized) meaning of the lived experiences of African American males by locating their experiences within a specific historical, economic, political, and sociocultural context. This is an important feature considering that Black men's experiences are largely and objectively negative, oppressive, nonaffirming, and depotentiating.

Hence, clinical interventions (individual, couple, family, or group work) with African American men that are driven by an integrative critical practice perspective must also integrate the "deconstructionist" quality inherent within the critical consciousness perspectives. That is, practitioners must empower Black men to become agents of their own choices by first encouraging them to tell their individual stories and then helping them to deconstruct (immobilizing and marginalizing narratives) and later reconstruct these stories in a way that empowers them. This restorying process must also be directed at multisystems (i.e., macro and micro) levels of intervention activities and outcomes, lest we become coauthors of denial and hence the "gatekeepers" of the status quo in our own (clinical) practice with African American men.

NOTE

1. The terms therapy and counseling are used interchangeably throughout this chapter and the book. In addition, the terms therapist, counselor, practitioner, and clinician are also used interchangeably. We acknowledge that some disciplines make a distinction between the processes of counseling and therapy, with the former helping process being a less intense version of clinical practice than the latter helping process.

Chapter 5

COUPLE THERAPY WITH AFRICAN AMERICAN MEN

The African American conjugal dyad is the most neglected subsystem in the clinical practice literature. Even within the clinical practice literature on the various dyads and subsystems within the Black family, the clinical literature on African American couples is quite sparse. Needless to say, clinical practice literature specifically exploring male (gender) issues in conducting couple counseling and therapy with African American men is practically nonexistent.

This chapter is an attempt to articulate clinical issues that are salient in the conjugal relationships of African American men and their partners. Hence, in keeping with the focus of this book, this chapter is not intended to be a complete examination and discussion of gender issues facing both African American men and women. For the sake of a more holistic and contextualized treatment of this topic, however, this chapter does examine issues that are generic to conducting couple counseling and therapy with African American couples.[1] Therefore, the primary focus and intent of this chapter is to articulate and examine clinical issues that need to be considered in couple therapy involving African American men.

Specifically, this chapter examines the impact of the unique sociocultural issues on the dynamics of the conjugal relationships of African American men. Clinical issues in engagement, assessment, and intervention that clinicians face in couple therapy with African American men as a result of these unique sociocultural factors are presented.

SOCIOCULTURAL FACTORS AND THE AFRICAN AMERICAN CONJUGAL DYAD: BACKGROUND AND OVERVIEW

The sociological and psychological research literature on African American marriages concludes that Black male-female relationships are no more problem ridden than male-female relationships within other ethnocultural groups (Aldridge, 1991). Current research shows, however, a significant decline in marriage, a significant increase in divorce, and an increased separation between marriage and childbearing among Blacks (Dickson, 1993). Sociologists interpret these statistics as being more indicative of the unstabilizing impact of the economy and unavailability of Black men for marriage (in light of enumerable social problems) as opposed to a statement about the quality of marriage relationships between Blacks (Dickson, 1993; Gibbs, 1988; Wilson, 1987).

Regardless of the previous statistics, it is important that practitioners and social scientists be aware of, understand, and address sociocultural factors that operate to **uniquely** impact the dynamics of African American couples. A review of the literature reveals the following factors in American society that profoundly impact the conjugal relationships and thus inform the worldview of African American couples and marriages (Aldridge, 1991; Boyd-Franklin, 1989; Braithwaite, 1981; Wimberly, 1997b):

1. Racial oppression of African American men and women
2. Bicultural challenges or pressures involved in living in two cultures at the same time
3. Sexism and gender socialization issues
4. Culturally dystonic modes of connecting within the conjugal relationship and uncritical assimilation of dominant (Eurocentric) cultural values into the conjugal relationship
5. Capitalism and effects of class differences within (Black) male-female relationships
6. Scarcity of Black men
7. Negative and stereotypical (societal) images of Black men
8. Extended family issues
9. Religious values and spirituality
10. Africentric ideology and cultural strengths

These unique sociocultural factors form the foundation for the bulk of this chapter, which examines the dynamics of African American couples, the impact of sociocultural factors on the clinical process, and implications for couple therapy.

CLINICAL ISSUES IN COUPLE COUNSELING
WITH AFRICAN AMERICAN MEN
Engagement of African American Men in Couple Therapy

In the previous chapter, we examined the critical therapeutic task of engagement of Black men in individual therapy. This chapter extends the prior discussion to issues of engagement of African American men within the context of couple therapy. Dr. Nancy Boyd-Franklin (1989) articulates, "Black men in particular, resent the feeling of being 'summoned' to come in [for couple therapy]" (p. 230). Boyd-Franklin encourages Black females to avoid ultimatums to get Black men to receive couple therapy and further suggests that therapists call the men directly and not use the women as messengers. We suspect that this advice derives from the knowledge that African American women are more apt to already be involved in the social service and mental health delivery systems than are Black men. Hence, additional (potential) gender-related power dynamics may be exacerbated by the Black male's fear of entering a situation in which his partner may have established unequal leverage (in reference to the issues to be dealt with, etc.) in light of the partner's preexisting relationship with the therapist and the service delivery system. These fears are not unrealistic given the uneasy relationship that African American men typically experience with social service and mental health delivery systems. Their experiences with these systems are frequently characterized by coercion, dread, apprehension, exclusion, paternalism, avoidance, or all these (Leashore, 1981; Parham & McDavis, 1987).

Hence, we recommend clinicians take the following steps toward engagement of African American men in couple therapy:

1. The practitioner should tell the female that he or she will be calling the male partner; the practitioner should specifically elicit the male's point of view regarding the therapy and so on.

2. In the initial telephone conversation, the practitioner should express an interest in establishing a separate time to get to know the male, especially if the female has already been engaged in an individual therapy or counseling process.

3. In cases in which the therapist has had no prior contact with either partner, we suggest that the initial phone conversation regarding (couple) therapy be held with both parties to avoid any unbalancing of therapeutic alliances. This measure is especially crucial in light of the factors articulated in the previous discussion.

4. In the initial (individual) interview that is conducted in anticipation and in preparation for the actual couple therapy, practitioners are encouraged to first explore the Black male's prior experiences, apprehensions, and expectations with regard to social service and mental health delivery systems in general, the counseling or therapy process, the therapist and his or her race and gender, how the therapist plans to handle any prior working relationship with the partner, and the practitioners' attitudes toward African American men and their unique experiences as males and as spouses.

5. In the initial (conjoint) couple interview, practitioners should emphasize to the African American couple their interest and intent to effect a multisystems or ecosystemic interventive approach to ally apprehensions that the couple may have about the "therapy chamber" being used a vehicle for "blaming the victim" when real external social problems are present.

6. After the initial individual and conjoint interviews, therapists are strongly encouraged to be reflective of potential transference and countertransference issues that arise and to challenge themselves with regard to ethnocentric notions and biases resulting from their own sociostructural racial or gender position—especially those that may be unique to working with African American couples in general and with Black men in particular. Female clinicians are especially encouraged to initiate discussion of gender issues, to ally fears that the male may have (or expectations that the female may have) regarding alliances that may develop based on gender.

We are aware that the previously outlined steps represent sound clinical practice for all couples, regardless of ethnocultural membership. These steps, however, are carefully articulated here because they are viewed as crucial engagement strategies in working with African American men in couple therapy in light of the unique clinical issues frequently presented by African American men.

General Clinical Issues in the Assessment of African American Couples in Therapy

Boyd-Franklin (1989) emphasizes that there is no such phenomenon as **the** African American couple or family, and that each couple or family should be evaluated with their own set of problems and concerns. Clinicians should also be prepared for an **elongated diagnostic phase** in couple and family therapy with African Americans because of the unique and complex societal factors facing African American men that need to be understood with reference to their implications for couple therapy.

There are several factors that contribute to the prolonged assessment phase that is necessary in couple work with many African Americans. For instance, many clinicians observe that African American couples are more likely to enter the counseling process via a child-focused concern (Boyd-Franklin, 1989). Additionally, many African American couples may enter counseling when the presenting problem is financial and they are not necessarily seeking couple counseling. The therapist's task in these situations is to carefully consider the couple's initial interpretation and even attempt an intervention to deal with the initial presenting problem (as deemed appropriate) as a gesture toward building trust and credibility with the couple. The therapist is encouraged to get the couple to redirect these initial complaints, however, if indeed the therapist believes that the presenting problem is merely the beginning of more complex dyadic difficulties.

Other ecological realities (i.e., racism and poverty) also serve to extend the assessment phase in couple and family work with African Americans by virtue of their complicating impact on the lives of these individuals. For instance, economic instability may have operated to undermine prior relationships and thus result in longer and more complex social histories that need to be taken and understood by the practitioner. In addition, larger, dense, and more complex and varied familial networks will also likely result in a longer assessment phase. Therefore, it is imperative that clinicians discard existing temporal templates for completing the assessment process and truly allow the couple's unique history to dictate the length of the diagnostic phase.

Sociocultural Factors and the African American Couple: Impact on Couple Dynamics and Implications for Couple Therapy

Racial Oppression

The noxious influence of racism on the interpersonal relationships of Black couples is probably one of the most widely documented factors in the social science literature. The omnipresent and deleterious impact of racism on the African American conjugal dyad cannot be overemphasized. Paying particular attention to the impact of race and racial oppression is especially important in light of scenarios in which many Black couples present for counseling and are adept at camouflaging stress and pain they are experiencing at the hands of racial oppression. Hence, counselors may erroneously assume that institutional and individual racism is not a major factor in the dynamics of the couple.

It is particularly important for counselors to be cognizant of the "traditional male code" that may dictate that the (Black) male should suffer in silence and opt to deny, avoid, or suppress his anger and rage about racial oppression. Hence, it is important for practitioners to assess several clinical issues resulting from the effects of racial oppression and its impact on the African American conjugal relationship. First, practitioners must not allow other relationship factors to detour discussion about racism, in that the couple may prefer not to deal with such a "weighty" issue. In our clinical supervisory and consultative experiences, we have observed counselors collude with Black couples in avoiding this topic. Additionally, practitioners need to be prepared to deal with one partner turning on the other when this topic is discussed—often out of feelings of exasperation and a need to locate a source for their anger and frustration. Practitioners are reminded that Black couple members have the dual burden of dealing with their own individual racist experiences and the racist experiences of their partners.

African American couples' reaction to racism and the pain that it causes may take many different forms. As in any other affective or behavioral response to stress, some reactions are more apparent, severe, enduring, or all three than other reactions. In our clinical and supervisory experiences, we have witnessed the stress of racism and oppression resulting in mild (temporary) adjustment disorders or (recurrent) major depression. We have also worked with African Americans for whom we suspect their personality development is profoundly impacted by the chronic stress of racism. Predictably, these individual reactions typically have a significant impact on the conjugal dynamics, if only in that it adds another layer of stress and issues of which the African American couple must contend. Other

more complex conjugal dynamics may emerge, as in situations in which one partner may be irritated or angry with the other for avoiding or internalizing racist situations or merely not handling the situation in the way that he or she would have
elected to do so. Certainly, couples may also experience pain in relation to racism
as one partner realizes that some of his or her pressing emotional needs will not
be dealt with because his or her partner is too overwhelmed and distracted by
racist situations. The following vignette illustrates how the pain of racism
affects African American couples and how these issues can be handled in couple therapy.

Wayne and Carol are an African American couple in their thirties.
They married right after graduating from college. (He received his MBA
and she received her degree in journalism.) They have both been very
successful in their careers; early on, however, Carol experienced some
difficulty in getting decent news assignments. She has always attributed
this to racism and that she believes her dark complexion, short kinky
hair (a source of insecurity despite her husband's obvious physical attraction
to her) and "invisible ceiling quotas" on Black women in high-profile
positions in journalism work against her. Wayne has been especially supportive of Carol in her struggle with the "light skin, long hair" issue and
personally gets angry as they both watch Black and Brown women who
fit this description get the more high-profile assignments. Carol's "in-
your-face" style in dealing with issues of racism (and other issues) has
been a mixed blessing for her with regard to her career and her marriage.
Carol's directness was one of the qualities that most attracted Wayne to
her, and he believes she compliments his "strong, silent" demeanor.
Carol enjoys the intensity of their emotional relationship and believes
that Wayne's more laid-back, attentive style compliments her needs as
well, especially when she returns home from what she describes as
"doing battle with White folks."
Wayne is considering leaving the firm at which he currently works
and starting his own. He has grown weary and pessimistic about ever
making partner, despite his ability to attract some of the highest grossing
accounts. Carol was supportive of this move a few years ago but is now
wanting to start their family and is nervous about "cash flow" at such a
critical time. Wayne knows his market and feels that the time to move is
now, lest his competitors (including his current firm) edge him out. They
are now at an impasse regarding the timing of the pregnancy. Carol feels
strongly about not being a first-time mom at age 40; and Wayne recognizes that he is never going to break into the inner circle of all White
males at his firm.
Carol is silently angry at Wayne and believes that he should have
been more outspoken regarding his aspirations earlier on with the firm or
should have left. She believes that he did not explore all his options at
his job, because they are always being invited to social functions and
weekend getaways with the "power players." Carol believes that Wayne's
pleasant, ambassador-like demeanor (a quiet confidence) and his striking
physical appearance (Wayne is more than 6 feet tall with bronzed complexion and piercing green eyes, and he has a strong, squared jawline
with high cheekbones), coupled with his obvious competence, make him
a perfect "affirmative action" partner. Wayne becomes very angry when
Carol makes reference to his less aggressive style and more exotic physical features as a possible marketing tool because he really identifies with
Carol's pain when they both agree that she has been shunned due to the

combination of her (very African-looking) physical appearance and aggressive demeanor.

The issues of Wayne's entrepreneurial interest, Carol's wanting to start their family, Carol's continued frustration with her news job, and their anger at each other have caused them to stop being supportive of each other on a daily basis. They entered couple counseling because both believed that they did not know how to bridge the gap that had developed between them and are afraid of continuing to move in opposite directions.

Their therapy focused on getting them to talk about prevailing societal stereotypes of Black men and women—given certain physical features and personality styles—to help them regain the empathy that they obviously once had for each other's unique position and to get rid of some of the anger that had developed. Their counseling also encouraged them to revisit and reflect on Africentric values, which would help them to see the gestalt instead of the smaller picture, with the hope that some of the principles of *collectivity, interdependence*, and *mutuality* would begin to reshape their perception of the situation and hence guide their actions. (This therapeutic move was, in part, inspired by the fact that this couple was very Africentric in their dress and recreational activities. Hence, the therapist anticipated their receptiveness to these ideological principles and goals.)

In the vignette, one can see how getting the couple to process their reaction(s) to racism can be an ideal opportunity to initiate mutual dialogue that will well serve the African American couple and encourage them to become supports for each other in a (racially) hostile environment.

Black men's awareness of racism in the workplace and resulting fear of occupational and economic failure may cause them to feel a need to work extra hours and result in their becoming "visiting dignitaries" to their spouses and children. These types of complaints should be evaluated in light of the impact of racism, which can result in a "hyperinternalization" of the "traditional male code." African American women, however, may also give way to the (American) capitalist ethos and conform exclusively to marketplace values. This may result in both partners laboring under demanding work environments that can cause them to neglect their marriage and hence operate to frustrate the growth of African American marriages (Aldridge, 1991).

Practitioners need to consider giving the African American male time alone in counseling to confront and manage fears regarding perceived failure as sole provider in the traditional male role. This therapeutic measure is seen as helpful so as not to interfere and possibly tilt the power dynamics within the conjugal relationship by giving the impression that the therapist is showing more empathy to the plight of the Black male and thus "siding" with the male and that the Black female should somehow "just deal with it." Individual sessions may also allow the male to be more open and forthcoming with his feelings of failure or vulnerability or both within traditional (societal) gender expectations. It is also recommended, however, that this issue eventually be brought back to the conjoint couple counseling session to encourage feelings of empathy within their mate and create a climate more conducive to negotiation.

Bicultural Challenges

Being bicultural refers to living in two cultures simultaneously; for African Americans, it is a sense of being both African and American at the same time. Most theorists agree that having the proper balance between African American heritage and assimilation into American culture is essential for healthy psychological functioning (Aldridge, 1991; Wimberly, 1997b). (Dubois [1961] refers to this phenomenon as having a "double consciousness".) Theorists also agree that uncritical assimilation into dominant cultural values can cause a great deal of stress and strain on relationships between Black males and females (Wimberly, 1997b). For example, issues of "emotional cut-off" within extended families may result as the individual begins to feel "too different" from family members and distances himself or herself from family members, thus causing additional strain on the conjugal relationship. Additionally, the couple may begin to neglect their cultural ties to the Black community and possibly weaken (potential) systems of social support.

The extent to which one partner has achieved a higher level of assimilation and acculturation into mainstream society (compared to the other partner) is another important consideration for the clinician. Very disparate levels of acculturation and assimilation can be especially problematic for Black couples and can have a significant impact on the power dynamics and conflicts. These acculturative differences (within the conjugal dyad) can account for many ensuing conflicts over issues of child rearing, recreation, place of residence, friendship network, and so on. In essence, power struggles and conjugal conflicts within Black male-female relationships should always be assessed to determine if "acculturative tensions" and "acculturative conflicts" within the conjugal dyad are indeed playing a role.

Compounding the previous scenarios are situations in which individual partners may be dealing with *invisible loyalties* (Boszoremenyi-Nagy, 1987).[2] We expand this concept to include ***invisible cultural loyalties.*** Invisible cultural loyalties may be very potent sources of strain on African American couples; therapists may discover that these bicultural and acculturative differences or conflicts may have intergenerational familial origins. No doubt, resolving these familial-based ledgers, debts, or (cultural) commitments, which may date back over several generations, can be a clinically complex and painful process for the couple. The following case vignette illustrates some of the issues presented in this section.

> Kenneth and Marian have been married for 15 years and they have one child (age 16) from this union and adult children from previous marriages. They have experienced chronic conflict over childrearing issues and how to recreate, and at times take issue with each other's selection of friends. It appears that the theme in these tensions and conflicts can be described and categorized as ***acculturative tensions*** and ***acculturative conflicts.***
>
> Kenneth comes from a "working-poor" family with strong ethnic ties to the African American community. His mother is a well-known and respected lay-community activist. Kenneth's ethnic identity can be described as being "culturally immersed," with only a few very selective areas of behavior being acculturated or assimilated. His (extended) fami-

ly has also adopted many ethnic traditions, such as the outdoor dedication of newborns to God and the universe, the celebration of Kwanzaa, and that most of the marriages in this family feature a definitive African flavor.

Marian is a member of the third generation in her family to attend college. Marian's ethnic identity can be described as being a more bicultural and integrative style, as is reflective of her family's values. Two of her four siblings are interracially married, and Marian's mother (a retired teacher) is a member of a prestigious Black women's social organization.

For the most part, this couple has been able to avoid major rifts in their relationships as a results of their different cultural and ethnic styles, but both admit that they are not as close as they could be in many regards.

Sixteen-year-old Tiffany (the father wanted her to be named Ebony) is beginning to seriously consider the college of her choice. Kenneth and his extended family are hoping that she will attend an historically Black college. (Kenneth's grandmother left a $50 U.S. savings bond to Fisk University when she died—she was a cook there many years ago.) Marian prefers that Tiffany attend a Big Ten university because she believes there are more curriculum offerings, and Tiffany has yet to settle on a major. (Marian's parents attended the University of Wisconsin-Madison and continue to be very active in the local alumni chapter.)

This couple actually presented with the complaint that they fear that they are drifting apart and their differences are becoming less tolerable, especially regarding childrearing and recreational activities. Kenneth becomes concerned when he does not see Tiffany socializing with Black friends or listening to "Black" music. This gets Marian quite angry with Kenneth, and she believes that he is a closet racist. They also admit that they are very close to their respective extended families, and that many times their (potential) divisions are fueled by their extended families.

Their therapy was focused on reframing their difficulties from personality differences and getting them to see that these differences are more culturally based and very likely reinforced by their perspective families of origin. As this couple moved through a psychoeducative process of understanding different cultural and ethnic identities, they were also encouraged to work on developing a positive appreciation for differences in this regard. The next phase of therapy entailed the exploration of family of origin issues with reference to the aforementioned concepts of invisible cultural loyalties. As it turns out, this therapeutic move was very powerful and very effective in that it helped the couple to see how powerful forces were entering into their conflicts. This insight empowered them to rethink some of their own choices in this regard and to consider the overall needs of their own family of procreation and conjugal dyad. It should be noted that it was important to conduct individual sessions with each partner to enable them to explore family of origin issues without the influence or intrusion of the other partner so as to give each of them the space to freely examine their issues.

Africentrism: Building on Cultural Strengths

We take the ideological position that African-based cultural values should drive the couple therapy and counseling goals with African Americans. African-based cultural values should be used as guiding principles that have the potential to facilitate important problem-solving processes, such as negotiation and compromise. The following are Africentric principles recommended for incorporation into couple counseling with Black couples:

Interdependence and collectivity: the importance of working together for the mutual good of the relationship, with the philosophy that all contributions to the relationship, family, and community are equally important

Humanism and spirituality: the ability to allow a concern and a commitment for one's partner to override one's own agenda and concern for self

Harmony with nature: an acknowledgment and acceptance of the natural flow and rhythm of each partner's developmental life cycle, which inevitably introduces changes in one's partner's needs and issues that should be affirmed by the other

African American couples should also be encouraged to build on the many ethnocultural strengths, such as flexibility in conjugal roles, strong kinship bonds (that can especially well serve young Black couples who need mentors and conjugal role models), a humanistic orientation, and a commitment to religious values (Billingsley, 1968; Braithwaite, 1981; Hill, 1972; McAdoo, 1978; Nobles, 1978; Stack, 1974; Staples, 1971).

Asante (1981) notes that there are four aspects of an Africentric relationship that should be nurtured and developed within Black male-female relationships: sacrifice (each partner is willing to give up certain aspects of himself or herself for the advancement of an Africentric people), inspiration (the productive and creative maintenance of the collective cognitive imperative), vision (establishing a purpose outside of and beyond the daily considerations of living), and victory (deriving pleasure out of the sense of importance of the relationship for the sake of the advancement of African peoples).

Hopson and Hopson (1998) rearticulate these Africentric principles with a different spin. They suggest that African American couples become "soul mates" in the relationship and pursue a more fulfilling relationship, self, and an empowered, thriving community. These goals are achieved largely through an open, active, and proactive examination of the impact of racism and sexism on the conjugal relationship (Hopson & Hopson, 1994). (In the evolution of their thinking and ideology, Hopson and Hopson [1998] take on a decidedly spiritual, if not religious, orientation to their approach to couple counseling with African Americans [discussed in the following section].)

Wimberly (1997b) reinterprets these same Africentric values as he emphasizes mutuality, androgyny, and egalitarianism (in guiding gender role behaviors) as ideological and spiritual goals in the Black male-female relationship. Within this ideological position, couples work together to survive the stressors of racism, oppression, (White male) sexism, capitalism, and harsh socioeconomic realities. These factors create a sociocultural context that gives rise to gender role behaviors that are more culturally syntonic and eventuate the unique responses and emphases as observed within African American couples (Wimberly, 1997b).

Religious Values and Spirituality

We contend that a spiritual and religious worldview and the integration of religious principles and values into the clinical or counseling process are implicitly discouraged in most professional (clinical) schools and training programs. This marginalization of religious values in the counseling process can serve to fragment the spiritual, psychological, and emotional realms of African Americans. Wimberly (1997b) encourages African American couples to examine the spiritual context of their relationships because he holds that a religious worldview is a constant in the African American heritage.

The decision to address or ignore the spiritual and religious aspects in counseling with African American couples is a subject that has been hotly debated within the social science literature. Critics of the Judeo-Christian influence, such as Asante (1981), boldly assert that "the church is the single most tragic influence on Black male-female relationships" (p. 76). From a decidedly contrasting ideological and spiritual perspective, Wimberly (1997b) is one of the few theorists who challenge the tenets that the church, Christianity, the Judeo-Christian ethics, values, or principles, or any of these influences have undermined the African American marriage. Rather, Wimberly asserts that it has been more of an issue of how Christianity has been distorted and misused.

Hopson and Hopson (1998) also embrace spiritual and religious values in their orientation to couple therapy with African Americans as they advocate the use of the concept of the "power of soul." Hopson and Hopson explain that African Americans have a unique soul—a deep sense of connectedness, strength, faith, focus, and passion to act on their innermost feelings. Thus, therapists of African American couples are urged to explore the spiritual, if not religious, realm of the couples' relationship to help them express positive feelings, to communicate more effectively to resolve conflicts, and, most important, "to talk to God through prayer" (p. 1).

Sociocultural Factors and the African American Male: Impact on Couple Dynamics and Implications for Couple Therapy

The "Traditional Male Code"

We take the view that adopting dominant (Eurocentric) societal images of masculinity and femininity can hinder the growth of both African American males and females individually and the growth of their conjugal relationship. This position is taken in light of the fact that gender role identity is a socially constructed paradigm. Hence, the notion of a single "male ideology" (i.e., men should behave, think, and feel in a certain way) greatly contributes to gender role strain in marital relationships (Levant, 1997).

The notion of an "essentialist nature of masculinity" is particularly confining for African American men, who face additional external pressures in achieving traditional gender role performance that can challenge these rigid notions of masculinity. White psychologists such as Ronald Levant (1997), however, are actively questioning the fit and function of traditional gender roles, functions, and behaviors for White males. Rather, practitioners faced with the challenge of dealing with these issues in couple counseling with Black men are encouraged to empower Black men to explore more culturally syntonic role behaviors that have a greater potential to complement the adaptive roles that Black women have had to take on in response to their own unique sociocultural pressures.

Practitioners need to encourage the mutual discussion of gender role strain and the nature of contradictory messages internalized by Black males and females in a manner that does not undermine their self-esteem. Therapists also need to consider allowing cultural and religious values to take on a primary role in attempting to mediate issues of gender role strain with Black men in couple counseling. We reemphasize the positive role that religion and culture can play in processing these issues.

For example, it may be helpful for the practitioner to get the couple to examine their own notions of the essence of masculinity and femininity and to examine ways that their own definitions coincide with or are incongruent with dominant (Eurocentric) societal norms, values, and behaviors. Next, couples should be helped to review some the philosophical, spiritual, and ideological materials that exist for African American couples that are based on Africentric and religious principle. Armed with this new cognitive information, couples should then be encouraged to co-create their own gender narratives that include role prescriptions that take into account their individual needs, lifestyle choices, and available options given their mate's strengths and limitations.

Sexual Dysfunction, Infidelity, and Domestic Violence and Abuse

The stress of harsh ecological realities that face many African American men along with societal messages that attempt to socialize all men to internalize the traditional male code may combine to create situations in which issues of domestic violence and abuse, infidelity, or sexual dysfunction surface as primary presenting problems. The experiences of some Black men may result in the adoption of dysfunctional "hypermasculine" behaviors that likely assist in setting the stage for domestic violence and abuse, infidelity, and sexual dysfunction. The clinician's task is to determine the source(s) of anger, rage, and feelings of anomie and alienation that may be operating in the dynamics of these problems. Furthermore, clinicians need to consider if restrictive ego defense mechanisms, such as repression, suppression, sublimation (of anger), displaced aggression, denial, avoidance, or all these have been (over)relied on as primary coping mechanisms by these men.

In the case of infidelity or sexual dysfunction as presenting problems with African American men, clinicians are encouraged to explore issues regarding midlife crises and negative responses to a closed or traditional model of marriage that may be fueled by the "scarcity" of Black men, especially as perceived by Black women. These unique sociocultural factors can complicate other developmental and external stressors common to the experiences of African American men. The social science literature has widely documented the maladaptive response of compulsive "womanizing" as an attempt to offset the "zero image" of

Black men (Bowman, 1989; Majors & Billson, 1992). These issues, coupled with the athleticizing and sexual (societal) stereotypes of Black men, create a fertile climate for problematic behaviors as infidelity and sexual dysfunction to develop and flourish.

Wimberly (1997b) proposes that "African American women have ignored their own needs for self-development and care for self to wage a war on behalf of African American men" (p. 113). In essence, this position renders many African American women very vulnerable to abuse and exploitation in their conjugal relationships. It is imperative for counselors to tread in these waters very carefully, leaving intact the humanistic values and Africentric orientation of Black women while separating out and eliminating the dysfunctional and abusive aspects of their relationship dynamics.

Again, it is therapeutically important to conduct individual sessions with both partners and to continue couple counseling to deal with these issues effectively. In individual sessions with the female partner, the practitioner needs to explore "cultural messages" that may cause her to feel obliged to "suffer in silence" in attempts to be the quintessential "strong Black woman." In individual sessions with the male partner, the therapist needs to explore how the man may have fallen into acting out (negative and dysfunctional) societal stereotypes of Black men. Furthermore, these individual sessions can be used to encourage Black men to unveil fears and issues that may be unique to them that add additional layers to the problematic aspects of being socialized according to the traditional male code.

Negative and Stereotypical (Societal) Images of Black Men

One of the central clinical interventions in couple counseling with African American men is to empower the couple to challenge, demystify, and then re-create their own narratives about Black men. This clinical task is especially imperative if the partners in African American couples are to be helped to understand their individual narratives as opposed to the negative societal narratives that are often handed (or forced) on both male and female African American partners. Black couples should also be helped to uncover how the dominant discourse of politicized knowledge of Black men (i.e., negative assumptions and binary descriptions of Black male masculinity) have operated to adversely impact their conjugal dyadic issues and conflicts. Practitioners need to be aware of and intercede in situations in which the African American couple collude on false or dysfunctional (Black) male narratives.

Facilitating Black couples in challenging culturally constructed ideologies regarding traditional male-female gender roles (i.e., strength as a desirable masculine trait and sensitivity and humanism as desirable feminine traits) should be viewed as an important clinical task in couple counseling involving African American men. It is important that clinicians explore these issues, regardless of whether either partner initiates this as a relevant concern. Black couples should be encouraged to build on their heritage of cultural strengths that have historically allowed them to engage in flexible conjugal roles and defy rigid and stifling societal gender roles and prescriptions.

Sociocultural Factors and the African American Female: An *Africana Womanist* Perspective on Their Impact on Couple Dynamics and Implications for Couple Therapy

Not all Black women who are sympathetic and supportive of the "women's liberation movement" refer to themselves as *Africana womanist;* some prefer the terms "womanist," "Black feminist," or simply "feminist." The term Africana womanist, however, is widely used compared to feminist because many Black women believe that this term highlights the unique issues of racism and sexism that interact to profoundly impact the lives of African American women (Hudson-Weem, 1993). This section sets forth an Africana womanist perspective on couple counseling with Black male-female couples. Our decision to include such a section in a book on social work practice with African American men in part reflects our own ideological biases and a conceptual awareness that there are many "self-proclaimed" Africana womanists who take a decidedly different view of Black male-female relationship dynamics and thus likely approach couple therapy with African Americans with an additional set of lenses, so to speak. This section is an attempt to share these lenses with others because we believe that one does not have to be Black or a female to take on an Africana womanist position in therapy.

The power dynamics within African American couples is vastly different in some significant ways. The differences in power dynamics and in their underlying issues are largely due to the cumulative effects of racism, (White male) sexism, the (American) capitalist ethos, the scarcity of (available or marriageable) Black men, the "endangered" plight of African American men, and the common socioeconomic class differences between Black males and their Black female partners. What can be particularly confusing and misleading about the power dynamics and other gender issues within Black male-female relationships is that on the surface, or to the "casual" or untrained eye, these gender dynamics can appear to be no different than gender issues or power dynamics found within White couples. This is not to imply a homogeneity or lack of acculturative or assimilative differences existing within African American couples. Certainly, African American couples exhibit the full range of conjugal behaviors and dynamics as exhibited in other ethnocultural groups. There are distinct and unique differences, however, that are also in part due to African American women's unique sociopolitical (Africana womanist) philosophy.

Specifically, African American women may prioritize their feminism (or womanism) differently than White women or women from other ethnocultural groups. That is, the Africana womanist views (female) gender issues as having secondary importance and significance to their race position in American society (Hudson-Weem, 1993). Another key central to the difference in their womanist prioritization of race and gender is the presence of racism and racial oppression within the sociocultural context of African American men. That is, given the hierarchy of economic, political, and social power in the United States (in which Black men are decidedly on the bottom rung), some Black women may view their conjugal issues and gender issues qualitatively and quantitatively different than do

White women. The Africana womanist is cognizant of her mates's societal position—on the bottom rung of the socioeconomic ladder—and hence realizes that her mate is not the (societal) oppressor but rather is a victim of White male institutional oppression. Hence, these sociocultural differences can operate to create vastly different power dynamics within the conjugal dyad of African Americans.

In our clinical experiences with African American couples and in individual counseling with Black women, we have observed Black women who create a nurturing, even emotionally indulgent, relationship environment with their mates. In essence, these Black women put their needs on the "back burner" in acknowledgment of the stress and harshness of racism on the egos of their Black men. (This humanistic stance is certainly in part derived from the wider Africentric cultural values of African Americans, but it is also fueled by Black women's awareness of their mates' endangered plight and precarious societal position.) We have also observed, however, occasions in which anger and resentment begin to set in, with Black women believing that they are not receiving the same amount of effort, understanding, compassion, and support from their mates that they believe they are giving. Hence, anger is often internalized, and this same anger often goes "underground" in the relationship, creating significant problems for the couple.

There are additional forces that operate to compound this difficult situation. For example, the experiences of racism tend to harden the emotional side of Black men, and to cope Black men may opt to emotionally insulate themselves. In essence, they become less affectionate toward their mates, thus making it more difficult to continue being "largely on the giving end of the relationship," as stated in complaints from some Black women.

Compounding this difficult conjugal situation are the not so unusual socioeconomic class differences between Black males and their Black female partners, with Black women having higher earnings than their mates. Black male-female power dynamics have long been unbalanced due to these societal factors, and Black couples have long since had to revisit and renegotiate gender roles and the division of household tasks. It takes a very self-assured, if not "liberated," male not to be threatened by his wife's earning potential and to successfully renegotiate the division of labor in the household along traditional gender lines. Counselors are encouraged to empower these couples and challenge them to be creative—that is, use part of the wife's earnings to launch a small business for the family.

The issue of the scarcity of available or marriageable Black men may result in some Black women perceiving that they have limited choices and thus believing that they have to take Black men "on Black men's terms" rather than on their own terms. Thus, racial and ethnic loyalty exhibited in the relationship by Black women, as discussed previously, may be misconstrued by their mates as a sign of weakness or an indication that it is acceptable for the male not to work as hard to meet or affirm the needs of Black women in the conjugal relationship; thus further complicating this already overworked and overburdened dyad.

Virginia Satir's **Human Validation Process Approach** (1986), because of its inherent health-promoting process within the couple (and family) and its central focus on the building of communication that affirms the self-worth and inherent potential of family members, is an excellent fit with Africentric principles and with many Black couples' (especially Black mens') need for positive self-affirmation. This communication model of therapy can be especially helpful in exploring traditional (societal) gender role models and in exploring and challenging (affective and behavioral) gender roles and rules prescriptives for Black men that may not be working for them, given their own individual needs and the needs of their mates.

Sociocultural Factors and the African American Extended Family: Impact on Couple Dynamics and Implications for Couple Therapy

It is difficult for African American couples to survive without connectedness to the extended family (Wimberly, 1997b). Maintaining a connection to the African American family is an important vehicle for the Black couple in that this relationship enables the couple to stay in touch with African American cultural traditions and values, a vital source of comfort and strength for the couple. Hence, being relationally connected to the cultural heritage through extended family and cross-generational relationships has often made the difference between surviving and not surviving in a racist and hostile environment.

As a result, many African American couples may present to therapy with "intense" and complicated extended family relationships. Although these relationships generally are crucial sources of social support, they can also be sources of tension, stress, and conflict for the conjugal dyad. Thus, extended family relationships can undoubtedly be a "double-edged sword" for the African American couple. It is imperative, however, that clinicians not pathologize these close relationships and be careful not to (over)assess dynamics of *fusion, enmeshment, symbiosis,* "too richly cross-joined," or other concepts that characterize a degree of closeness that is dysfunctional. This is not to say that there are never instances in which there is a degree of "overcloseness" between Black couples and their extended families that does not work well for either the couple or the extended family. We caution practitioners, however, to be cognizant of ethnocentrism and cultural bias in their assessment of these relationships.[3]

According to Framo (1981), the most powerful obstacle to change in couple therapy is people's attachments to their *parental introjects* (psychological representations of external objects and their imprints or memories of parents or other significant figures). Hence, troubled marriages are seen as contaminated by *pathogenic introjects* (largely from past familial relationships) (Framo, 1981). We expand on the family therapy concept of *negative (familial) introjects* and introduce the notion of *negative (societal) introjects* for consideration. It is especially important for therapists to explore with both African American males and females *negative introjects* internalized about Black men not only from their families but also from society at large. This therapeutic task serves to free the partners to respond to each other as they truly behave rather than on their resemblance to internalized negative societal or familial introjects. Clinicians need to help the couple gain insight by becoming aware of how they have internalized (identified with) objects (family members) from the past. In view of the closeness within many Black families, it becomes a critical clinical task for African American couples to gain insight into how these family members continue to intrude on (or could enhance) current relationships. The following case vignette illustrates these dynamics.

Charles and Vanessa presented for couple therapy upon the wife's discovery of his extramarital affair with a coworker. They were married right after high school when Vanessa discovered that she had become pregnant. (They attended the same college but had to drop out—on the insistence of both sets of parents—in their second semester.) They now have three latency-aged children and work at good-paying, blue-collar positions.

In actuality, at first Charles would not agree to couple counseling; he stated through a message from his wife, "I don't need anybody else pointing fingers at me and telling what I did wrong." At this juncture, I stepped up my engagement efforts with him and made several brief phone calls to him until he agreed to attend individual and not couple counseling to deal with his own issues (his wife was attending weekly individual counseling with one of the authors). At the beginning of his individual sessions, we primarily talked about his guilt about having the affair, which was compounded by the fact that he had "fallen in love" with his coworker. As we made progress with his issues of guilt and grief at the loss of this relationship, he appeared ready to enter the couple counseling process. Vanessa was also ready for the couple counseling aspect of this therapy process in that even though she was still quite angry, she appeared to be in a place where she could put her anger aside long enough to engage in the couple counseling.

Even though this was Charles's only infidelity, Vanessa was chronically quite suspicious of him. Upon discovery of the affair, it was as if years of hostility and anger exploded from her. The therapy revealed that Vanessa's father was discovered to have an entire separate family living in a nearby small town. Vanessa's mother had discovered the other women and three children (Vanessa's half brothers and sisters). Vanessa's mother gave him an ultimatum, and he chose to live with the other family. (Vanessa was only 8 years old at the time and has not seen him since.) Ironically, a similar scenario played out in Charles's family of origin. He reports watching his mother struggle to be a single parent to him and his brother and vowed he would never abandon his children as his father had. Thus, it was an easy decision for Charles to make to drop out of college, marry Vanessa, and get a job.

Neither of them ever went back to college. My impression of their relationship is that they had outgrown each other or at least grew in different directions and no longer really enjoyed each other's company. It was as if there was no "zing" left in the marriage. Vanessa seemed to have redirected her energies to her children, frequent visits with extended family, and church activities. Charles busied himself with sports activities and learning how to do major home improvement projects.

Within their couple counseling, it was very difficult for Vanessa to get past her own (negative) narrative of all Black men. Charles, however, was not helpful in the therapist's attempt to challenge these negative (familial) introjects about African American males. It appeared that given his own family of origin experiences with Black men, Charles, within his masculine identity development, had also incorporated negative (societal) introjects about African American males. (Charles had very few close male friends.)

A combination of individual sessions that were primarily focused on
family of origin issues and couple therapy, which blended the two
processes, were eventually helpful to this couple. Within the couple therapy sessions, the couple was encouraged through a broader retelling of
their family narrative and personal stories about other (Black) men in their
families. This therapeutic measure assisted them to co-create a healthier
(societal) narrative about Black men, and a healthier (familial) narrative
about Black men. The end result was a willingness to embrace the possibility (on both their parts) that the potential did exist for them to rebuild a
more thriving, monogenous marriage.

Nancy Boyd-Franklin (1989), in her critical contribution to the field of couple and
family therapy, highlights the importance of giving special attention to helping
Black couples negotiate *boundaries*[4] between their conjugal dyad and their
extended families. This therapeutic move can be an especially tricky one in light
of the need to preserve these important relational connections; this point cannot
be overemphasized! Practitioners need to help African American couples find
their own way in this regard to effect boundaries that work for them as a couple.
The question, "Does the nature of these (extended family) boundaries work well
for this couple?," is indeed the central clinical question to be dealt with, and it
must be posed to the practitioner and to the clients. Posing the question in this
form can help therapists become more aware of their own (ethnocentric) biases
and notions of "closeness" in relationships with one's extended family.

Triangles[5] are important in marital assessment of the presenting problem of
many African Americans because of the emphasis on and closeness within these
extended families. The potential exists for Black couples to draw others into their
conjugal conflict (Wimberly, 1997b). Again, caution should be exercised by the
clinician in detriangulating the couple from (familial) third parties because it is
important that there not be permanent damage done to these familial connections
as sensitive issues are confronted.

In conducting couple work with African American men, it is important to
explore issues of rigid and constrictive, nonfunctional masculinity, and negative
stereotypes regarding Black men (derived from unresolved, conflicted, or ambivalent relationships with other Black men in the family [perhaps transmitted cross-
generationally] and through acceptance and internalization of negative societal
images of Black men). These distorted, negative images of Black men may have
been transmitted to **both** male and female partners. Bringing these issues into the
couple's awareness and allowing and encouraging them to examine and demystify these notions and issues can be an extremely important therapeutic move for
African American men in couple therapy.

The clinical issue of invisible loyalties and Black couples in therapy has
been previously mentioned. We expound on the clinical issues in this regard,
however. Black men—especially if they are spiritually or occupationally successful or both—as a result of strong support from their families of origin, can
be particularly vulnerable to allowing invisible (family) loyalties to interfere
with their conjugal relationships. This situation may be amplified within highly
successful, strong Black families that strive to maintain their sense of (family

and ethnic) history, family connectedness, family loyalty, and ethnic loyalty, especially if the extended family views these characteristics as part of the families' strength and survival strategies. Certainly, practitioners would not want to encourage a sense of ingratitude or aloofness with their clients to these highly functional family values.

Therapists may need to help the couple negotiate and resolve these invisible family and cultural loyalties in regard to the aforementioned acculturative tensions or acculturative conflicts, however, to ease tension and facilitate a more harmonious conjugal relationship. Additionally, clinicians will need to help the couple negotiate how they can show their gratitude to their extended families and to their communities while exploring and realizing new options that present in their own individual, conjugal, and familial experiences.

Family therapy may be indicated for the couple and for the extended family (as an adjunctive clinical process to the couple therapy) to help the wider familial system come to terms with "family goals" and unresolved conflicts that may hinder the growth of its individual members. To this end, concepts such as *family projection processes* and *multigenerational family transmission processes*[6] can be used as an umbrella in which to explore a entire rubric of family therapy processes, such as invisible family loyalties, invisible cultural loyalties, acculturative tensions, acculturative conflicts, negative (familial) introjects, negative (societal) introjects, and triangles (or rather *interlocking triangles* in which there is an additional intergenerational or cross-generational component to the triangulation process).

"KICKIN' IT": COUPLE THERAPY WITH YOUNG, UNMARRIED AFRICAN AMERICAN MALES

We decided to include a section on couple counseling that specifically addresses the issue of nonrelational sex because of the importance of this social phenomenon amid vastly changing values and sexual behavior. Levant and Brooks (1997) describe nonrelational sex as a self-involved, narcissistic way of experiencing sexuality and a tendency to experience sex primarily as lust without any requirements for relational intimacy or emotional attachment. We view nonrelational sex as a problematic feature of (**idealized**) male sexuality in that it is a vehicle for masculine validation and not mutual validation in romantic relationships (Levant & Brooks, 1997).

This section explores one type of romantic relationship, more frequently involving young African American males. These romantic relationships or liaisons with women are referred to as *kickin' it*.[7] The term kickin' it is interpreted here as reference to a sexual or romantic relationship between the opposite sex wherein the parties have not yet reached a stage of commitment to the relationship. There may or may not be an agreement for exclusive dating, but generally this term declares a more "relaxed" relationship. Our critique of this phraseology is that this characterization (of the relationship) has a decided impact on the sexual or romantic relationship. To refer to a relationship as just kickin' it generally implies that there is little or no commitment. Furthermore, this characterization operates to "downplay" the relationship between the two people and thus serves to ease the tension with regard to the level of intimacy within the relationship. Our experience with young Black couples who use or allow this term to be used to describe their relationship is that the females are likely to experience more discomfort and discontent with this amorphous description of their romantic relationship than are the males.

Indeed, the misogynistic lyrics of contemporary "gangsta rap" are an important deleterious influence on our youth and their values and attitudes toward women and relationships (McClean, 1997). In actuality, by current moral standards, if a young Black male defines his relationship with a women as kickin' it, despite the relationship's nonpermanent and noncommitted nature, he may be considered a rather conservative, right-wing moralist compared to the violent, degrading, and sexually mutilating relationships revered in the music of gangsta rappers.

The traditional male code, which may encourage the nonrelational sex syndrome, is no doubt also partly responsible for this dubious and frequent problematic relationship arrangement uniquely termed kickin' it. Nonrelational sexuality is closely linked to the traumatic socialization of boys in which displays of emotion are discouraged and emotional intimacy is equated with the loss of autonomy (Levant & Brooks, 1997; McClean, 1997). Hence, in situations in which emotional insulation, toughness, and the restrictive expression of emotions are viewed as potential coping mechanisms by young impressionable males facing virtual "extinction," it is easy to understand how tempting this nonmutually validating relationship style may appear.

It is therefore incumbent on clinicians to explore with these young males their hypermasculine and destructive behaviors and provide them with alternative paths in which to vent apprehension, anger, and rage. Hence, the clinician's task is to help them to experience (ego) validation—without the exploitation of young women. In turn, females need to be encouraged to defy the traditional male code in their relationships and not to internalize their maltreatment as a statement of their inherent worth.[8]

We acknowledge that practitioners seldom have access to this young, unmarried African American population. There are practice opportunities that exist in special settings, however, such as within some of the newer programs targeting adolescent parenting (pregnancy prevention or assistance to teen parents—for both mothers and fathers). Other opportunities exist within the newer programs for African American men, such as "rites of passage" programs and paternal involvement programs. In light of this situation, practitioners are encouraged to develop more programming for young, unmarried, African American males. (The reader is directed to Chapters 7, 9, and 10 for further discussion of program planning and development, group and community interventions for African American males.)

CONCLUSION

Employing the integrative critical practice approach, as advanced in this book, can be an important tool in helping the clinician avoid conducting couple therapy involving African American men in a "vacuum." The critical practice approach attends to the following central clinical tasks facing those who engage in couple therapy with African American men: empowering African American couples to challenge false or dysfunctional Black male narratives and helping them to coconstruct culturally syntonic (male-female) gender narratives, attending to the factors that inform the worldview of African American men and their partners, assessing and addressing the ecological (life space) and unique developmental issues and tasks facing African American men, and infusing and capitalizing on the cultural strengths and Africentric values of African American couples. It is posited that addressing these central and critical clinical tasks can facilitate the overall provision of culturally tailored couple therapy to African American men.

NOTES

1. In keeping with the general clinical focus of this book, couple therapy issues with interracial and gay or bisexual couples will not be addressed in this chapter. This omission is not to be construed as an ideological or philosophical statement about these couples. For similar reasons, only a limited discussion of special issues in couple therapy (i.e., domestic violence and abuse, sexual dysfunction and infidelity) is presented in this chapter.

2. *Invisible loyalties,* also referred to as *relational indebtedness* or *family ledgers,* are concepts that describe what an individual perceives to "owe" one's family of origin. This indebtedness can date back several generations and can also be a result of multigenerational and cross-generational unresolved familial conflicts or unrealized goals within the family (Boszoremenyi-Nagy, 1987).

3. Chapter 6 is devoted to African American men, their families, and implications for family therapy

4. *Boundaries* are an emotional barrier that protects the family or couple from the environment, thus maintaining the integrity of the family as a system and intrafamilial boundaries that operate to protect the separateness and thus integrity of the various subsystems and dyads within the larger family system.

5. *Triangulation* is the process of bringing third parties into the conjugal dyad for the purposes of detouring or avoiding conflict, taking pressure off the relationship issues, and lowering the intensity or anxiety within the conjugal dyad (Bowen, 1978).

6. Bowen (1978) describes the processes of *family transmission* and *family projection* as the mechanisms by which parental (unresolved) conflicts are transmitted to an individual's family of procreation through the process of

projection. When this projection process occurs over several generations, the process is referred to as *multigenerational familial transmission* or projection. The reader is referred to Chapter 6, in which this topic will receive full treatment.

7. We thank Mr. Troy Harden, a Loyola University Chicago graduate student in social work, for assisting with the conceptualization of the term *kickin' it.* This term is also used by many young, urban Blacks to refer to merely "hanging out" with friends or an evening of social activities with platonic (same or opposite sex) friends in which there is no sexual or romantic relationship.

8. We acknowledge that the discussion of young Black males and their relationships with women takes on a decided negative colorization. The discussion reflects only one aspect of relationship issues or styles of young Black men. Our research and clinical and personal experiences with young Black men reflect a broad range of relationship issues and styles as well as an indication that there are many young Black men who are involved in healthy, mutually respectful, and satisfying relationships with women. Our decision to explore one type of relationship style (i.e., kickin' it) should not be construed as indicative of the state of relationships of all young Black males.

Chapter 6

FAMILY THERAPY WITH AFRICAN AMERICAN MEN

The enormous contribution of Dr. Nancy Boyd-Franklin's book, *Black Families in Therapy* (1989), fills a tremendous void in the clinical practice and social science literature. We are facilitated by this important scholarship, which enables us to promptly focus on clinical issues in conducting family therapy with African American men. Thus, we will not attempt to summarize or restate the **generic** clinical issues in conducting family therapy with African Americans; we refer the reader to Boyd-Franklin's (1989) classic work, even though it has been 10 years since its publication.

This chapter illuminates, clarifies, and examines family therapy issues with African American men, their fathers ("father figures"), their children, and their extended families. General clinical issues that arise in family therapy with African American men are also addressed.[1]

BACKGROUND

The societal realities of racism and poverty pervade the life experiences of the families of African American men. Hence, African American men find themselves amid a collective group of kin and nonkin who are typically overwhelmed and burdened with their own issues. The multiple external stressors faced by the fathers, mothers, siblings, children, and assorted (blood and fictive) relatives of African American men create complex and sometimes fragile familial relationships. Because of the precarious position of African American men in our society, combined with their weakened systems of familial support, African American men need family therapists who are well versed in their complicated (sociocultural) familial dynamics. This population also needs practitioners who can translate this knowledge to the family therapy process. In this chapter, we attempt to further refine the clinical skills of family therapists and other practitioners working with African American men.

A "CRITICAL PRACTICE" APPROACH TO FAMILY THERAPY WITH AFRICAN AMERICAN MEN

Stanley Witkin is a major proponent of the critical constructionist perspective (which is one of the conceptual/theoretical/philosophical perspectives that undergirds the critical practice approach as advanced in this book.) Witkin (1995) views critical constructionism as a useful (organizing) framework for family social work, albeit the practice implications (e.g., techniques) of this framework still need to be refined. The critical constructionist approach is a heuristic (problem-solving) framework out of which the important activity of family social work may develop its distinctive approach. This approach is more an attitude or philosophy than a particular method (theorists using this approach tend to downplay technique).

As outlined and developed in Chapters 2 through 5, the critical constructionist perspective is not only an attempt to interpret social reality but also a framework for recognizing the inherently political nature of social explanations for human conditions. The critical constructionist perspective, with its emphasis on language as a vehicle to empower or "restory" the problems in one's life (Laird, 1993), has the potential to legitimize the perspective(s) of African American men and their families. Black men and their families are empowered, within this approach to family practice, to address and confront dysfunctional and destructive internalized (dominant) social meanings of presenting problems, thus freeing them to construct new meanings and thus consider alternative options or solutions to their problems (Goldenberg & Goldenberg, 1996).

The postmodernist influence on the critical constructionist perspective, with its emphasis on examining gender biases, gender stereotypes, and deconstructing subjugating gender narratives, is a comfortable epistemological fit within a family practice approach with African American men and their families. Engaging the entire family in the deconstruction of invalidating (societal) narratives of African American men can be a powerful and extremely beneficial family therapy exercise. Getting African American men and their families to engage in "externalizing conversations" (White & Epston, 1990) that encourage them to map the real effects of "politicized" knowledge about Black men, and getting the family to examine whether their gender stories of African American men correct these larger social prescriptions for gender role performance for Black male development, can be a powerful therapeutic activity.

The critical constructionist perspective is one of the central components of the critical practice approach as advanced in this book. In this chapter, several of the core principles, guidelines, and techniques that emanate from the critical constructionist perspective are articulated, interwoven, and applied to family practice situations with African American men..

African American Men and
Their Extended Families in Family Therapy

African American men are likely to turn to their families first for support. Hence, it is necessary to ascertain the strength of internal family support systems. Supporting and strengthening the families of African American men is an important therapeutic task toward facilitating the overall well-being of Black men. To this end, it is important to encourage African American family members to continue their tradition of flexibility and adaptability of family roles, including important childrearing and household tasks. In a similar vein, we encourage practitioners to help single parents reorganize their families in line with the historical tradition of the "collective will." Specifically, single parents should strive to create extended and augmented family systems with the goal of soliciting close familial relationships with blood relatives and fictive kin.

Practitioners also need to encourage and facilitate the strengthening of familial relationships with male relatives (kin or fictive kin). Kunjufu (1996) boldly asserts that "mothers lack knowledge of masculinity" (p. 6), which is not to imply any inherent shortcoming or pathology of female-headed families. Rather, we interpret this statement as a plea for all Black parents (especially single female parents) not to ignore the need for male mentoring and role modeling in their boy's development.

Young Black males are likely to hear many different messages from their families regarding the families' expectations of them as men. Some of these messages may be experienced by African American males as quite conflicting and confounding. For instance, sayings such as "Now you're the little man of the house" (a statement sometimes addressed to preadolescent or very young adolescent males on the departure—through death, divorce, or desertion—of adult Black males in the home) can be quite confusing when juxtaposed with other statements such as "You're just like your (no good) father."

To some extent, as a community, African Americans are aware of the double messages and double standards of male versus female responsibility and expectations, as embodied in the familiar cultural saying, "We raise our daughters and love our sons." This statement implies that more responsibility and higher expectations are placed on the females in Black families. The implication for negative *multigenerational transmission* and *family projection processes* in light of these destructive sentiments and their impact on both Black men and women, especially as Black boys and girls move into their own nuclear families and conjugal roles, is an important issue that warrants exploration with African American families. To this end, family members should be encouraged to **use their personal story and self-narrative to understand the "meaning metaphor" of their experience of the culture,** paying special attention to oral stories about family traditions, customs, rituals, and folklore (Laird, 1993). Practitioners need to be aware of the implications for family practice once individuals have deciphered (for themselves) these cultural meaning metaphors.

Critical constructionists suggest that practitioners should not strive for consensus from the family and **encourage multiple meanings of the families' experience of culture** (White & Epston, 1990). Hence, in exploring familial and cultural messages about African American men with their families, practitioners should encourage individual family members to explore within their own experiences and search for the strengths of Black men while confronting debilitating narratives that reinforce undesirable behavior. Within this cocreation of the "meanings" that are attached by various family members, practitioners should not cause the African American male or his family members to feel at odds with each other if they have different narratives and varying interpretations of the meanings of family and cultural oral stories.

Rather, family practitioners need to explore and amplify family legacies that are growth facilitating while discouraging those family messages and legacies that are growth inhibiting. Unfortunately, because of the onslaught of the advertisement industries' glorification of the use of alcohol and tobacco and early sexuality in the Black community, these have become "rites of passage" for too many African American youngsters. To wit, families, especially poor Black families, need assistance from counselors in creating positive, growth-producing rites of passage activities for young Black males.

Family rituals have been lost to many poor, young African American males and their families in these times of economic retrenchment. New family rituals need to be revived because these activities help families order their time, provide continuity, mark boundaries, communicate values and shared meanings, and reinforce and shape "age"-appropriate roles for these young men. The saying, "A culture without rituals is a dead culture," applies in this situation. Practitioners should suggest family reunions and **help families to construct or reenact missed rituals,** especially where there have been "emotional cutoffs" or "disengagements" of various family members over time.

African American Men and Their Fathers
and Father Figures in Family Therapy

In a review of the clinical practice literature in the past 30 years, we did not locate one journal article or book that addressed the issue of conducting family therapy with adult African American men and their fathers and their father figures. Nor did we locate any sociological or descriptive human behavior theory literature on this subject. In contrast, the issue of the effectiveness (or the perception) of the paternal role function(s) of African American males (across age and social class lines) is one of the most well-researched areas in the social science literature on African American men. Despite this fascination or perhaps even valid emphasis on this area of family behavior, the clinical literature addressing practice concerns with Black men, their fathers, their children, or all three is nonexistent.

The strategy of having adult Black men and their fathers and father figures perform a systematic and comprehensive exploration of their perceptions, reactions, and generalized feelings about their father-son relationship and feelings about themselves as men (and as Black men), as well as attending to multigenerational issues involving the Black men in their families, can no doubt be very powerful. The possibility for "male bonding"—that is, collaboration and support in cocreating positive narratives about themselves as Black men, fathers, husbands, brothers, uncles, and friends—is quite exciting. Practitioners are encouraged to **use circularity and reflexivity in questioning** these men to promote open dialogue about taboo or previously neglected areas (Ceechin, 1987).

Extending this therapeutic experience could entail the inclusion of the "multiple fathers and father figures" typically involved in the lives of Black males. (We often speak of the "multiple-mothering" pattern within Black families but fail to recognize that a parallel pattern exists for many males and females who are also "fathered" by an extended family system of blood and nonblood male relatives.) Again, practitioners are cautioned against striving for consensus from the men regarding the meanings that they may create or cocreate within the various dyadic groups. The following vignette illustrates some of the dilemmas and practice principles described in this section.

Mark (a 28-year-old African American male) entered therapy as an effort to reconnect with his biological father, who did not raise him. Rather, he was "fathered" by a man who is a very close friend of the family. Mark had not felt the need to resolve his many angry and ambivalent feelings for his biological father until two situations simultaneously occurred. First, his "play" father recently confided in him that he was diagnosed with inoperable lung cancer and did not expect to survive the year. Next, his girlfriend of 5 years announced that she was pregnant with his child and intended to raise the child (with or with out Mark's assistance). Mark had mixed feelings about his girlfriend's pregnancy that were related mostly to relationship issues that he believed needed resolution before he could entertain the idea of marriage to her.

Mark now felt the need to reconnect with his biological father for the sake of his unborn child, with whom he fully intended to play a central role. Mark was already beginning to feel the empty space that was going to be created on the pending death of his play father. It was agreed on by both Mark and the therapist that both fathers (biological and surrogate) would be invited for an extended conjoint family therapy session. (In prior individual sessions with Mark, it was believed that he had made enough progress in putting aside his anger and resentment for lost years with his biological father to engage in a constructive session with him.)

The men were encouraged to tell their stories about how Mark came to be parented in the fashion that evolved. Mark, Sr. volunteered to talk first. What emerged from his story was a narrative in which he viewed himself as inept in the parenting role as a 19-year-old, and after the breakup from Mark's mother he slowly disappeared into the background because Mark's mother quickly remarried a much older gentlemen (she was then 21 years old and her second husband was 31 years old). Mark, Sr. reported feeling woefully incompetent in comparison (his stepfather was a college graduate). Mark did not develop an attachment to his stepfather, however, and Mark's mother divorced him after 4 years of marriage.

Mark was surprised to hear that his father felt so inadequate in comparison to his stepfather; Mark believed that his father was a superior role model because his stepfather was impatient, inconsiderate, and a heavy weekend drinker (despite his academic and occupational success). Mark, Sr. never knew Mark's view of him because Mark's mother was too proud and angry to allow any information to leak outside her immediate family.

Mark's play father was aware of his stepfather's ill-tempered ways and excessive drinking and very early stepped in and spent a lot of time with Mark to shield him from his stepfather's mood swings and drinking binges. Mark's play father was surprised that Mark, Sr. was not aware of their home situation; as a result, had just "written him off" as one of the many "deadbeat" dads. (Mark, Sr. had always paid child support but rarely spent time with him, except on holidays at extended family gatherings.)

Mark, Sr. was surprised to learn that Mark wanted a stronger connection with him and confided that his stepfather, his play father and the other men in Mark's life all seemed to "have it going on." Mark, Sr. also confided that he should have swallowed his pride and asserted his parental rights despite his own feelings. Mark, Sr. had remarried and raised three children (two boys and one girl). None of the children that he raised, however, had "turned out very well," and Mark, Jr. was the highest functioning of all his children. Mark, Sr. confided that the only child he did not rear was also the only one of his children that would be considered successful. As a result, he developed a negative paternal image of himself. He also avoided seeing Mark, Jr. because doing so reminded him of his failure as a father.

The remainder of the interventions centered around their exploration of family stories, beliefs, and attitudes toward Black men, especially Black men as fathers and husbands. These stories were analyzed regarding their impact on the men's lives and the choices that they made regarding these roles. This "marathon" (3-hour) therapy session ended with the three men making plans (bonding) regarding the unborn child and the roles that they all planned to play in the child's life.

African American Men and Their Children in Family Therapy

The dyadic relationship of African American men and their children has similarly suffered from a lack of attention within the clinical practice literature. Fortunately, however, social science research in this area has flourished (moving beyond its former narrow boundaries that typically explored only issues of child support and expanding to an exploration of interpersonal father-child relationship variables) and as a result has propelled important policy and programmatic initiatives on behalf of this vulnerable dyad (see Chapters 8 and 9).

One of the most important and potentially therapeutic tasks that clinicians can perform for Black men and their children is to be able to provide a forum in which fathers can affirmatively counter the negative societal (and possibly familial) image(s) of the African American father and the Black male. Therapists should strive to empower this dyad to seek a "we-ness" (an "us against the world" stance) in their relationships. This dyad should be encouraged to regularly discuss issues of racism and the politics of being Black (and male) in America. The ultimate goal of these therapeutic tactics is to facilitate an environment in which Black fathers and their children have the opportunity to cocreate their own narrative about their relationship without intrusion from outside forces.

Practitioners need to be aware of the multiple influences of their cultural background (e.g., gender, race, ethnocultural, and class) and engage in a self-examination of their values. This self-exploration will greatly facilitate their ability to conduct father-child explorations of the perceived importance of various roles and functions relative to the performance of Black men as fathers. This therapeutic task is especially critical in light of prevailing societal perceptions of the "peripheral" nature of the performance of Black men in their roles as fathers. Clinicians need to be clear on who gets to define which roles as peripheral (or essential). It is important that therapists not *collude* with other members of the family system who may share their worldview regarding Black men as fathers, especially if these views run counter to those of their male clients. It is equally important that practitioners empower Black men and their children in deconstructing traditional notions of "acceptable" paternal behaviors. Practitioners need to ensure that they and their clients move away from the dysfunctional, restrictive "traditional male code" definitions of paternal roles and functions and facilitate their reconstruction of more functional, culturally adaptive (i.e., Africentric) alternative behaviors.

For example, practitioners need to encourage Black men to initiate frank discussions with their children on their perceptions about African American men as males, fathers, husbands, or employees, and so on. Next, practitioners need to encourage this dyad to engage in a mutual dialogue and to share their views specifically about the father in a caring, respectful, and nonconfrontive manner that encourages additional dialogue. It is vital to facilitate this dyad to share (or maybe for the first time to discover) the source or sources of their perceptions, attitudes, and feelings about Black men in various roles. Finally, practitioners must empower the men to cocreate their own narratives about Black men as fathers that are much more accurate, affirming, and ego syntonic. The following vignette illustrates several of the issues and dilemmas discussed in this section.

> Jason Green is an 11-year-old African American male, initially referred by his mother because of concern regarding his sexual identity. She reports that he steals money from her to buy beauty supplies (wigs, plastic nails, nail supplies, and other professional hair supplies) and then proceeds to work on the wigs and sometimes glues the fake nails to his own nails. The latter behavior is very distressing to her.
>
> Although his mother is financially and occupationally secure, she has a very (emotionally) ambivalent relationship with her only child, Jason. Their relationship fluctuates from long periods of intense conflict (I suspect even physical at times) and emotional *disengagement* to periods of emotional *fusion*. During the periods of conflict, the mother threatens to kick him out of the house or "make him go live with his father." Jason often retorts that he would prefer living with his father rather than deal with her emotional ups and downs. At this juncture, the mother reminds him that his father lives in a garage, in which he fixes cars and has no real furniture or traditional household appliances. During one of the mother and son skirmishes, Jason ran away to his father's house and the mother (enraged) vowed to let him stay there as a punishment.
>
> As the therapist, I asked the mother's permission to bring the father and son in for family therapy—as she continued to be the legal guardian. This was a particularly important therapeutic move in that Mrs. Green

was quite critical of this intervention, volunteering negative information to thwart my interest in effecting a family intervention with the father-son dyad (i.e., the father's living quarters were unsuitable and void of many everyday conveniences and undesirable "characters" often hung around the garage; the mother suspected that the father sold drugs on the side in his garage).

In the initial interview with the father and son, I noticed a very healthy, affectionate, and close emotional relationship between them. I had never seen Jason so happy, carefree, and elated. Neither of them attempted to pretend that their living situation was anything less than ideal. They both explained, however, how they accommodated to get their needs met (regarding cooking, laundering, etc.). Jason added that he would rather make these accommodations to live with his father, who admittedly lived a very marginal economic existence, especially in comparison to the mother. (I admired that Mr. Green, who showed up for the initial interview in heavily soiled clothing and disheveled hair, offered that he did not apologize for his appearance or his speech—he spoke in very broken English compared to the mother's standard English). We began our family therapy sessions, which spanned over 2 months, and Jason also began individual sessions. (The mother refused to receive individual therapy or continue her family therapy sessions with Jason.)

Indeed, what was most significant about this intervention was that, given all the signals that many practitioners receive about Black fathers from society and their professions that define the yardstick by which to evaluate a "good enough" father, as well as a whole host of negative countertransferences that many practitioners struggle with regarding African American men, it would have been quite easy not to attempt an intervention with this father or support a live-in relationship with him and his son—especially in contrast to the mother's middle-class comforts. In summary, the family therapy of the father and son focused on perceptions of self, especially of them as males, and deconstructing some of the negative images about Black men that they received from society at large and from their own families.

African American men who parent nonbiological children (especially those who do not have a legalized marital relationship with the children's mothers) may need help in clarifying their roles with these children. These fathers may need help in soliciting the maternal family members' cooperation and acceptance, in light of their nonlegal status with the mother. It is important that practitioners search for cultural strengths, especially dormant or underutilized strengths, that can empower the father. The ecomap can be an especially important tool in this regard (Hartman & Laird, 1983). As interventions are implemented, however, the practitioner is cautioned to **present intervention or other suggestions for change as ideas** and not to take or usurp the responsibility for change from the father (Laird, 1993; Saleebey, 1997).

Additionally, these men may need help in negotiating with other social service and governmental systems that may present as *gendered obstacles* to their parenting because of their ambiguous paternal status. Never-married, noncustodial fathers should be empowered to take over parenting if necessary. (See Chapters 8 and 9 for an in-depth discussion on policy and programming issues on this topic.)

Special Issues in Family Therapy With Young or
Adolescent African American Fathers

Family practice social workers should not misconstrue the young or adolescent African American father's inability to financially provide for their children as peripheral (Ho, 1987; Hopkins, 1973). Rather, creative approaches should be used to involve these young fathers during family therapy with other family members. Extended family members should be encouraged to acknowledge the innovative ways that these young men are fulfilling their roles as fathers. Additionally, the families of these young men may need help in separating out their anger and disappointment regarding paternal role behaviors that fall below expectations. That is, family members may need help in sorting out paternal role behaviors that fall within the young father's control and those that are beyond his control. Ultimately, these young men need the ongoing support and encouragement from their families if they are to successfully negotiate these difficult circumstances.

The mother should also be encouraged not to draw the children into her conflict with the young or teen father; and she should be helped to separate her feelings about their relationship with the father and recognize her children's need to have a positive relationship with their father. Both parents should also be encouraged not to denigrate the children's perception or image of either parent. Practitioners should pay special attention to messages that African American mothers send to their sons about their fathers.

These complex (coparent) relational ties must be maintained throughout the children's lives. To this end, couple conflict mediation skills may become an essential interventive tool for practitioners with this population, given their immature (social and emotional) developmental stage. This mediation process (which can make use of traditional divorce or conflict mediation and divorce counseling skills) should attempt to refocus their relationship issues to specific life concerns and decisions that must be dealt with on behalf of their children. In addition, these young parents must be equipped with necessary basic problem-solving and communication skills so that, as they continue their coparenting relationship throughout the years, they can address (likely unresolved) conflicts and tensions that may have built up from their early years of recklessness and immaturity. (See Chapter 5 for a detailed discussion on addressing communication issues within the conjugal dyad.)

This parental dyad should be encouraged to search for strengths within each other's parenting. They should be encouraged to amplify situations in which the partners perform in some outstanding manner in fulfilling their parental responsibilities; Saleebly (1997) refers to this technique as the **exception, survival, or possibility questions** in order to discover [client] strengths.

General Clinical Issues in Conducting
Family Therapy With African American Men

Engagement

In Chapters 4 and 5, we examined the clinical issues involved in engaging African American men in the counseling and therapy process. Here, we do not reiterate these issues but rather explore the issue of engaging the family system and the separate subsystems of the families of African American men.

Apprehension and distrust of counseling professionals attempting to "meddle" in family matters, "emotional cutoffs" from family systems, oppressive work schedules, or all three may make the engagement process of African American men in family therapy very difficult. Central to the task of engagement of the entire family (extended and nuclear) system of African American men is one key dilemma.

This dilemma is an ethical one and is rather straightforward in that practitioners are challenged to work harder to engage all the subsystems of the families of African American men. That is, clinicians are confronted with the ethical dilemma of whether to take the easy way out (i.e., work with family members that initially present or those that, with a little encouragement, are willing to receive therapy) or to make a genuine effort to engage family members who are initially resistant to the notion of receiving family therapy, especially African American male members of the family.

Two clinical strategies may enhance the engagement process with African Americans in general and with African American men in particular. The first of which is to avoid placing textbook "familial templates" on the family memberships of these complex and large systems. That is, the practitioner must allow the family members who do enter therapy to inform him or her of the important members in the family. Practitioners are reminded that the extended and augmented nature of African American families is typically rendered even more complex when one considers the following factors: the fluidity of family membership (i.e., fictive kin change occasionally); the flexibility of roles that dictates that, given a certain issue, some family members may be more central than others; many of the more "powerful and influential" members may not initially present for therapy but rather send a "proxy" who may act as a go-between or "messenger" between the therapist and himself or herself; and that none of these factors or scenarios are necessarily dictated by household membership. If clinicians allow their initial outreach efforts to African American families to be informed by these unique factors, it is likely that engagement of African American family members (for those who initially enter therapy and for those who hesitate) will be enhanced. Clinicians who **take a nonhierarchical position in the client-worker relationship and become more of a cultural consult** to Black men and their families, adopting the philosophy that the family members are the real experts, may avoid initial resentment of family members because African American families are especially attentive to and cognizant of "outsiders" deciding who makes up their family system and who is important to the resolution of family problems. Showing this initial respect to African American families may operate to motivate others (especially Black men) to enter family therapy because some of their initial apprehensions about the paternalistic attitudes of professionals may be allayed.

The second clinical strategy that may operate to enhance the engagement process of African American men (and other allusive members) in family therapy is for the clinician to be willing to work with Black men in some nontraditional ways, at least initially (i.e., be willing to communicate with them on the phone and keep them apprised of details discussed in sessions with other family members). In this way, they can also be used as consultants in gaining information or direction, given their intimate relationships with others. At the very least, therapists will be able to develop an ongoing relationship with these men and have another chance at motivating them to become an active participant in the therapy process.

Assessment

One of the most important clinical dilemmas in conducting assessments in family therapy involving African American men is that of challenging preconceived notions of the importance of the familial membership and the roles of African American men in their families. The clinical task in accomplishing this, however, involves conducting a skillful assessment of the various subsystems of these families and engaging these various dyads, subsystems, and *invisible triangles* in the important therapeutic tasks of *joining* and *accommodating*[2]. Therapists are encouraged **to use an ethnographic (anthropological) approach to studying families** and to "view the family as tiny societies that over time, seem to develop their own systems of meanings and beliefs, their own mythologies and ritual practices, and their own cultures" (Laird, 1993) (p. 80).

Guided by one of the most important practice principles and guidelines emanating from the critical constructionists perspective or approach is the need for **clinicians to search their own "privileged ways of knowing"** and examine their practitioner biases (Laird, 1993; White & Epston, 1990). That is, practitioners need to examine how they come to understand and to "know" the African American family, especially perceptions regarding the Black men in these families. Practitioners may find it necessary to deconstruct distorted, erroneous, and destructive perceptions and biases about the role(s) and function(s) of African American men in their families. More accurate, strengths-oriented perceptual and knowledge bases about African American males will then need to be reconstructed by practitioners with the assistance of their Black male clients.

Next, practitioners need to conduct a careful assessment of the various subsystems and dyads within the African American family, paying special attention to the presence of Black men, who may exist in important and powerful invisible triangles. Black men are always present in Black families (physically, emotionally, spiritually, and via the collective communal). Sometimes, however, through our filtered lenses that internalize media-induced overstatements regarding the absence of Black men in African American families, we as practitioners render their presence invisible in our assessments and in our interventions. The critical constructionists offer a very helpful way of avoiding the use of outdated, distorted, or irrelevant information about African American families. That is, critical constructionists recommend that clinicians **should not derive their "clinical understandings or meanings" from "expert" knowledge or global assessment schemes;** rather, meaning should be cocreated by the family and the practitioner within the clinical setting (Laird, 1993; White & Epston, 1990).

Boyd-Franklin (1989) encourages the use of genograms to gather family information; she cautions therapists, however, about attempting to formulate genograms too early in the clinical process, before important "joining" activities occur. We suggest that practitioners consider engaging in "cultural joining"—that is, attempting to enter into the life space of African American men—paying special attention to how gender, race, and social class issues may impact their life experiences both within and outside of the family. Practitioners also need to make special note of how the narratives of Black men may differ from the narrative meanings assumed by their own family members, which has the potential to cause considerable pain and an increased sense of anomie, alienation and isolation from an important system of social support—that is, their nuclear and extended families.

Again, clinicians are cautioned not to attempt to "complete" the genogram, or any other diagnostic activity, too early in the clinical process, especially in the initial interview with African American families (Boyd-Franklin, 1989), because Black families are acutely aware of the often negative and distorted perceptions about African American men and thus may unwittingly collude with therapists to conform rather than to create their own narratives about how they experience the Black men in their lives. That is, Black family members may not feel like "going through the hassle" of convincing and educating a practitioner about their worldview.

The membership, structure, role(s), and function(s) of African American families have been widely documented as being complex, diverse, dense, dynamic, and (at times by necessity) fluid (Billingsley, 1968; Hill, 1972; McAdoo, 1978; Stack, 1974; Staples, 1971). These characteristics are an inherent part of the strength, resiliency, and adaptiveness of African American families and are especially descriptive of the role(s) and function(s) of African American men in families. Practitioners need to piece together an interactional, dynamic, and fluid picture of the rich gestalt that is a more accurate portrayal of Black men's roles and functions in their families. Linear family diagrams, family maps, and genograms conforming to "textbook templates" are not likely to capture the essence of or the real impact that Black men have on their families.

Finally, African American men may seek social services for issues that may not appear to be directly related to family problems (e.g., occupational problems). It is important, however, that practitioners make diagnostic connections between these specific presenting problems and broader family issues. We are not suggesting an etiological (causative) connection with the men's individually expressed presenting problem and family dynamics but rather that the clinician attempt to understand the interconnectedness of these two systems and their relative impact on each other.

Intervention

We challenge family therapists not to attempt to make important structural, emotional, or psychological changes within the African American family without the Black male present in the therapy process. In the previous section, we acknowledged that the engagement process in family therapy with African American families should be given primacy and may have to be elongated to include Black men because of the presence of invisible triangles involving Black men and their *invisible presence* that family practitioners have coconspired to create. To this end, practitioners may have to abandon the obligatory and perfunctory practice of weekly (1-hour) scheduled family counseling appointments. Practitioners may opt to schedule two or three strategically planned, longer family therapy sessions to accommodate unrelenting work schedules or other environmental realities. Other options that practitioners may want to explore are home visits, the use of phone calls for briefer planning sessions, and the use of letters by African American men to other family members, especially when geography is an obstacle.

Cultural or *therapeutic joining* (e.g., the technique of exploring the receptivity and flexibility within a family system to make changes that are most syntonic or familiar to the family system) with African American men in family therapy can be achieved by inclusion of important cultural, religious, and/or civic Black male figures from the community. These persons can also serve as expert cultural consultants to the therapist and thus lend credibility to the counseling process.

Speck and Attneave's (1973) "network therapy," although it has not received much attention or elaboration in the clinical family therapy practice literature in recent years, can serve as a important vehicle for inclusion of these important and influential (indigenous) African American male community, religious, and/or civic figures in a very profound way. Their inclusion in the actual family therapy process may also spark a regeneration or reconnection of ties that may have become dormant throughout the years. (It is conceivable that these persons will continue to reach out to these men, even after the actual family therapy session is completed. Perhaps these well-connected persons may be inspired to instigate special programming for African American men in their various arenas of influence.)

Speck and Attneave's (1973) network therapy can also be used to include often neglected and ignored male members within Black men's larger kinship and friendship networks. The inclusion of the larger social network of African American men (especially male members) in family therapy can be an important resource for practitioners, especially because of the strong nonkin or fictive kinship bonds that frequently develop within Black families (Boyd-Franklin, 1989). Social network therapy can serve as a powerful interventive tool with its emphasis on reconnecting and strengthening bonds that are culturally based and potentially gender affirming.

CONCLUSION

Throughout this book, we have emphasized the importance of using a critical constructionist perspective within an ecological framework while incorporating Africentric values in the provision of counseling, therapy, and social services to African American men. The result is an integrative critical practice approach, perspective, or framework to family work with African American men that encourages practitioners to allow their family therapy and practice to be guided by a vision of social justice. This perspective is especially crucial to family-based interventions with African American men in its potential to move family practice beyond the narrow conceptualization of family-based problems, and it has the ability to integrate the roles of therapist and advocate. Also, an ecosystemically based model of family intervention assists practitioners in paying special attention to critical, unique developmental "stress points" that may threaten the familial relationships of African American men. Finally, the infusion of Africentric principles in family practice, such as an emphasis on *familial interdependence, collectivity,* and *cooperation,* may help prevent practitioners from marginalizing African American men in their family practice efforts.

NOTES

1. The reader is referred to Chapter 5 for an in-depth discussion of concepts relevant to couple and family therapy. The concepts defined and examined in Chapter 5 were selected because of their special relevance in couple and family therapy practice with African American men.

2. *Joining* is the therapeutic tactic of entering a family system by engaging its separate members and subsystems and gaining access to the family system to explore and ultimately to help modify dysfunctional aspects of that system (Minuchin, 1974). *Accommodating* is similar to the technique of joining in that the therapist works to "blend" into and make personal adjustments to adapt to the family style in an effort to build a therapeutic alliance with the family to understand family themes and myths. The reader is referred to Chapter 5 for a definition and review of the basic concept of triangles and its relevance to couple and family practice with African American men. The term *invisible triangles* is taken from the concept of triangles in the family theory literature (Bowen, 1978). We reconceptualize the concept of triangles and coin the term invisible triangles to refer to the existence of a third person, in an emotional system, who exerts a powerful but not always apparent force on the systemic or dyadic relationship system.

Chapter 7

GROUP WORK WITH
AFRICAN AMERICAN MEN

The quality of being human for Africans is embodied in the South African phrase *"Umutu ngumtu ngabanye abantu"* ("A person is a person through other people") (Louw, 1995). Within the African worldview, the individual exists so that the group can survive. Consequently, an individual can only be understood through the life of the group (Nobles, 1980). Furthermore, the African model of human relationship emphasizes the importance of group and community needs over individual aspirations (Roberts, 1994). Key to this perspective is the belief that self-identity can only find expression and fullness in connection with the communal whole or through other people.

Within the contemporary African American community, the sense of group or collective identity is retained from its African origins. This group perspective is evident in the family, church, and a variety of social groups and institutions within the African American community. These institutions provide communal support and a sense of peoplehood through mutual group associations.

Groups exist as an integral part of the social and ecological milieu of African Americans. They have served a vital and critical role in the lives of African Americans. Group affiliations historically provide a bulwark for African Americans against the forces of racism, poverty, and oppression. Mutual-aid groups have been the cornerstone for the tradition of self-help within the African American community. African Americans have maintained a sense of collectivity and group consciousness, and groups have provided continued and regenerative resources for collective empowerment.

Given the significance of groups within the African American community, group work practice can be a powerful resource for social work interventions with African American men. Three factors contribute to the potential significance of group work practice with African American men. First, African American men, especially poor, young African American men, may need an ear—someone to listen to them. Extrafamilial support is especially important within this young, urban population because of the "burnt bridges" and the "emotional cutoffs" that may have occurred as a result of their earlier years of recklessness, as discussed in Chapter 3. Second, low-income African American men are often isolated in poor Black communities, given the presence of gangs and the resultant peer pressure to join or affiliate with gangs. Finally, negative "narratives" passed down by society through the mass media and possibly intergenerationally within their own families have a profound impact on many African American men. These men may need assistance in confronting these negative distortions, which may have been internalized by them. Groups can provide this assistance.

Groups can be a source of personal and collective empowerment for African American men. Social work groups can enable African American men to achieve a sense of connection with each other and reconnection with the broader African American and national community. Groups can provide the opportunity for African American men to reconstruct personal and collective narratives. Groups can mobilize African American men to be the authors of their own personal, social, political, and economic destiny. Finally, groups can provide the means for African American men to develop skills for functioning effectively in key life roles, such as parents, husbands, and employees.

In this chapter, we examine how groups can be utilized as a intervention approach with African American men. Different types of groups and other subsequent group issues particularly relevant in group work practice with African American men will be discussed. In this chapter, we examine groups from an Africentric perspective. We also provide an overview of the requisite skills needed by both African American and non-African Americans group leaders in working with groups of African American men.

AFRICAN AMERICAN MEN AND THE "COLLECTIVE" IDENTITY

The sense of group identity is integral to the African American community. The experiences of African American men have often mitigated against their sense of connectedness with each other and a larger communal consciousness, however. There have been no enduring institutions within the African American community other than specific religious faith communities, in which African American men can meet, bond, and talk with each other on an ongoing basis about life and personal growth issues. Scattered opportunities may exist outside the African American community, however, through the military or within organized athletic activities. Within the African American community, however, such organized opportunities for male bonding are extremely limited.

Admittedly, this experience is not unique to African American men. The traditional male code restricts men from sharing personal concerns within an association of men. Such emotional expressiveness violates certain "rules" of the "male code," which promotes a sense of emotional isolation and disconnectedness in relationships with other men. These factors appear to provide a compelling argument against the viability and effectiveness of groups for men in general and for African American men in particular.

Contrary to widely held views, in some respects African American men depart (at least ideologically) from this model of restricted emotional expressiveness. Research evidence suggests that African American men tend to rate expressive males more favorably than nonexpressive males (Roberts, 1994). Additionally, African American men tend to describe their closest male relationship as having "brotherly" qualities. This reflects a common expectation among African American males that close friendships should reflect the trust, caring, openness, and honesty associated with one's brother. As Roberts (1994) examines some of the problematic interactions between African American men, however, he states, "Unfortunately, the majority of the evidence suggest that Black men are not getting [or giving] what they desire and expect in relating to each other" (pp. 387-388).

"Tribeless Black Men"

Many African American men have existed on the margins of the African American community and have been described as *tribeless black men* (Frazier, 1939). The tribeless black male is the African American male whose life reflects a state of marginality away from the center of African American life. These men are described as tribeless because they live a life of tenuous and temporary relationships with men and women. These men, who were migrants when E. Franklin Frazier wrote his description of them, are bereft of any connection to the "black collectivity." These tribeless men, because of their experiences with poverty, racism, and oppression, live a life of indifference to intimacy and connection. They are the personification of the state of existential alienation described by Fanon (1967); as are African American men who have experienced long-term poverty and described in contemporary terms as the underclass (Martin & Martin, 1995).

The Gang as Collective Identity

Another group of African American men, especially poor, young African American males, are being seduced toward group consciousness through gang affiliation. These young Black men have been the primary subject of contemporary professional literature. Gang affiliations, although satisfying some of the need for a collective identity, do not reflect the sense of connectedness with the broader community of African American men or connectedness with the African American community. In actuality, gang affiliation and gang behaviors represent a detachment from the social praxis of African Americans in that the primary focus of their relationship with other African American men and with the African American community as a whole is through crime and deviant and destructive behaviors.

AFRICAN AMERICAN MEN IN HUMAN SERVICE GROUPS:
AN OVERVIEW

The social science and clinical practice literature on social group work with African American men is quite sparse. There has been little written about the experience of African American men in human service-related groups. Much of the relevant literature describes the role of social control and rehabilitation in groups with African American males. This literature discuses groups for "involuntary" or mandated clients whose dysfunctional, problematic, and criminal behavior requires a form of "social control" or "social rehabilitation" often under the guise of therapy.

Populations that have been the target of social control or rehabilitative groups include adolescent males (including teen fathers), men in prison, men in alcohol substance abuse recovery, men who batter, and "uninvolved fathers" (Fagan & Stevenson, 1995; Harvey & Coleman, 1997; Williams, 1994). Group participants have usually been low-income men. Group involvement for these men is often required by courts, social service agencies, or hospitals. In these instances, group services may be the treatment of choice not by the men themselves but by the referral agencies.

In recent years, however, there has been a proliferation of concerns about "rites of passage" or "manhood development" programs for African American men (Watts, 1993). These programs are focused on identity development issues and life skill development. Such programs, however, have primarily been directed toward African American adolescent males. The focus of these manhood development programs has been to establish nurturing relationships that engage and expose young men to opportunities and avenues for personal advancement, build competencies needed to pursue life and career opportunities, and build self-esteem (Watts, 1993). These programs have typically been grounded in an Africentric cultural value framework.

Hence, the significance of the group experience for African American men is beginning to be reevaluated within the African American community. This has been especially true since the *Million Man March* in 1995. During the Million Man March, there was a clear exhortation to African American men to join male and community groups. There was also the recognition among the march participants of the power of groups to impact change and to create change within the community. The Million Man March also increased the consciousness and awareness of how "personal reality" is shaped by political and cultural realities.

AN AFRICENTRIC AND EMPOWERMENT FRAMEWORK
FOR GROUP WORK PRACTICE

Of profound concern for many African Americans is the irreparable crack in the foundation of the spirit of "collectivity" and group consciousness. Racism, oppression, and poverty have produced a profound fracture in the community and group spirit. The result of this fracture has been the psychosocial and existential alienation as described by Fanon (1967). Fanon posits that "anti-Black racism" and anti-Black male racism has resulted in the Black male's alienation from the self, the significant other, the general other, his African culture, and the creative social praxis (Bulhan, 1985).

The Principles of Nguzo Saba

Social theorists propose that the lack of group consciousness in the African American community is a reflection of a cultural crisis in that there is a need for a socialization process or value system to resurrect a sense of cultural collectivity. To address this issue, an Africentric value system known as *Nguzo Saba* ("Seven principles" in Kiswahili) was developed by Dr. Maulana Karenga (1996), a professor and author of Black studies. Dr. Karenga saw the need for Africentric socialization to regain the sense of collectivity and cultural connection to Africa. These seven principles are the minimum moral set of values that African Americans need to reconstruct their history, humanity, and community.

The seven principles of *Nguzo Saba* have been incorporated by social scientists and social workers (Crawley, 1996; Harvey & Colemen, 1997; Oliver, 1989; Pack-Brown, Whittington-Clark, & Parker, 1998) as the necessary value base for providing social and human service intervention with African Americans. These principles have been used as the basis for "manhood development" groups. The following are the seven principles of *Nguzo Saba* in brief:

Umoja (unity) encourages striving for unity in family, community, nation, and race

Kujichagulia (self-determination) encourages self-identity as a people and an individual the ability to be able to define one's self.

Ujima (collective work and responsibility) encourages collectivity building and maintaining the African American community and making the burdens of African American males and females those of the African American people and community.

Ujaama (cooperative economics) encourages building and maintaining African American businesses and profiting from these businesses.

Nia (purpose) encourages collective work for the building and developing of the community.

Kuumba (creativity) encourages doing whatever is possible to create beauty in the community.

Imani (faith) encourages belief in African American people, parents, teachers, leaders, righteousness, and the victory of the African American struggle.

Nguzo Saba provides a unique framework for guiding group work practice (Harvey & Colemen, 1997; Pack-Brown et al., 1998). *Nguzo Saba* also provides a frame of reference for group workers in the African American community in that these principles form a conceptual bridge that supports group activity and community building. Finally, these principles form an integrated whole including the individual, family, and community as integrated units and speak to a commitment to the principle of togetherness and collective action *(Umoja* and *Ujima).*

The principles of *Nguzo Saba* can also give direction and structure to group work efforts with African American men. One of the fundamental keys for groups with African American males is to empower the men to create self-affirming narratives that counter the hegemonic narratives that perpetuate the state of "tribelessness" *(Kujichagulia)*. Grounding a group in *Nguzo Saba* enables the participants and the leader to examine group processes and outcomes in connection with larger systemic and ecological concerns. For African American men, the prime systemic concern needs to be connection with other African American males, the African American community, and the broader American community *(Ujamaa, Nia, Kuumba, and Imani)*.

One of the most important features of *Nguzo Saba* is that it speaks to the need for self-help and self-empowerment. As a cultural and value framework for group work practice, *Nguzo Saba* is clearly congruent with an empowerment and an "Africana womanist" perspective in group work practice.

An Empowerment Perspective

As outlined and discussed in Chapters 2 and 4 through 7, a "critical practice" approach addresses the need for African American men to confront the dominant narrative that marginalizes the African American male experience. An empowerment model of group practice (Garvin & Reed, 1994; Garvin & Seabury, 1997; Lee, 1994; Solomon, 1976) would support such goals. The empowerment model encourages an awareness of the African American male's relationship to the larger environment and the experience within a historical, cultural, and political context.

The empowerment perspective allows African American men to gain an understanding and mastery of their status within the dominant social order. This perspective gives attention to achieving a critical consciousness by understanding the impact of sociopolitical realities on their lived experiences. From an *Africana womanist* perspective, there is also an acknowledgment of how the lived experiences of African American men are "raced" and "gendered," as in the case of African American women. As a basis for group practice, African American men, who share a common experience, would be able to draw from a collective group and mutual resources for personal and collective empowerment (Lee, 1994).

An empowerment perspective is also strengths oriented in that it acknowledges the preexisting capacity to modify situations that hinder personal and interpersonal fulfillment (Fagen & Stevenson, 1995). A strengths perspective in group work with African American men counters the deficit perspective, which tends to reinforce negative stereotypical views of Black men.

TYPES OF GROUP WORK PRACTICE WITH AFRICAN AMERICAN MEN

The empowerment perspective along with the principles of *Nguzo Saba*, can undergird an array of types of social work groups with African American men. The level of empowerment and employment of *Nguzo Saba* may differ according to the type, purpose, form, structure, process, dynamics, and phase of group development (Lee, 1994). Regardless of the type of group, *critical practice* and empowerment orientations allow the participants to understand the link between individual circumstances and societal conditions. Furthermore, an empowerment-oriented group can help members achieve a sense of solidarity with each other.

Issues in Different Types of Group Work Practice

Within the critical practice and empowerment perspectives, groups can address critical challenges for African American men, including developing a culturally syntonic sense of masculine identity, confronting racism in the workplace, establishing working relationships with spouses and other significant women, managing anger, negotiating personal value conflicts, gaining job readiness skills, developing more effective parenting skills, managing more healthy lifestyles, gaining overall self-improvement, managing stress, and developing conflict resolution skills. This list is not exhaustive; it does address some of the primary life domain concerns of African American men, however.

These challenges can be addressed in a variety of group types. We broadly classify the types of groups for African American males as (a) manhood development groups, (b) self-help and support groups, (c) psychoeducational and life skills development groups, and (d) counseling or psychotherapy groups. This topology is not a rigid classification system because the primary focus of a specific type group can be (and perhaps should be) integrated with the goal and focus of another type of group. For example, although a group may have as its primary focus manhood development, it may contain elements of self-help and support. Such a group may also give attention to the development of life skills. A psychotherapeutic group for African American men may correspondingly have as one of its goals the enhancement of a sense of Black masculinity or manhood development.

In the following discussion, we describe the goals and purposes of the previously mentioned group types. Following these descriptions, contemporary examples of actual groups or programs that exemplify the aforementioned characteristics will be presented. These examples, of course, are not meant to be exhaustive of the types or range of potential groups for African American men.

One of the unique and common characteristic of the examples presented here is that a broad-based Africentric cultural framework is used to guide the groups' purposes, goals, and processes. In one of the groups, the principles of *Nguzo Saba* are explicitly articulated as the value and cultural basis for group and program activities. In the other groups, the principles of *Nguzo Saba* are not explicit in defining the group purpose or in guiding the group process; the spirit of *Nguzo Saba* is present, however.

Manhood Development Groups

The purpose of manhood development groups is to facilitate the development of constructive African American masculine identities. These groups are often developed in community-based human service organizations or within churches.

Manhood development groups have typically focused on adolescent males as they make their transition into adulthood. These groups provide opportunities and avenues for personal advancement and help males develop competencies needed to be successful in adulthood. The desired outcomes of these groups are to enhance one's identity as an African American male and to build self-esteem. This process is accomplished through nurturing and supportive relationships between adult African American men and adolescent or preadolescent African American males.

Within this broad classification of manhood development groups are two types of groups: rites of passage groups, and mentorship groups. The rites of passage group is a small group model that many African American social work practitioners advocate as a method for inducting African American adolescents into a sense of responsible communal consciousness (Harvey & Coleman, 1997; Long, 1993; Perkins, 1986; Warfield-Coppock, 1995). Rites of passage groups provide a structured (small group) format for learning skills, attitudes, behaviors, and values that support a strong sense of responsible manhood. Generally, this effort is grounded in the principles of *Nguzo Saba*. These attitudes, behaviors, and values are supported by experiential and ritualized activities and events to promote their inculcation, internalization, and integration.

In mentorship groups (mentoring is often a one-on-one activity), the group process may not be as formal, structured, or ritualized as in a rites of passage group. A mentorship group, however, does provide the opportunity for a group composed of both adult males and young males to interact in an open and relatively unstructured format and to discuss topics that pertain to key developmental, life, and survival issues for the young African American males. A significant outcome of this group type is that the generational gap can be bridged between adult and youth. Across this generational bridge and support, information sharing can traverse. Additionally, rather than a singular adult mentor in a leadership role, the mentorship group provides a structure for multiple or situational leadership, depending on the topic or activity.

In both groups, the adult male has key leadership responsibility, although there may not be a formal group "leader" who guides the group throughout its life. In the rites of passage group, the adult leaders are the "elders" or those males who, by virtue of their life experiences, have the responsibility to instruct, support, and preside over the "initiatory" rituals. The elders have the role of confirming the "new adult male" as he makes his "transition" from childhood to adulthood. In the mentoring groups, the mentors are guides, teachers, advisers, and confidants who confirm the "Dreams" of the young male group participants. These dreams contain the heroic self-images that give shape to the young males' aspirations to be special people in the world of adults (Gooden, 1989).

The elder and the mentor are both impacted in important ways as a result of this helping relationship. The "helper theory" principle of Riessman (1965) states that "to help another is to help oneself." Thus, as the elder and mentor engage in the external process of support, affirmation, and confirmation of young men's identities, this interactional process can reaffirm or confirm the development of the leaders' sense of masculine self. In essence, this process can solidify the leader's sense of who he is and what he can be as an African American male role model.

Leadership in rites of passage groups or mentoring groups can be a very empowering experience for adult male participants. In addition, the group process can mitigate against generational and *emotional cutoffs* that have unfortunately developed between older adult African American men and young African American males. (The current generation is the first generation of African Americans in which the elders actually fear the young.) Hence, potentiating dialogues need to be established between these generations. The chasm between adult African American men and African American youth can be bridged by cocreating a structure in which mutual understanding and the empowering of each other's world is achieved.

Responsible African American Men United in Spirit Academy and the Young Warriors: Developing Black Men. Two examples of manhood development groups are the Responsible African American Men United in Spirit Academy (RAAMUS) (Gee, Walker, & Younger, 1997) and the Young Warriors (Watts & Abdul-Adil, 1997). Both programs prepare boys for formal rites of passage programs and provide some of the support, information, and guidance traditionally provided by fathers and other males. As stated earlier, such groups are primarily targeted toward adolescent males. These groups, however, have a significant impact on the adult male "elders" who initiate the young men into African American male adulthood. Additionally, unlike more conventional psychosocial interventions that focus on personal development, the RAAMUS and Young Warriors groups are attentive to the cultural and sociopolitical status of African American males (Jagers & Watts, 1997).

The RAAMUS program gives primary attention to promoting academic motivation. The Young Warriors program is focused on helping adolescents develop critical thinking skills to broaden their social, political, and cultural awareness or a state of critical consciousness. The Young Warriors group goals explicitly reflect this purpose:

1. Developing critical consciousness skills
2. Learning about manhood and how African American manhood is constructed in contemporary society
3. Developing cultural awareness, including both African and African American cultures
4. Increasing the understanding of and participation in community development and social change

What is significant about these groups is that not only do the groups focus on initiation into manhood but also these groups are concerned with constructing and evolving a new concept of Black manhood. Additionally, these manhood groups simultaneously engage in a critic of existing concepts of manhood toward the development of critical consciousness.

Support and Self-Help Groups

Lee (1994) describes one of the principles of the empowerment perspective as follows: "People who share common ground need each other to attain empowerment" (p. 208). Self-help and support groups provide the format in which those who share common conditions, experiences, or problematic situations can join together for common support. These groups become the arena in which one can get help, support, and mutual aid from those who have had similar experiences. In this supportive environment, a sense of personal and collective empowerment can be generated.

Self-help groups can provide both personal growth and collective action via mutual support among the members (Katz and Bender, 1976). Following the Million Man March, many African American men returned to their communities and formed self-help groups. These groups focused on mutual support as the men shared their struggles with the alienating and oppressive experiences of being African American men. These groups began to define strategies for collective action and advocacy, thus truly merging the personal with the political (Kunjufu, 1996).

Self-help and support groups can facilitate the emergence of critical consciousness through mutual discussion and problem solving. Self-help and support groups help to mediate some of the stress resulting from the experiences of role strain as described by Bowman (1989). Self-help and support groups allow African American men to name and confront their experiences. These groups can also be the means in which African American men overcome the psychoexistential experiences of alienation resulting from racism and oppression.

The role of group leader in a self-help support group is primarily that of an organizer. The leader can bring people together in terms of their common need. A group leader must recognize that, in a self-help group, peer solidarity is more significant than group structure or group hierarchy. In the case of groups with African American men, the principles of *Nguzo Saba* become the cultural milieu that both creates the climate for the group process and shapes the rationale for the "coming together" for mutual self-help and support.

"Men as Teachers": A Support Group for African American Men. An example of a support and self-help group is described by Fagan and Stevenson (1995). This group, called Men as Teachers, provides a forum for low-income African American men associated with Head Start programs to discuss parenting concerns. Fagan and Stevenson found that the primary focus of discussion in this group is the men's felt need, as African American men, to control their own destinies. The men also expressed the need to challenge racism and assume a collective responsibility to help other African American men and children.

One of the significant outcomes of this study is that the men in the community who were not affiliated with Head Start and did not have children wanted to join the group (Fagan & Stevenson, 1995). This group is viewed by the African American male participants as providing a place where African American men can talk about parenting issues and other themes particularly relevant and salient to their own lived experiences. Most important for these men is the experience of helping each other and having an impact on their community through the engagement of other men in the group program.

Psychoeducational and Life Skills Groups

Psychoeducational and life skills groups provide the primary function of socialization and psychoeducational instruction in life skills that enhance functioning in key life roles including being a parent, spouse, or employee. These groups can operate in a variety of settings. The group participants can be both voluntary and "involuntary" clients.

In addition to the role of socialization (and possibly rehabilitation), these groups may have as their primary purpose developing the kinds of skills needed to help people function more effectively in the social order. These types of groups have special relevance for the African American male. Such groups may provide the kinds of skills needed to help tribeless black men reenter the communal life of the broader community. That is, these groups can operationalize the principles of *Nguzo Saba* by the development of job readiness skills, effective parenting skills (especially for marginalized low-income [never-married] noncustodial fathers), money management skills, political awareness, and community-building skills. The skills and information provided in an educational group are not just those that enhance personal achievement and success. The skills and information for African American men should also promote communal involvement and investment.

Key to the development of an educational and skills-building group is the role of the group leader. Understanding the group process is a key requirement along with understanding the experiences of African American men. In addition, group leaders should use African American men and African American organizations outside the group to assist group members. This involves using African American male leaders from the church, community organizations, and other civic or social groups. These men can be the bridges from the isolative existence of the group participants to a more productive entry into the broader community.

Choices for Fathers: Developing Life Skills. There are several programs and group efforts that demonstrate various elements of a psychoeducational and life skills development group. One of the authors had the opportunity to conduct research on such a group program called "Choices for Fathers" (Rasheed, Fitzgerald, & Howard, 1996). This program provides low-income, noncustodial fathers with an opportunity to contribute to the emotional and financial support of their families. These goals are accomplished through a variety of groups and workshops in the following areas:

1. Job readiness and placement services
2. Effective parenting classes
3. Adult education classes (i.e., GED and the ABE diplomas, etc.)
4. Rites of passage groups
5. Parent-child (group) activities and field trips

6. Health and dental services

7. Self-help and support groups mixed with counseling and psychotherapy concerns

8. Professional mental health services (i.e., individual, couple, and family)

Choices for Fathers, although primarily oriented toward life skill development, provides a range of group-oriented services, including rites of passage, manhood development training, and psychosocial support and self-help. This program clearly incorporates the principles of *Nguzo Saba* into the fabric of its activities. *Nguzo Saba* not only informs the rites of passage components but also these principles are infused throughout all phases of program and group activities. The group participants are continually and deliberately exposed to the principles of *Nguzo Saba.* The desired outcome of such exposure is that the participants achieve a sense of cultural self along with the requisite life skills needed to enhance the economic survival of themselves and their families.

Counseling or Psychotherapy Groups

Therapy groups are focused on helping group members examine and change behaviors, emotions, or thoughts related to some problem in functioning (Garvin & Seabury, 1997). In the experience of many African American men, "problems in functioning" are often defined by external authorities. Thus, many therapy groups for African American men have the onus of social control or rehabilitation. To confirm this experience of therapy group for African American men, Sutton (1996) states,

> Most African American men enter group psychotherapy unaware of its benefits, unaware of why they were referred, and with reservations about the value of any form of psychotherapy. In low-income settings, participation is often required by courts, social service agencies, and hospitals because clients risk loss of freedom or sustenance. ... They may be cajoled and threatened by wives, parents, employers, and others to join group therapy as a last-ditch effort to make a change. (p. 134)

Chapter 4 describes many of the concerns of African American men regarding engaging in individual therapy. The same issues are evident regarding involving African American men in group therapy. In fact, many of the conditions that are stated for clinical practice success with individual therapy are also applicable to group therapy. As stated in Chapter 4, mental health practitioners must move beyond deficit and punitive approaches to mental health intervention. Successful mental health interventions, including groups, must embody an empowerment and culturally sensitive and oppression-sensitive approaches that promote a sense of critical consciousness. With these conditions for successful interventions in mind, a psychotherapy group for African American men should also give attention to the following (Lee, 1990):

1. Provide the opportunity for the participants to critically analyze the images of African American men and reassess their notions of masculinity within an African American perspective

2. Provide a forum for the healthy ventilation of feelings of anger and frustration associated with the sociocultural challenges to African American manhood

3. Provide a format for the members to develop and share proactive strategies to challenge self-destructive and high-risk behavior patterns

4. Enable the participants to develop the requisite attitudes and skills for individual contributions to the optimal development of African American men and the African American community

Basic to the previous conditions is the assumption that therapy groups for African American males can be racially homogenous with African American leadership (preferably male). Given the human service settings in which group therapy takes place, it is likely that most therapy groups may be racially mixed and include both males and females. It is also likely that the group leader may not be African American. The salience of race and group composition is a critical factor in racially heterogenous groups (especially counseling-oriented groups). The factor of racial composition influences both group dynamics and group leadership issues. This is a critical issue that will be discussed later.

"Reflections on the Native Son": A Group Therapy Experience. Some psychotherapy groups, such as the Reflections on the Native Son therapy group, specifically address African American male issues (Lee, 1990). Reflections on the Native Son is described as a multisession, nontraditional, and innovative counseling group designed to

> Help Black men raise their level of masculine consciousness ... to develop a supportive therapeutic atmosphere that will enable a diverse group of African American men to explore thoughts, feelings, and behaviors associated with being Black and male in contemporary American society. (p. 131)

The group name Native Son is derived from the literary work, *Native Son,* by the African American author Richard Wright (1940). This title is apt for such a group because the novel describes the "emotions, suffering, frustrations, and yearnings that generally typify growing up Black in America" (Lee, 1990, p. 130). Such descriptions of the emotional plight of African American men inform the goals of this group, which are as follows (Lee, 1990):

1. To have group members reflect on the challenges associated with being Black and male and to have them reflect on their masculinity from an African American perspective

2. To have group members examine the psychological, social, and health hazards confronting African American men and their personal patterns of coping with them

3. To have group members examine roles, responsibilities, and relationships in their lives in an effort to gain a better understanding of their attitudes, values, and behaviors as Black men

4. To have members consolidate group cohesion and terminate the experience with a positive sense of Black manhood

This group is not problem specific but gives attention primarily to the conscious-ness-raising of African American men. As such, this group can be implemented in a variety of settings. Critical in the implementation of this group is group compo-sition and leadership. One of the key (and most obvious) elements for the success of this group is the maintenance of racial homogeneity and Black male leadership.

The racial composition of a group is indeed important to the group process and the attainment of group goals. The experience of the participants within the group is clearly influenced by the racial composition of the group. Understanding the impact of group composition is also crucial for successful group leadership.

The Salience of Race and Group Composition

Moreno (1934) was one of the first researchers to discuss the impact of racial ratios in small groups. His concept of "racial saturation point" described the num-ber of out-group members that an in-group can accept within its boundaries (Robinson, 1995). Brayboy's (1971) research noted that Whites are reluctant to become members of groups in which they are a minority. Davis (1984) points out that African Americans appear to prefer groups that are 50% Black and 50% White (contrary to White participants, who prefer an 80% White to 20% Black ratio).

A recent study suggests that groups containing equal numbers of Black and White participants may exacerbate racial confrontation and tension between the Black and White participants (Davis, Cheng, & Strube, 1996). This phenomena can be explained as a thrust for racial group dominance by either of the racial groups. Even more significant is that the struggle for dominance is more apparent in racially heterogenous male groups than in female groups.

Davis (1984) recommends that racially heterogenous groups should have at least two African Americans in the group so that each may help to validate the experiences of the other. The sole Black male group member may find that instead of gaining support and strength from the group he is quite isolated in these group treatment situations (Ahmad, 1990).

Although crucial for all multiracial groups, issues of composition may have a unique significance for African American men. All Black male groups tend to cre-ate an excellent environment for increased group involvement due to an increased level of trust by group members and greater (potential) identification with values and themes discussed in the group (Williams, 1994).

In a racially heterogenous group, however, especially in the initial phase of group involvement, African American men may be apprehensive, vigilant, and racially sensitive, especially to what they perceive as negative stereotypes of African Americans and African American males as perpetuated by group mem-bers or group leaders or both (Sutton, 1996). In cross-race and mixed-gender groups, African American males, being cognizant of stereotypes and myths about the "aggressive Black male" or the "highly sexualized Black male," may be apprehensive in expressing personal issues regarding anger, intimacy, sexuality, or all three.

Finally, if African American men perceive White group members as active (or even passive) participants in terms of social oppression, African American men are likely to put up their defenses. African American men may also be quite hesitant in expressing angry feelings regarding "White privilege" and Black disfranchisement in a racially heterogeneous group, however. These responses are truly adaptive but may reflect a degree of distancing from other non-Black group members. This distancing will become a major issue for the group leader.

Leadership Issues for Group Practitioners

Working with African American men in a psychotherapy or counseling group presents many challenges for a group leader. Some of these leadership challenges are not only unique to a psychotherapy group leader but are also relevant for any leader who undertakes group work with African American men. Basically, group leaders must attend to the cultural and racial issues brought forth in groups. Group leaders need to be particularly attentive to ensure that the issues brought to groups by African American men are validated and not merely tolerated or, in worse-case scenarios, subordinated, rejected, or even excluded.

A successful group leader with racially heterogenous groups must be comfortable in using his or her knowledge, skills, and sensitivity when confronted with racially sensitive issues. One approach for group leadership is particularly applicable to racially heterogenous groups (Davis, Galinsky, & Schopler, 1995). This model, designated RAP,

> assumes that effective outcomes of any multiracial group requires that leaders carry out three essential tasks. First, they must recognize (R) the critical importance of the racial dynamics of the group and their own ability to act. Second, they must anticipate (A) the source of racial tension and help members deal with the tension. Third, they must be prepared to problem solve (P) if issues become problems. (p. 160)

Recognizing the salience of the racial dynamics in a racially heterogenous group requires the group leader to be engaged in an ongoing self-assessment and assessment of the group, its members, and their environment. In addition to this recognition, the group leader must anticipate potential sources of tension in composing the group, formulating the purpose, and structuring the group's work together. Finally, the leader must be able to intervene whenever there are incidents relating to racial tension by involving group members in confronting and resolving problems within and outside the group (Davis et al., 1995).

The RAP model prescribes an extensive outline of the skills required for effective multiracial group leadership. To reiterate this outline is beyond the scope of this chapter. It is suggested, however, that RAP does represent a viable model for multiracial group leadership.

Other group practitioners and theorists have also developed and articulated the competencies required for multiracial group leadership (Leong, 1992; Pack-Brown et al., 1998). The following are some of these competencies as adapted for group work with African American men:

1. Group leaders need to understand the concerns of African American men via the literature on African American men.

2. Non-African American group leaders need to take the time to learn African American values. Group leaders also need to be aware of the impact of cultural issues on the group process.

3. Group leaders need to approach interpersonal problems of African American men from a collective rather than an individual orientation.

4. Non-African American group leaders need to view the men as experts of the own lives and thus serve only as cultural consultants on the African American male experience.

5. Group leaders should use African American men and African American organizations outside the group to assist with group members using African American male leaders from the church, community organizations, and other civic or social groups.

6. Group leaders should focus on the "multiple ways of being" a Black male while recognizing the commonality in the group experience of racism.

7. Group leaders should help the men deconstruct the "politicized knowledge" of African American men and empower them to construct individual narratives rather than strive to adhere to monolithic notions of Black masculinity.

Any group leader who considers leading multiracial groups that include African American men should familiarize himself or herself with various group leadership models such as the RAP framework (Davis, 1995; Leong, 1992; Pack-Brown, et al., 1998). These leadership models, along with an awareness of the dynamics of being an African American man, can enhance the leadership effectiveness with groups.

SUMMARY

Groups for African American men should strive to develop cultural and gender identity, racial and gender pride, and collaborative relationships with other African American men and to facilitate the overcoming of alienation from significant others in their lives. These groups should also build on the inherent, but sometimes dormant, strength of African American men and seek to mobilize personal and communal resources. These objectives can assist African American men in reaching the goals of personal, collective, social, and communal empowerment.

Group leaders must be acutely cognizant of the social realities and experiences of Black men. That is, group leaders need to be sensitive to the personal and institutional experiences with racism and be willing to explore the extent to which presenting problems are influenced by economic deprivation, anger, rage, and frustration. Lack of such an exploration can contribute to trust problems between

African American group members and the group leader (Sutton, 1996); this is especially the case in which the group leader is White.

CONCLUSION

As with any group, groups for African American males should establish goals that relate to their own ecological, cultural, and developmental needs and not goals that are socially imposed or goals that represent social oppression. These groups, regardless of goals or types (manhood development, support or self-help, psychoeducational, and counseling or psychotherapy), should address issues of developing a critical consciousness. That is, as group leaders facilitate the group process, they should be sensitive to the cultural and *gendered* meaning of interactions and tasks. In essence, leaders need to emphasize the fact that these tasks should not be limited by either racism or sexism. Finally, the group leader must be willing to address the issue of racism as it presents in covert and overt ways, whether it is explicitly presented or not in group work practice with African American men.

Part III

MACRO PRACTICE ISSUES AND STRATEGIES

Chapter 8

POLICY ISSUES OF LOW-INCOME
AFRICAN AMERICAN MEN

The history of social welfare policy in the United States has been one of benign neglect with respect to low-income men. The benign neglect of this group of men has reduced them to psychological, economic, and social impotence. That African American men in the inner city are disproportionately represented among low-income men and low-income fathers is an important consideration that merits further study regarding the focus of social welfare policy.

In this chapter, we examine ideological, theoretical, and conceptual analytical frameworks that have been used to guide and develop policy for low-income African American men and fathers. We also explore policy issues that adversely affect the lives of low-income African American men. Obstacles to the paternal role functions of low-income African American fathers and low-income, unmarried or noncustodial fathers will also be discussed. Finally, we present suggestions for future directions for policy making that should be based on the needs and strengths of low-income African American men and fathers.

IDEOLOGICAL, THEORETICAL,
AND CONCEPTUAL ANALYTIC FRAMEWORKS

There are several positions that attempt to explain the prevalence of social problems among African American males. These ideological positions are viewed as conceptual analytical or theoretical frameworks that serve to ultimately direct and mold policy. Thus, it is important for social scientists, policy analysts, politicians, and journalists to understand and acknowledge the ideological assumptions and biases that profoundly give direction to policy making activities. Four of these positions are briefly outlined here.

The *genetic inferiority* position views social problems as a result of inferior genetic traits that predispose persons to engage in higher rates of problematic behavior (Jensen, 1973). Proponents of this position typically disregard the role of systematic racial discrimination. This perspective has been criticized for failing to provide evidence of a specific genetic trait that causes major problems (Montagu, 1941). It has also been noted that advocates of this perspective tend to differentially apply it in explaining the causes of social problems among various racial and ethnic groups (Archer & Gartner, 1983).

Advocates of the *culture of poverty perspective* argue that poverty, social disorganization (i.e., the breakdown of community institutions, family, church, and school), and inadequate socialization of children are the primary causes of high rates of social problems (Banfield, 1970; Moynihan, 1965). The major flaw in the logic of this position is its failure to explain why only a small number of group members engage in problematic behaviors if, as the theory suggests, all group members have internalized values and norms that conflict with mainstream values and norms (Hill, 1972).

The *racial oppression position* holds that historical patterns of political disenfranchisement and systematic deprivation of equal access to educational and employment opportunities have induced a disproportionate number of Blacks to engage in illegitimate means to achieve mainstream values and goals (Cloward & Ohlin, 1960). A major criticism of racial oppression theories is that they tend to overpredict the number of Blacks who are likely to become involved in problematic behavior (Oliver, 1989).

The *structural-cultural perspective* offers an alternative explanation of social problems based on the interrelationship between structural pressures and cultural adaptations. This position argues that the high rate of social problems among Blacks is the result of structural pressures and dysfunctional cultural adaptations to those pressures. Two variations of this perspective are set forth by Wilson (1987) and Oliver (1989). Wilson argues that historical patterns of racial discrimination and the technological transformation of the economy have produced disproportionately high rates of joblessness, female-headed families, poverty, drug abuse, and crime among African Americans. Oliver articulates this position as a failure among African Americans to develop an Africentric ideology in the face of White racism and as the result of structural pressures (i.e., political, economic, social, and cultural) and various patterns of racial discrimination.

With the exception of the structural-cultural position, we contend that the major theoretical and conceptual analytical frameworks used to guide and formulate policy for low-income African American men possess inherently negativistic assumptions about Black men. The end result of social policies developed within these ideologic frames are policies that are paternalistic and do not build on the strengths of this population.

POLICY ISSUES ADVERSELY AFFECTING LOW-INCOME MEN

Federal policy has often had a disproportionate effect on the lives of African Americans. The federal retreat from programs and policies in the 1970s, especially in areas of employment, education, health, and family stability, contributed to the deepening of social problems in the Black community in the 1980s (Taylor, 1995). Such reversals in federal initiatives have had a particularly adverse effect on the quality of life of young Black men as evidenced by several social indicators (Gibbs, 1988). Black males are worse off today than they were two decades ago (Gibbs, 1988; Taylor, 1995). The shift in emphasis of federal policy in the past 20 years has contributed to the current crisis among young Black males in the inner cities (Taylor, 1995).

The structural unemployment of Black men has reached virtual epidemic proportions. A contingency of policy analysts assert that employment and job training programs were never designed to address the more serious structural problems that the Black poor encounter in gaining access to long-term employment. Rather, these programs are attempts to ease the deprivation among the poor and prevent the possibility of mass insurgency (Piven & Cloward, 1971).

Other theorists propose that the high unemployment rate among many inner-city, poor African American men results from the interaction of three structural factors: *spatial mismatch, skills mismatch,* and racial discrimination (Kasarda, 1989; Moore & Laramore, 1990). The spatial mismatch hypothesis contends that high African American unemployment rates are the result of a mismatch between inner-city residence and the location of jobs in the suburbs. This position holds that urban employment opportunities that provide good wages for less skilled workers are becoming increasingly scarce while central-city employment is becoming concentrated with high-skilled jobs, in information-intensive industries, which are filled by better educated suburbanites. The existence of a skills mismatch can be seen in statistics showing the lower educational attainment of Blacks compared with Whites, which contributes to their higher rates of unemployment. Indeed, most unemployed youth are Black inner-city high school dropouts. Beyond spatial and skills mismatch, discrimination still presents a significant barrier to employment for African Americans. Once Blacks are employed, occupational discrimination contributes to constraints in upward career mobility and to lower wages compared to those of Whites.

Other barriers to employment for poor African American men include low self-esteem, "streetwise" attitudes, low literacy levels, substance abuse, police records, gang activity, low skill levels, and chronic illness (Chicago Institute on Urban Poverty, 1993). Employers will not hire men with these problems when better qualified applicants are available. Additionally, there are often not enough job training and placement services in the neighborhoods of these men to meet their needs. Finally, discrimination in hiring and recruiting and discrimination on the job have all been cited in the research literature as significant structural barriers to employment (Laseter, 1997).

Wilson's (1987) work focuses on the relationship between poverty and family stability in the African American community. He asserts that due to the structure of the welfare system, women have no incentive to live with or marry men who do not have enough income to bring the household above the poverty level. Thus, the inability to find employment undermines marital stability and further decreases the African American male's sense of self-worth (Testa, 1989).

Many low-income African American men have major medical, dental, and mental health problems (especially major depression, and alcohol and drug problems) likely related to long-term poverty (Gibbs, 1988). These problems prove to be complicating factors for these men by causing them to miss days at work, and at times they threaten newfound employment. Health and mental health reform efforts that include wide coverage and a large federal financial role are needed to address the needs and challenges of this population.

POLICY ISSUES ADVERSELY AFFECTING LOW-INCOME AFRICAN AMERICAN MEN'S ROLE FUNCTIONS AS FATHERS

One of the most pressing issues facing African American men are policy issues that exist as obstacles to their role functioning as fathers. As a function of their disadvantaged economic status, low-income men inadvertently rely more on social policies to support and facilitate their roles as fathers: thus, they are also more vulnerable to these same policies. Fathers are a missing element of social policy in the United States, however (Levine, 1993). Existing policies at state and local levels often minimize rather than increase possibilities for coparenting and father involvement (Gadsden & Smith, 1994). Contemporary legal and social policies in the United States do not facilitate paternal participation; in fact, most existing practices functionally serve to limit and restrict opportunities for male involvement (Lamb & Sagi, 1983).

Generally, policy discussions on "father issues" and "father involvement" have been largely limited to the financial contributions of the father to the family. Only recently has research begun to focus on the impact of father involvement on children's psychosocial well-being and cognitive development: this is especially the case in the literature on the African American father-child dyad (Gadsden & Smith, 1994).

Much of the early social science research on poor African American fathers is based on a *cultural-deficiency* theoretical perspective and imposes a middle-class, Eurocentric definition of paternal involvement (Rasheed & Johnson, 1995). These theoretical perspectives result in narrowly conceptualized paternal involvement and role behaviors that characteristically portray and assume African American fathers to be emasculated, ineffectual members of the parental dyad in the African American family.

Research has also failed to address several compelling policy issues that come to bear on fathering (Cromwell & Leeper, 1994). Beyond child support enforcement, there is little consensus about the range of policy questions that bear directly on fathering. Gadsden and Smith (1994) suggest that policymakers should conduct analyses on political issues that can add to our limited understanding of the cultural contexts in which African American male development and fatherhood occur. These analyses could then contrive opportunities to improve the problem.

Low-income married fathers, be they custodial parents or not, derive some support with their parenting efforts from the law by virtue of their marital status because state public assistance and child welfare programs provide for children and their custodial parents (if they were married when their children were born) regardless of the gender of the remaining (previously married) custodial parent. Additionally, low-income "intact" families (in which both the mother and the father are present in the household) are also eligible for state support and various public assistance programs, however limited these resources may be. Hence, poor, never-married, custodial fathers fall within the cracks of existing social policies. It is also worth noting that married fathers tend to have higher incomes than their unmarried counterparts (Lamb & Sagi, 1983).

Poor, never-married, custodial fathers have similar problems and experiences as do low-income single mothers, even though their numbers are few. There are no special sanctions, policies, or procedures that address their unique needs and situations, no doubt in part a result of prevailing societal norms and laws that favor mothers over fathers. To date, little is known about poor, never-married, custodial fathers. This population is not publicly visible, and we speculate that prevailing community and societal norms do not lend much encouragement or support to this population. It is evident that pubic policy needs to focus on supporting these fathers.

Policy Issues of Low-Income, Unmarried or Noncustodial Fathers

Social welfare policy has neglected the plight of low-income men in their parenting capacities as noncustodial fathers. Systematic barriers convolute the already difficult problems facing low-income noncustodial fathers in supporting their families. Family policy has ignored low-income, noncustodial fathers and thus poorly serves the best interests of their partners and children as well.

There has been a dearth of work written for the academic audience that addresses family policy issues regarding African American fathers, especially low-income, noncustodial fathers (Gadsden & Smith, 1994). Social researchers and policymakers however, know very little about the lives and social conditions of low-income fathers. Even less information is provided by the social sciences regarding the lives and social conditions of poor, unmarried or noncustodial fathers.

Minimal attention has been paid to the context within which noncustodial fathers fulfill or fail to fulfill their responsibilities to their families. Research has offered little understanding of these factors within families, communities, social institutions, and the cultures that support or undermine fathering for different groups. This is especially true of poor, inner-city, noncustodial African American fathers (Cromwell & Leeper, 1994). Policymakers need to pay closer attention to how current policies may have a deleterious impact on factors of race, gender, class, and custody status. Furthermore, the field should seek to understand how these unique factors combine to affect the personal circumstances of these men, which in turn may affect the provision of financial and noninstrumental support to their children.

Conventional governmental policies designed to enforce child support are of minimal value typically because social structural factors have severely limited employment opportunities (as discussed previously.) These structural factors are decidedly detrimental to the African American community (Marsiglio, 1989). A more pragmatic approach would be to attempt to maximize the potential for long-term child support rather than short-term support. This could be achieved by crediting economically disenfranchised fathers for their efforts to finish high school or college, receive job training, or both (Marsiglio, 1989). Levine (1993) offers an interesting and equally pragmatic viewpoint. He believes that the core issue and primary focus of social policies and programs should be on "father absence" and not on "money absence."

Recent welfare reforms, such as the Family Support Act of 1988 (FSA) and the Personal Responsibility and Work Opportunity Reconciliation Act of 1996, focus mainly on lifting single mothers out of poverty and have provided little assistance to noncustodial fathers in increasing their income or in developing relationships with their children.[1] These reforms attempt to make noncustodial fathers more responsible for their children by increasing child support but provide little assistance to noncustodial fathers in increasing their income or in developing relationship with their children.

As a result, these men are often characterized as "deadbeat dads" primarily due to their inability to financially support their children. This problem disproportionately affects low-income African American men who are also noncustodial fathers because employment is the first step in increasing the ability of these men to support their children. Taylor (1995) believes this crisis is the result of a shift in focus in social policies and programs targeting the Black community from one of blaming the system to blaming the victim.

A significant problem that many of these unmarried, noncustodial fathers face is that there are no "safety net" programs to help them get on their feet. These men have never been viewed as the "deserving poor." Rather, they are typically viewed as "able-bodied" adults without children. Societal perception is that these men should "just go to work!" As a result, there are no entirely federally funded or joint federal and state grant programs for low-income, noncustodial fathers.[2]

Children of low-income African American fathers are disproportionate among the rolls of Aid to Families with Dependent Children (AFDC), no doubt a function of the father's dire state of unemployment. These policies need to be reexamined in light of the structural issues of unemployment and underemployment of these fathers. The following quote, taken from an ethnographic interview with an unmarried and noncustodial father, who had recently secured (minimum-wage) employment, addresses several issues that need to be examined more closely within this population (Rasheed, et al., 1996, p. 61)[3]:

My daughters lost, when I started paying child support through the Aid [referring to AFDC] ... I was never one to sit around and not bring in some kind of money, but I never had a regular [mainstream] job until now, I've always had side "hustles" to make ends meet ... that's all I could find or qualify for in my neighborhood. ... Now I can't afford to give my kids any money directly out of my pocket, you see after they take the child support directly out of my check, I barely have enough money to get to work and back until the next paycheck and pay my rent ... my kids don't understand, they think I don't care any more, because they don't see me bringing over groceries or clothes anymore or giving them some spending money ... the part that's the hardest is that I can't really afford to take them any where any more when they visit me, so we just sit around the house and they think that 'cause I have this new job that I'm making all this money and keeping it to myself. ... I showed their mother my pay stub, so she could see what they were taking out and what I had left to live on, 'cause she was riding me too, when I stopped giving her money directly. ... Now she's angry with me as she gets less money from the welfare, and now I'm also giving her less money ... talk about a no-win situation!"

Few states operate programs designed to assist unemployed noncustodial parents (most of them fathers) obtain employment to help them with child support obligations (Furstenberg, Sherwood, & Sullivan, 1992). Additionally, the Job Opportunities and Basic Skills (JOBS) program further undermines paternal involvement in that it supports the family by providing employment assistance to mothers but not to noncustodial fathers. Although low-income fathers are eligible for programs funded through other sources, such as the Jobs Training Partnership Act, they usually are not AFDC recipients. Therefore, they are not eligible for the JOBS programs.

Compounding the situation, many low-income, unmarried fathers have been affirmatively pushed out of their children's households via the policies of AFDC programs. AFDC policies seem to be oblivious to the fact that these men are the fathers and the husbands of a largely poverty-stricken population (i.e., children of single mothers). These unmarried or noncustodial fathers experience the entire litany of problems that all low-income people face. In addition, they are faced with unique obstacles as noncustodial parents. A particularly critical concern is the tearing down of many single residence occupancies; many low-income, noncustodial fathers live in very crowded conditions, and others are even homeless. This is not a very conducive environment in which to build self-esteem or encourage father-child reunification. There need to be programs that have connections with public housing authorities to provide stable living arrangements for these low-income, noncustodial fathers.

Legal Issues of Low-Income Unmarried or Noncustodial Fathers

In the state of Illinois, there are two separate (and unequal) court systems— one for married parents and one for unmarried parents. The Illinois Constitution covers equal treatment of children, whether they have married or unmarried parents, but does not cover equal treatment of their parents. The children of unmarried parents have their cases heard in cramped, crowded courtrooms in downtown office buildings or at police stations; whereas children of divorced parents have their cases heard in Chicago's main civil courthouse at the Daley Center. In addition, vital support services, such as home studies, psychiatric evaluations, mediation services, couple and family counseling, court reporters, emergency intervention, and guardians, are not offered to unmarried parents. This discriminatory practice lends support to the contention that the courts have taken a middle-class view of divorce and do not view low-income and unmarried men as real fathers in that the main purpose of divorce appears to be property settlement and child support. To this end, through the efforts of a local paternal demonstration and evaluation project, the Paternal Involvement Demonstration Project (PIDP), a lawsuit was filed by the Legal Assistance Foundation of Chicago (LAFC) (*Comerford vs. Gomez*, see Rasheed, 1998a). This case is a hallmark case. The LAFC filed a federal class action against the Circuit Court of Cook County to challenge the separate and unequal treatment of children who belonged to unmarried parents. The LAFC also drafted and advocated for changes in state and/or federal laws and regulations regarding child support, employment, and training opportunities. In addition, the LAFC advocated against in-state and federal laws and regulations that would harm low-income, noncustodial fathers and their children. The LAFC consultants were also successful in negotiating changes in administrative rulings with other integral governmental agencies, such as Earnfare and various local child welfare agencies.

State departments of public assistance need to expand their thinking beyond child support enforcement; they need to make important administrative changes that reflect more sensitivity to the issues of these fathers and begin to reach out to low-income, unmarried or noncustodial fathers because these fathers typically encounter situations in which paternity establishment and child support litigation processes mitigate against paternal involvement and unnecessarily heightened intrafamilial conflict. This is a particularly unfortunate scenario because an important first step toward empowering poor, noncustodial men as fathers is the establishment of legal adjudication of paternity.

For example, in the state of Illinois, the State Attorney office will represent the mother's interest but not that of the father. That is, only the mother can file with the State Attorney's office to get the father adjudicated. The cost to get paternity adjudicated can range from $200 to $1,000, clearly a factor that makes this process prohibitive to poor unmarried fathers.

There are many other inherent obstacles to these men working the system themselves. For example, poor reading skills or illiteracy, as well as fear and intrepidation of the court system, often result in an uneasy relationship. At the time of the writing of this book, the LAFC was trying to establish paternity without going to court, but there were still many administrative and legislative kinks to work out.

Many poor, unmarried or noncustodial fathers do not know their legal standing with their biological children (Fitzgerald & Rasheed, 1998; Rasheed, 1998a). Many men assume that there is legal significance to their children bearing their last name or the father's surname appearing on birth certificates when, in fact, these mean nothing in regard to the establishment of legal paternity for unmarried fathers. Very few fathers know that they have to sign a form, called the "hospital consent to paternity," when the child is born.[4]

In the state of Illinois, the Department of Child Support Enforcement (DCSE), mothers, and fathers with physical custody can get legal help in establishing paternity. Noncustodial (PIDP) fathers have previously been turned down. The LAFC threatened to sue DCSE. Although it took 11/2 years, the DCSE finally yielded in June of 1995, when they established a Noncustodial Parents Unit for Men. This unit was created to provide legal assistance to men who want to establish paternity, regardless of whether they are on AFDC or not.

There are a host of policies that serve to threaten recently reunited low-income families. For example, in the state of Illinois, these fathers have to go to court to get child support abated. Many of these men do not know that they must do this, nor do they know that public assistance agencies should not continue to take monies out of the father's check for families that receive welfare. As a result, these fathers can build up significant arrearage. In some cases, monies are taken out of the father's check even though the father is living in the home and actively contributing his entire income to the families' well-being. This practice often creates undue financial hardships on these families and can create tensions with current employers, who may take a dim view of wage assignments of its employees. The LAFC attempted but failed to get an amendment passed to this statute. At the time of the writing of this book, however, the LAFC continued to work directly with the Illinois Department of Public Aid (IDPA) to try to get an administrative rule that will have the same effect.

Finally, in the state of Illinois, The Parent's Locator Services checks for the social security and driver's license numbers to obtain child support payments from noncustodial parents, but they will not check to find children for noncustodial parents (most of them are fathers) who are currently paying child support. At the close of the PIDP project, the LAFC continued to try to get an administrative rule from the IDPA to change this policy.

The legal obstacles faced by low-income, noncustodial fathers that undermine their involvement with their children certainly cannot be addressed by the social service delivery system because the paternity enforcement and child support mechanisms are administered under the judicial system. Public policy researchers and other professionals, however, can begin to link their professional activities to policy-advocacy projects (Rasheed, 1998a). By doing so, we can begin to create vital and potentially effective "interlocking feedback loops" within the realms of our various ongoing professional activities.

Future Policy Directions

In summary, what is needed on the contemporary policymaking agenda are comprehensive social policies that encourage and support African American men as fully contributing members of their families and society. Central to this task are access to high-quality education; massive educational reform that creates better linkages between elementary schools, high schools, and colleges; a commitment to full employment; a higher minimum wage; and continued opportunities for skills update and job retraining.

As a profession, we continue to educate and socialize social workers according to intraprofessional boundaries. For example, we view clinical practice versus community practice or practitioners versus researchers versus policy advocates and so on as separate and distinct areas of social work practice. As a result, we have mistakenly viewed social change and social action as not being a primary concern for all areas of social work practice. These professional divisions of labor are especially unfortunate for the neglected (and at-risk) population of African American men. We challenge the profession to unify these intraprofessional boundaries, and we also challenge social workers to create interlocking feedback loops between the various areas of practice, research, and policy in their regular professional activities and responsibilities.

Bruce Jansson (1994), in his widely used text on social policy theory and practice in schools of social work in the United States, strongly advocates that social workers who engage in one-on-one counseling and in clinical practice "be conversant with social policies and be able to seek changes in them, both to help clients and to advance the interests of the profession" (p. 1). Jansson also argues that one-on-one counseling efforts can be facilitated by attempting to change policy in agencies, communities, and legislatures.

The National Council of African American Men (NCAAM), founded by Richards Majors and Jacob Gordon, is the first Black male umbrella group in the United States to address the problems of Black males in America. NCAAM has become a "think tank" designed to educate the public on critical issues facing Black men in America and to help solve problems and shape public policy. Other national forums for research, discussion, and policy recommendations for African American men include the National Black Family Summit (founded by social work professor Dr. Augustus Rogers), the Children's Defense Fund, the National Black Child Development Institute, the National Association of Black Social Workers, and the National Council of Negro Women.

CONCLUSION

State and federal policies assume responsibilities primarily for women and children but not for fathers. This is a middle-class concept that does not even work well for middle-class families and certainly does not work for poor families (Lamb & Sagi, 1983). Policy making must shift from "seeing the parts to seeing the whole" (Austin, 1996). The "band-aid approach" that is in vogue in major social policy planning and political arenas in the United States has had an especially deleterious effect on Black men in general and on Black fathers in particular. Policy making must shift to a systemswide approach to make systemic changes in the African American community. Concomitantly, family policy changes must be made for low-income Black men and their families and not just for low-income Black mothers or poor Black children. Family policy must include all the dyads and subsystems within poor African American families.

Additionally, policymakers should consider whether they are imposing a monolithic, middle-class, Eurocentric definition of paternal involvement on low-income African American fathers. Thus, policymakers need to articulate or reframe policy objectives so that they can facilitate functional behavioral alternatives within the communities of these men. Contrary to widely held views, not all poor African American fathers are "noninvolved ghost dads," and many are struggling to be or stay involved with their children, despite societal or public policy obstacles (Rasheed & Johnson, 1995). In short, policies must strive to move the low-income African American male from his current position of invisibility in the policy arena.

Finally, family policy advocates must become aggressive and facilitate the development of primary and early prevention policies. This proactive approach is necessary particularly because of the grim social status indicators among low-income African American men who are fathers (Gibbs, 1988). Widespread joblessness, welfare dependency, and social isolation from mainstream institutions have deprived many poor African American men the opportunity to get work experience (Laseter, 1997). These societal and structural obstacles discourage self-sufficiency and in turn often discourage men from marrying, thus further undermining the African American family. The social science research literature continues to point to the solution that key to breaking the cycle of disadvantage in the African American community is a federal policy that seeks to address the employment and familial needs of poor African American men and not just poor African American mothers or poor African American children.

NOTES

1. When the FSA was implemented, the Young Unwed Parents Project sponsored by the Public Private Ventures and the Parents Fair Share Project of the Manpower Demonstration Research Corporation were demonstrations created out of the FSA with funding from the Department of Labor (Achatz & MacAllum, 1994). No other more permanent programs or measures were instituted.

2. Long-standing welfare payments for destitute men were slashed in 1991, when the Illinois Legislature eliminated the General Assistance (GA) (a public aid program for adults and non-custodial parents). GA is replaced by the Transitional Assistance (TA) program, significantly reducing already insufficient benefits. A new Earnfare program was designed to allow TA recipients to work for their grant, but only a few thousand part-time Earnfare jobs were created. Jobs are needed for an estimated 50,000 destitute, single men in Chicago who no longer have any income (Rasheed, 1998a).

3. All quotes from Rasheed (1998a) reprinted by permission of Transaction
    Publishers. "Obstacles to the paternal role functions of inner-city, low-
    income, noncustodial African American fathers," by J. M. Rasheed, *Journal
    of African American Men, 3,* 1998. Copyright © 1998 by Transaction
    Publishers; all rights reserved.

4. In cases in which the unmarried or noncustodial biological father has signed
    the paternity consent form, the court does not send a copy to the father. Thus,
    men are left without important documentation that proves their legal right to
    paternity. This procedure changed as a result of the collaborative advocacy
    efforts of the PIDP and the LAFC, and currently the courts routinely mail the
    signed paternity consent form and the birth certificate to both parents (see
    Rasheed, 1998a).

Chapter 9

PROGRAM DEVELOPMENT, IMPLEMENTATION, AND EVALUATION ISSUES IN PROGRAMS FOR AFRICAN AMERICAN MEN

Despite the general ideological aim of social service agencies and organizations, African American males are generally excluded or ignored (Leashore, 1981). Black men are characteristically viewed as "intruders" into the social service partnership. Thus, the provision of social services to Black men is typically characterized by a "negative approach"—that is, a relationship based on paternalism, coercion, exclusion, or all three. Black men are one of the least recognized and least effectively addressed populations in terms of social service and counseling programs (Parham & McDavis, 1987). As a result, social service agencies, by design or default, have combined with other sociohistorical and politicoeconomic forces to further marginalize African American men.

In this chapter, we present suggestions for program design, development, and implementation that can assist program architects in creating and evaluating programs for African American men that are more holistic, Africentric, and ecologically based. Next, we examine how *gendered obstacles*[1] in social and human service organizations have interfered with the role functioning of poor, noncustodial African American fathers. Finally, programming issues for poor, noncustodial fathers are examined.

PROGRAM DEVELOPMENT, DESIGN, AND IMPLEMENTATION ISSUES

One of the theoretical or conceptual streams of the critical constructionist framework (which provides conceptual, theoretical, and philosophical direction to

135

this book) is the postmodernist perspective, as discussed in Chapter 2. Program planners and agency administrators can learn from the postmodernists and their questioning of traditional intra- and interdisciplinary boundaries and artificial distinctions—that is, "who owns what problem." This reminds one of the authors of a personal conversation with Dr. Carol H. Meyer (October 1987) in which she stated that "a lot of social work practice is boundary work." What the author derived from this conversation is that one of our most important professional tasks is the need to locate the "natural" boundaries of the phenomenon or presenting problem(s) rather than to impose our own preconceived notions of where those boundaries are or where we would like them to be. The implication for agency administrators and program architects is that they must allow African American men to lead them to these natural boundaries and only then begin the work of assessing and planning for programmatic needs. This strategy, however, does involve a degree of trust and respect for the population that we serve.

In the following sections, we outline key program intervention strategies, principles, and guidelines that are suggested for consideration in conceptualizing, designing, and implementing social service programs for African American men.

Program Intervention Strategies

Use an ecosystemic framework to organize specific interventions and various program components. Consider using an integrative approach to individual counseling and psychotherapy, employing a wide array of models, including psychodynamic, cognitive-behavioral, psychoeducational and family systems. (See Chapter 4 for a more detailed discussion of this topic.)

Initially, many of the men may not be ready for "suggestions"; often, they just need someone to listen to them.

Use social network therapy and family-based intervention approaches with an emphasis on reconnecting and strengthening bonds between African American men, their families, and community support resources. (See Chapter 6 for a more detailed discussion of this topic.)

Job Training Partnership Act programs should be an integral part of on-site programs and services for low-income men.

Develop new (needed) services, such as mentoring programs, "rites of passage" programs, and peer group counseling for African American males. These programs have proved to be especially effective intervention strategies with Black males. Be sure to plan for important differences in occupational situations in developing these groups, however.

Couples' counseling or conflict mediation services or both may be especially helpful in assisting the parental dyad (as distinguished from the marital or conjugal dyad) to ventilate and perhaps resolve past differences, thus possibly facilitating coparenting efforts. (See Chapter 5 for a more detailed discussion of this topic.)

Principles in Program Conceptualization

Use the Africentric paradigm and values as an intervention paradigm as a way of understanding African American men's aspirations, strengths, and potential and for offering more positive direction for African American male development and socialization.

Focus all interventions on the "positive self" rather than on a constant reflection on pathology, negatives, and inferiority.

Empower African American men to explore and develop more culturally syntonic ways of being masculine and means by which they can "become men." Develop models of masculine identity and manhood that are in sync with African-based values of *cooperation, interdependence* and *collectivity, spirituality,* and *oneness with nature* as opposed to conflicting values of *materialism, competition, individualism,* and *mastery over nature,* which exacerbate conflicts related to manhood (Harris, 1995; Schiele, 1996). Models of Black masculinity should strive to ease the conflict between the cultural systems and dominant societal expectations of manhood and facilitate the Black male's negotiation of these two systems.

Reach African American fathers first as men and then as fathers.

Broaden the definition of father to include "father figures."

Rethink the prevailing conceptual and operational (class-bound and culture-bound) definitions of paternal involvement.

Guidelines for Program Development

Strive toward the development of comprehensive service centers, which integrate services, such as "mini-client-centered support systems."

Work with the mothers of the children; do not neglect one part of the familial subsystem for the other.

Retrain staff to work with this population because these men are relative newcomers to the social service delivery scene. Encourage staff to broaden their role as service providers; they need to become the teachers, fathers, brothers, sisters, and spiritual consultants to these men.

Identify the current extent of parental involvement before planning program components and intervention; do not make assumptions.

Consider providing services in "nontraditional" settings: For instance, civic centers, churches, YMCAs, and the client's home are potential sites for service intervention.

Develop an "entrepreneurial" philosophy to job training and placement for these men. Get the men to think and work toward true "self-sufficiency."

Consider a "holistic" approach to service provision; employ nutritionists, physical fitness experts, spiritual and religious leaders, and traditionally used consultants (i.e., licensed mental health clinicians, physicians, and lawyers).

Build the advocacy skills of staff and clients, and empower clients to engage in political participation, coalition building, and lobbying. Get the men involved in the larger community and enhance their position as role models while promoting system wide policy and program changes.

Build in community intervention strategies that can nurture community and economic development; involve fraternal, civic, religious, professional, and cultural organizations. Form partnerships with businesses and key governmental and social service agencies. (See Chapter 10 for a more detailed discussion of this topic.)

Employ aggressive, innovative outreach approaches that can help to reverse the strained relationship between African American men and traditional social service organizations.

CASE MANAGEMENT ISSUES

As a result of poverty, mental or physical disabilities, other impairments or long-term disabilities, or all these, some African American men may require extensive and protracted social services. These services can come under the broad rubric of *case management* services. The term case management is defined as the enhancement and optimization of continuous, long-term services that enable clients to maintain themselves in the community with their (long-term) disabilities or impairments (Rothman & Sager, 1998).

A comprehensive and intensive case management approach that recognizes the impact of myriad and complex environmental and cultural factors is critical to the provision of effective services for these men. Case management services for African American men need to effect a careful coordination of services that are also culturally sensitive. Case management services must address the following issues of this special population of "vulnerable" African American men; housing or homelessness, health and dental care, mental health problems (the services must be careful to assess major depression and substance abuse problems), legal issues and issues related to paternal adjudication, traditional job training and placement services, parenting classes (if the father has had little or no experience in rearing children), and advocacy assistance in navigating with central social service and governmental agencies (such as child welfare, public assistance, child support divisions, and the criminal justice system).

The issues of marginalization, stereotypes, and negative images of the African American male also impact these individuals to further complicate their already marginalized situations. Their social, mental, economic, physical, or all these disabilities render them especially vulnerable. Because of the duality of their at-risk status–continuity of care, parsimony, individualized services that address cultural differences, and client empowerment are important intervention principles that can assist this population in comprehensive psychosocial enhancement for community living (Rothman & Sager, 1998).

GENDERED OBSTACLES (IN SOCIAL SERVICE DELIVERY SYSTEMS) TO THE PATERNAL ROLE FUNCTIONS OF POOR, NONCUSTODIAL FATHERS.

Fathers, especially African American fathers, are the "neglected partners" in social work (Lamb & Sagi, 1983). Gender differences are an especially important consideration among low-income parents in that women as parents are generally better served by the social welfare system. Thus, there is a need for sex-neutral policies in social services and governmental agencies that facilitate fatherhood (Lamb & Sagi, 1983). The examination of gendered obstacles in social service delivery systems becomes even more essential in comprehensively addressing the needs of low-income, noncustodial African American fathers when the dual dele-terious impact of both race and gender factors is considered. Potential racism and sexism factors compound an already weakened position because of their disad-vantaged social class and custody status.

The literature reports case studies of incidents in which social service agencies and other organizations differentially enforce documentation requirements for use of services by these poor, noncustodial African American fathers (Rasheed, 1998a). For example, clinics and hospitals are reported to require these fathers (who routinely care for their children for extended periods of time) to present legal documentation of their relationship or guardianship status with their children that authorizes them to consent to medical services for the children. These fathers typically express anxiety and apprehension about caring for the children when they are ill due to prior hassles that the men have experienced. In contrast, these men are painfully aware that female relatives or unrelated female caretakers are not questioned about their relationship to the child as long as they can present valid and current "green cards" when seeking these services. These organization-al practices operate to make "child-keeping" difficult for these poor, noncustodi-al fathers and serve to inhibit paternal involvement for this population.

Other examples of gender-based (service delivery) discrimination that emerge from the study by Rasheed (1998a) are reports that there is only one homeless shelter in the Chicago area (the Salvation Army) that will take in a father and his biological children without a verifiable birth certificate or proof or documentation of the relationship of the father to the child. Birth certificates and other documen-tation are not required of adult females with children in other Chicago-area shel-ters. In effect, there simply are not many shelters (for parents with children) that can or will accommodate fathers, even with proper documentation. These shelters are not equipped to accommodate both sexes because of their close quarters.

Social services generally, as in the case of child welfare and permanency plan-ning services, have failed to incorporate African American men as significant par-ticipants in the service delivery process (Leashore, 1997). The child welfare sys-tem typically overlooks poor, unmarried, noncustodial fathers as a resource. There are many institutionally based gendered obstacles to these men's parenting efforts within this system.

For instance, these men frequently report difficulty in gaining access to their children once the children enter the foster care system (Rasheed, 1998a). This problem is especially evident for fathers whose paternity status has not been adjudicated, as is often the case for this young, never-married population. Even the newer "Kinship Care" or "Relative Foster Care" programs overlook noncustodial, never-married fathers as a resource in that criteria to qualify (i.e., being able to produce a lease with one's name on it or legal adjudication of paternity) systematically exclude this poor, unmarried population by virtue of the various qualification criteria. For example, many of these men have experienced long-term unemployment; as a result, names are not listed on rental leases. This same study also shows that many of these men live with relatives or friends or do not live in dwellings that meet child welfare standards (Rasheed, 1998a). These practices are particularly discriminatory and inequitable in light of the fact that mothers would not be denied custody of their children merely due to unemployment and thus lack of (suitable) housing. Rather, it is more likely that mothers would be given special grants and housing assistance to enable them to provide for their children.

Fathers report anger regarding the fact that other relatives are allowed weekend and unsupervised visits as these relatives often have not established paternal adjudication, a very costly and thus prohibitive venture (Rasheed, 1998a). Traditional foster care criteria is also relaxed for relatives (but not for poor, unmarried biological fathers) to allow them to have custody of children through the Kinship Care or Relative Foster Care programs. These men are given less consideration and assistance than total strangers (i.e., traditional foster parents) in that traditional (nonkin) foster parents are frequently given housing assistance, parenting classes, and (if needed) rehabilitative case management and other social or mental health services if the assigned caseworker deems these services as necessary to ensure a safe and healthy environment for the foster child.

The following vignette, excerpted from an ethnographic interview held by one of the authors, illustrates several of these concerns (Rasheed, 1998a). This case involves a father whose children had been taken into The Department of Children and Family Services custody due to the mother's drug addiction. (She chronically left the children unattended for extended periods of time.) This father has a long-term and consistent relationship with his three children. He also serves as a father figure to the mother's other three children, who are the offspring of other males. This case is typical of many poor, unmarried fathers in that this man had fathered these children in his late teens, dropped out (or was "pushed out") of high school, never married, and he has a weakened social network (no doubt in part due to his long-term unemployment, brief history of drug abuse, and minor skirmishes with the law.)

This father poignantly describes his experiences with and reactions to the child welfare system as follows:

> I did everything they said [referring to the child welfare caseworker] ...
> Now they don't know what to do next... [meaning with him] ... Now I'm
> only a father, once a week for an hour, to my own children, in some

caseworker's office [he was referring to the fact that for the past 18 months, he had been trying to get custody of all six children, jumping through all of the appropriate "hoops"—that is, urine drops, parenting classes, enduring demeaning and abusive behavior of caseworkers; he had been limited to once-a-week visitation at the agency because caseworkers deemed that he did not have suitable housing for weekend visitation; he even went through the foster parent's training program and received his certification to ensure qualification for getting custody of his three "step" children] ... I feel my head about to explode when I see the "lowlifes" [foster parents] that they put my children with ... You wouldn't believe how much money and services they are willing to give to those "crackheads" to take care of my kids ... I lived with my kids until me and the mother split, but even after we broke up I still saw my kids every day, I would never move out of walking distance from them ... I could pull it together too if they gave me all them social case services and helped me with my rent until I found a decent paying job.

The epilogue to this vignette is that the children were eventually separated into several different homes. One of the children threatened suicide as a result of being separated from his entire family. Several other children began to display other signs of emotional and behavioral problems. After 2 years of foster care placement, the father was asked to become a traditional foster parent to the siblings of his biological children. At the close of this study, the father had not been able to gain custody of his biological children. This scenario illustrates how child welfare criteria do not address any special sanctions for poor, unmarried, noncustodial fathers.

In summary, the child welfare system is lagging in its understanding of the structure and functioning of many contemporary African American families. The child welfare system continues to build program and policy on the dated assumption that the central and pivotal figure in the African American family is the grandmother. Program and policy architects have ignored the impact of the enduring pattern of multigenerational teenage pregnancy, combined with epidemic proportions of drug and alcohol addiction among females in the Black community. As a result, today's Black grandmother is not necessarily the stable, mature, middle-aged grandmother of yesteryear. Rather, today's inner-city, poor grandmother could conceivably be a 28-year-old struggling with her own chemical or alcohol addiction or both and experiencing a host of other psychosocial problems.

Programming Issues for Poor, Noncustodial Fathers

There has been a recent burgeoning of demonstration-type pilot programs designed to deal with the critical social issue of strengthening the role functioning of young African American fathers. As the number of programs have increased, these programs have served to highlight the incongruities between public perception and the lived experiences of African American fathers (Gadsden & Smith, 1994). For example, Stier and Tienda (1993) show that noncustodial African American fathers have more daily contact with their children than do noncustodial White, Mexican American, or Puerto Rican fathers.

Programs have been redesigned for this population to include a more comprehensive array of social services while maintaining the traditional job training and placement services. These programmatic adaptations are designed to deal with the long-term psychosocial effect of unemployment on the men and their relationships with their children.

Furstenberg, Sherwood, and Sullivan (1992) raise a provocative question of whether programmatic interventions for noncustodial fathers should be driven entirely by the social goal of offsetting Aid to Families with Dependent Children expenditures because many of these program initiatives are specially funded, and program sponsors are typically concerned with immediate program outcome, especially the impact of program outcome on participants' increased ability to pay child support. Paternal involvement program success has often been (narrowly) measured by monetary support and legal adjudication of paternity. In-kind support (i.e., taking care of children or performing odd jobs around the house to help the mother save money on household repairs) is not typically operationalized in "program success" objectives (Rasheed & Johnson, 1995).

Research reports present evidence that reveal that the ways in which programs for young fathers are structured (and also policies that define our child support enforcement, employment and training, and public assistance systems) are out of touch with the real-life circumstances of young fathers (Achatz & MacAllum, 1994; Rasheed, 1998a). Self-sufficiency is arduous for these fathers, and even the most helpful program intervention is not likely to result in immediate financial gain for the children. Furthermore, ethnographic reports of paternal involvement programs present compelling evidence that the nation's major social policies do not promote effective programming for young, poor, noncustodial fathers (Achatz & MacAllum, 1994; Fitzgerald & Rasheed, 1998).

Specific Programming Issues for Paternal Involvement Programs for Low-income, Noncustodial Fathers

Here, we examine specific aspects of developing and implementing paternal involvement programs for low-income, noncustodial fathers. The issues and suggestions considered here are informed by the program evaluation experience of one of the authors (Rasheed, Fitzgerald, & Howard, 1996).[2]

Recruitment and Retention Problems. Difficulty in recruiting participants is a significant problem for programs targeting poor, young fathers. The staffs of these programs typically must expend much more effort on recruitment. This unexpected situation certainly has an impact on these often modestly funded demonstration-project service sites because overworked direct service staff must also become involved in recruitment efforts.

A major factor in the difficulty of recruitment of these men stems from the social isolation and sparse social networks characteristic of persons who have suffered long-term poverty and unemployment, as is frequently the case with this population. Thus, the "word-of-mouth" recruitment strategy that many of these programs rely on is greatly hampered (Gadsden & Smith, 1994).

The program dropout rate is typically very high for this population. These young men drop out for several reasons, but frequently the high drop-out rates can be traced to one or two issues: (a) their lack of trust in project staff, and (b) an inability to see immediate improvements in their financial situation as a result of the program—their primary reason for joining these types of programs.

Training, Education, Employment, Income, and Child Support Issues. Programs for low-income men have considerable difficulty in locating jobs (and "living-wage" jobs) for the men; these programs also receive minimal assistance from local job training and placement centers. These programs however, must become proficient at placing participants in employment. It is clear that an integrated service provision approach of programs employing a full-time "employment specialist" to identify job leads or possible job openings and to maintain relationships with employers is optimal.

The structural problems that have exacerbated unemployment and underemployment with this population also work to confound other psychosocial problems that the men already have (i.e., lack of job skills and training, "on the job coping skills," and substance abuse problems). Many of these men need continued "job readiness" consultation in their initial job placements because these men typically have little or no experience in relating to others in a formal setting, outside of their early school experiences. Important job readiness interventions include teaching more formal communication skills, providing instruction for handling problematic interpersonal situations on the job (i.e., feelings of alienation or a sense of not belonging), and providing guidance for appropriate dress.

Health, Mental Health, and Substance Abuse Issues. Many of these men frequently have significant alcohol and drug problems that developed from a need to relieve major depression. These problems frequently cause the men to miss days at work and likely result in their being fired. The ability of program staff to assess these situations and to intervene quickly can make the difference in a successful job placement. Additionally, developing close and effective working relationships with nearby drug or alcohol programs and health providers can prove to be a key element in program success (especially considering the fact that many of these men present with long-standing and unattended medical and dental problems).

Other Psychosocial Environmental Issues. Weakened and often nonexistent systems of social support are characteristic of this population. Long-standing drug or alcohol problems or both, gang affiliations or membership, and periods of skirmishes with the law all too often serve to sever the ties of their already weak and overburdened network of family. Program staff will need to focus on restoring these systems of social support in light of scarce community resources.

Paternal Adjudication and Other Legal Issues. Poor or low-income noncustodial fathers are often very unclear as to their legal standing with their biological children, as discussed in Chapter 8. Programs should consider hiring lawyers who can be instrumental in helping these men navigate the complex (and costly) court system. Many of these men will likely never be able to establish legal adjudication of their paternity without the assistance of these programs.

Father-Child Interaction. Parenting classes and general "rap" sessions within other group sessions can be used to help these men discuss and explore new techniques for improving or renewing their relationships with their children. Additionally, program administrators may consider sponsoring field trips; this strategy may prove to be a useful medium through which the program staff can observe and later provide consultation to the men about their parenting skills. These father-child field trips can also serve as a "safe" environment in which the men can "try out" the suggestions made in individual and group meetings.

Staffing and Training Issues. There is no clear consensus regarding the relative merit of hiring male versus female staff for these programs. On the one hand, the female staff may be able to do more outreach to the mothers of the children and to other female relatives, which can yield significant success. In addition, the men may feel less apprehensive of revealing "emotional" vulnerabilities to female staff. On the other hand, the male staff can provide important male-bonding and role-modeling opportunities for the men. We conclude that employing both sexes for programs for low-income, noncustodial fathers may prove optimal.

The issue of race or ethnicity in staffing similarly appears to be an inconclusive one. From one of the author's interviews with a paternal involvement project participant and staff, the overwhelming response was that "anyone with their heart in the right place, and a willingness to roll up their sleeves is welcome" (Rasheed, et al., 1996).

PROGRAM EVALUATION ISSUES

There is a large body of literature on the relative value of quantitative versus qualitative research methodologies in program evaluation. Although some researchers exaggerate the differences, most agree that they are mutually complimentary approaches (Reichardt & Cook, 1979; Sechrest & Sidani, 1995; Shadish, 1995). Indeed, Sechrest and Sidani point out that both approaches are empirical to the extent that they are based on observation.

Although optimal, researchers frequently do not have the liberty of deciding the relative emphasis on each approach prior to starting the evaluation. Programmatic changes and other unforeseen problems encountered by pilot demonstration service sites frequently require several midevaluation methodological changes (Fitzgerald & Rasheed, 1998). Program evaluators are commonly faced with the dilemma of how to salvage an evaluation when it becomes increasingly clear that the quantitative data are being "compromised" by necessary changes made by the demonstration service sites. The solution is often to increase the emphasis on the qualitative measures.

This trade-off, however, can introduce tensions between funders and the evaluators. That is, funders are typically not very interested in methodological issues of self-selection bias, diminishing sample size, and changing interventions. They are, however, interested in the researcher's ability to attribute "cause and effect" under tightly controlled quasi-experimental designs. Indeed, project funders, and the larger community, look to program evaluators for "definitive" answers and solutions to very "murky" social problems and issues.

Although evaluations of demonstration-type pilot programs are considered formative in many respects, rigid methodological constraints are often placed on the program evaluators by its funders and by the larger community. These contradictory goals result in a sticky methodological dilemma that is best articulated by Donald Schön (1983):

> In the varied topography of professional practice, there is a high hard ground where practitioners can make effective use of research-based theory and technique, and there is swampy lowland where situations are confusing "messes" incapable of technical solution. The difficulty is that the problems of the high ground, however great their technical interest, are often relatively unimportant to clients and the larger society, while in the swamp are the problems of greatest human concern. (p. 42)

In the program evaluation experience of one of the authors with a paternal involvement project for poor noncustodial fathers, the choice was to continue the evaluation in the "swampy lowlands" (Fitzgerald & Rasheed, 1998).[3] Changes were made in methodology (i.e., an increase in emphasis of qualitative over quantitative approaches) to provide meaningful input in the policy arena in which there was a sense of urgency to create effective programming (Fitzgerald & Rasheed, 1998).

We argue that in responsively and strategically using both qualitative and quantitative research approaches, evaluators are likely to gain a more comprehensive awareness and understanding of program participants' experiences in terms of program outcome and process data.

If the ultimate value of an evaluation is to determine the effectiveness of the program in achieving its goals and whether or how to replicate it we conclude that maintaining "responsiveness and flexibility" in the evaluation process is key to moving demonstration projects to more permanent status.

Finally, demonstration projects, if they are to consist of an evaluation and research component, must have a "pilot" year. This pilot year allows program sites to work out the "kinks" in their programming and allow sufficient time for recruitment of program participants. Service providers and other program staff also have more time to get to know one another to develop the important trust and confidence that would greatly facilitate the practitioner-researcher relationship. The previous measures can serve to minimize the methodological problems for the researchers (Fitzgerald & Rasheed, 1998).

CONCLUSION

In addition to incorporating the previously outlined program development strategies, guidelines, and principles in programming efforts for African American men, it is also important to incorporate in planning efforts crucial areas in which to target specific programs. Principally, we can rely on sociological, epidemiological, and psychological studies to guide our thinking in this regard. The following list provides critical areas and key organizations and institutions in which to target specific programming. Critical areas in which to target specific programs:

Unemployment

High school dropout or push-out and literacy programs

Housing problems

Teen pregnancy prevention and teen fathering programs (Note: The Department of Health and Human Services is using Head Start as the centerpiece of its "male initiative" to increase the involvement of young fathers and other males in the lives of young children [Levine, 1993].)

Coparenting skills

Leadership development and mentoring programs

Father-child reunification programs (Note: More than 60% of low-income African American children live in mother-headed households [Stier & Tienda, 1993].)

Gang violence, street crime, and homicide

Mortality and morbidity rates: prenatal, well-child care, HIV/AIDS, and suicide

Epidemic rates of alcoholism and drug abuse

Key organizations and institutions that profoundly impact the lives of Black men in which program planners need to develop creative linkages:

Job training and placement programs

Schools (elementary, secondary, and colleges)

Local housing authorities

Health care systems

Mental health systems, especially alcohol and substance abuse programs

Child welfare system

Criminal justice systems (i.e., courts and prisons) [Note: In the state of Illinois, it costs $30,000 a year to incarcerate one man; in addition, the prison system makes 37 products. One might wonder if a new form of "slave labor" is being developed.]

This chapter underscores the need for sex-neutral policies in social service agencies that can operate to minimize the impact of gendered obstacles in agencies and organizations as a central part of programming efforts for African American men. To this end, programs for low-income, noncustodial African American fathers need to respond to the complexities of supporting these fathers, especially young fathers, and to try to respond to the familial, personal, social, and systemic problems as experienced and negotiated by this population. Additionally, programs for low-income fathers need to acknowledge functional, adaptive, and alternate family structures and arrangements rather than narrowly focusing on preserving intact nuclear families.

In summary, all aspects of programming for Black men should acknowledge the structural pressures, contextual realities, and the cultural strengths of this population. If we are able to achieve this goal, then as professionals we have a good chance to facilitate the movement of African American men out of the margins and peripherals of social work practice.

NOTES

1. The concept, *gendered obstacles* in social service delivery systems, is coined by us to refer to program features or policies or both that are differentially enforced based on the gender of the client. This concept also refers to organizational behaviors or policies that systematically operate to inhibit or obstruct role functioning. These organizational behaviors or policies or both can be implicit or explicit, formal or informal, and serve to discriminate and give preferential treatment to one gender over the other.

2. A full presentation of the results of this study is beyond the scope of this chapter. The reader is referred to the final technical report of The Paternal Involvement Demonstration Project (No. 360), funded by the John B. and Catherine T. MacArthur Foundation (Rasheed, et al., 1996).

3. All quotes from Fitzgerald & Rasheed (1998) reprinted by permission of Elsevier Science, "Salvaging an evaluation from the swampy lowland," by J. Fitzgerald & J. M. Rasheed, *Journal of Evaluation and Program Planning, 21(2),* 1998. Copytight © 1998 by Elsevier Science; all rights reserved.

Chapter 10

COMMUNITY PRACTICE ISSUES
Creating a *Village* Around African American Men

Being a part of a unique community has long dominated the social consciousness of African Americans. This sense of "peoplehood" has emerged from a commonality of experience resulting from a collective response to the forces of racism and oppression. Notwithstanding the debilitating impact of these forces, the African American community has contained a reservoir of strength and resources that often go untapped and unrecognized. Relying on this communal strength, African Americans have historically formed communal associations to pursue the attainment of civil rights, individual choice, and the legitimation of claims for institutional and psychological liberation (Blackwell, 1975).

In this chapter, we turn our attention to the African American community as the location for social work intervention with African American men. We begin by exploring relevant definitions of community and the significance of community in the lives of people. This discussion is followed by a description of the various approaches to social work practice within a community context. We then examine the significance of community for African Americans.

The "village" construct is employed as our model of community (intervention). This model of community is derived from the African proverb, "it takes a village to raise a child." Although this proverb speaks to the communal responsibility for childrearing, it also addresses the community's role in providing nurturing and sustaining infrastructures for the development of all its people throughout the life course.

We examine how the *Village* community can embrace, sustain, and nurture the adult African American male. In this discussion, we also identify key elements that are necessary to undergird any community practice effort on behalf of Black men within African American communities. On the basis of these elements, we articulate how the *African American Village* can be restored or revitalized through collaborative partnerships with African American women and philanthropic, grassroots, and civic organizations. The role of the African American church in these partnerships is also given special attention.

We also address another vital partnership in "village restoration": African American men in partnership with other African American men. We refer to this partnership as the "community of men" (for men)—a subset community that can assume a vital role in revitalizing the *Village.*

We conclude this chapter by presenting existing programs that exemplify Village revitalization. In this discussion, we provide examples of community development organizations whose goals are to build a village around African American men. For example, in the "communities of men" groups, men are engaged in local and grassroot efforts at building the Village.

A SOCIAL WORK PERSPECTIVE ON COMMUNITY
The Role of Community

How does the field of social work define "community"? Definitions of community are vast and varied. Some define community as a geographic space. Others define community as a geopolitical or civic entity, and still others define community as a place of ethnic, racial, and emotional identity. (This sense of identity is grounded in some form of similarity, intimacy, and reciprocity among the members of a given community.)

In the plight of oppressed people, the community can assume a critical role in their struggle for empowerment. Hence, community can represent (Lee, 1994)

> the critical mediating structure between empowerment, liberation, and oppression. Community members can receive buffering and sustenance from community life; in return they are responsible for giving back; contributing to the strength, survival, and power of the community. As empowered people join together to address and act on community issues and wider political concerns, communities become empowered. In turn, empowered communities provide a growing place for empowering people. (p. 263)

The central question for the oppressed is how to develop communities that can become that "critical mediating structure."

Ideally, communities should be the site for personal and collective empowerment because they should be civic entities and play a major role in providing personal, interpersonal, and communal sustenance to their members. People are able to draw on these community resources, but they also have the responsibility to replenish the community with their skills and talents. Thus, the community becomes a civic entity as individual members empower each other.

Empowered communities are also sites for participation and belonging. A prerequisite for an empowered community is that its members have a sense of connection with other members. There must be a sense of shared membership in community life.

This sense of connectedness is achieved if a community has the following components: the capacity to allow each member to contribute to the life of the community; a belief that the community is enhanced through the collective effort of its members; a means or rituals for celebrating the results of consensual association; a common narrative that gives meaning to the past and gives direction for the future; and an explicit and common knowledge of the struggles, adversities, and suffering that bind the community as an entity (Lewis, 1992).

Defining a community in this broader context allows us to view community as a symbolic construction. A community thus becomes a system of values, norms, and moral codes that evokes a sense of identity within a bonded whole (Cohen, 1985). Finally, an empowered community gives its members a secure sense of self within the context of association with others and within a specific communal and narrative history. It is this understanding of community that undergirds our perspective of community practice with African American men.

COMMUNITY PRACTICE: STRATEGIES FOR INTERVENTION

As we understand the relationship between community, personal, and collective empowerment, the goal of the community practitioner is to implement interventions that facilitate the development of supportive and empowering communities (or critical mediating structures). One of the major conceptual frameworks for guiding community practice interventions was developed by Rothman (1987). Rothman conceptualizes three basic models of community practice: locality development, social planning, and social action. The significance of these models is that much of the social work literature on community practice is grounded in either one or a combination of these perspectives.

In summary, the locality development approach seeks community change through engaging a broad segment of people at the local level in identifying and solving their common problems. The second approach, social planning, involves the technical process of identifying social problems and facilitating the development and coordination of community agencies and services to address those needs. Social action is grounded in a social justice perspective; it is assumed that there is a marginalized or disadvantaged group that needs to be organized to affect the alteration, redistribution, and reallocation of needed resources.

As indicated previously, these three orientations have historically been useful in designing and planning community-based social work intervention. Some community practitioners and theorists, however, have raised questions about the suitability of these models for community intervention in communities of color. For example, Rivera and Erlich (1992) pointed out that for communities of color, Rothman's "color blind" approach may not be sufficient to plan and guide community interventions. Devore (1992) further suggested that Rothman's (1987) models make the assumption that most residents within a community have the ability, desire, and capacity for participation in community change. Such motivation for change may not be evident in some of the fragmented and impoverished environments indicative of many communities of color.

In communities of color, the following key factors need to be taken into consideration in planning community interventions (Rivera & Erlich, 1992);

> (a) The racial, ethnic, and cultural uniqueness of the people of a given community; (b) the implications of these unique qualities in relation to such variables as the roles played by kinship patterns, social systems, power and leadership networks, relation, and the economic and political configuration within each community; (c) and the process of empowerment and the development of critical consciousness." (p. 11)

In addition to the previously discussed factors, community practitioners in communities of color must be able to culturally, racially, and linguistically identify with their communities. In addition to understanding the ethnocultural realities of a given community of color, a community practitioner must have an analytical framework for understanding the political and economic dynamics within a community. Such an understanding can give the practitioner a sense of the empowerment issues within a community.

Another key consideration within communities of color and impoverished communities is that the community practitioner must identify approaches that are *capacity focused* rather than *needs oriented* (Austin, 1996). Many of the past community efforts in communities of color have been based on a deficiency-oriented model. This is reflected in the efforts of community agencies that heighten the community's awareness of community problems and the value of a particular service or intervention to solve these problems. As a result, many low-income communities are now an "enviornment of services" in which residents believe that their well-being depends on being a client.

An alternative approach to community intervention is developing strategies based on the capacities, skills, and assets of the given community. A capacity or *asset-oriented approach* requires that the community practitioner assess and map out the assets, capacities, and abilities residing in the community. The elements needed for Village restoration will then be made evident and can be utilized for community restoration.

With these factors guiding community intervention, it is clear that understanding the unique dynamics and characteristics of the African American community is integral to community practice. Additionally, a community practitioner in the African American community must develop strategies that promote a state of critical consciousness while enhancing a pride in a sense of peoplehood. A practitioner who has an understanding of the capacities, assets, and the unique social, ethnic, and cultural characteristics of the African American community can become a key partner in revitalizing the Village.

THE AFRICAN AMERICAN COMMUNITY AS THE VILLAGE
Characteristics of the African American Community

What are the factors that distinguish the African American community from other communities? Several social scientists have identified some distinctive characteristics of the African American community (Billingsley, 1992; Blackwell, 1975; Solomon, 1976). Geographically, many African Americans live in segregated neighborhoods in which most of their neighbors are also African Americans. These geographic communities, also known as "Black communities," although not always communities of choice are often marked by a sense of personal intimacy and social cohesion. In many instances, these geographic communities have also been marked by social, economic, and political isolation. These communities, however, have played an important role in shaping and reinforcing a sense of racial and cultural identity.

On a cultural level, the African American community can be described as representing multiple perspectives. Each perspective is shaped by the historical and traumatic experiences of enslavement. One perspective represents a deep and rich cultural connection with an African heritage. Another perspective reflects an assimilation of Euro-American culture. The third and most dominate perspective reflects a culture representing varying degrees and mixtures of both African and Euro-American cultural frames of reference. The final perspective represents a state of alienation and disaffiliation from any viable and sustaining cultural perspective. This perspective is representative of those who have no buttress against the forces of racism and poverty.

These perspectives are represented in the diverse lifestyles and cultural perspectives of individual African Americans. From these diverse perspectives, a rich and diverse community with a unique history and heritage has emerged. Correspondingly, a set of institutions and organizations that identify with this heritage have developed. These organizations and institutions form the sustaining and nurturing infrastructure of the African American community. Such institutions and organizations include African American churches, mutual aid societies, fraternal orders, women's clubs, unions, orphanages, senior citizen homes, hospitals, educational institutions, protest movements, and race consciousness organizations (Martin & Martin, 1985).

Grounded in the historical, social, and economic experiences of African Americans, these institutions shape the communal experiences of African Americans. They form the nucleus for the tradition of self-help within the African American community (Martin & Martin, 1985). As community-based institutions, they provide for the experience of collectivity because they are the repositories of the communal narratives. These community-based institutions provide the format for communal celebration, and hence they provide succor and care during individual and communal tragedies.

A Community in Crisis

To speak of tragedy within the African American community is to speak of a community in crisis. In the African American community, there are high and rising levels of unemployment and poverty (Gibbs, 1988). The available jobs are those with low earning and advancement potential. Entrepreneurship in terms of small business is limited. Within the community, there are disproportionately higher rates of imprisonment, unemployment, poverty, and lower educational attainment rates for African American males (Gibbs, 1988). These factors, coupled with a resurgence of discrimination and a reduced national commitment to affirmative action, place the African American community in a state of crisis (Austin, 1996; Comer, 1997).

Although our concern is the African American male, it is important to state that the crisis in the African American community is not just a crisis of the African American male. African American women are also victims of discrimination, sexism, and oppression, both within and outside the African American community. The increase of single heads of households and the growing feminization of poverty directly affect African American females.

Patriarchy Versus Partnerships in Village Building: A "Gender Agenda".
To address how the African American community can be more responsive to the African American adult male, attention must be given to the African American female. A more responsive Village involves building partnerships between African American men and women. It is important to note that such partnerships may necessitate effort at gender reconciliation between African American men and women. It must be made clear that a focus on African American men's issues must not enforce, foster, or perpetuate patriarchy and sexism within the African American community. Dr. Beverly Guy-Sheftall, a feminist scholar, in an address to the National Task on African American Men and Boys (as quoted in Austin, 1996), points out that community-building efforts for African-American men must include

> a carefully constructed gender agenda encouraging dialogue and healing
> between men and women: new criteria for effective leadership in our
> community; open criticism of blatantly sexist individuals, reclamation of
> our communities from a segment of the youth population who have no
> intention of behaving in human ways; telling young men that Frederick
> Douglass and W. E. B. DuBois fought for gender equality. We need
> diverse voices and points of view surrounding the important subject of
> black male identity formation. (p. 100)

Restoring and revitalizing the Village is not a return to a patriarchal social structure. The new Village must reflect a nonsexist liberatory partnership between African American men and women. The new Village must ensure that this partnership does not reflect a mere toleration of each other's presence but a working together in solidarity toward Village reconstruction.

In these community-building efforts, there must be recognition that there are unique situations in which the African American male must be the prime target of intervention. Furthermore, in these situations, African American men must be empowered to assume a primary role in the implementation of interventions. This sentiment is articulated in the "Mission Statement" for the *Million Man March* (Madhubuti & Karenga, 1994), which states that African American men must

> Declare our commitment to assume a new and expanded responsibility in
> the struggle to build and sustain a free and empowered community, a just

society, and a better world. We are aware that we make this commitment in an era in which this is needed as never before and in which we cannot morally choose otherwise.

In doing this, we self-consciously emphasize the priority need of Black men to stand up and assume this new and expanded responsibility without denying or minimizing the equal rights, role, and responsibility of Black women in the lives and struggles of our people.

Our priority call is to Black men to stand up and assume this new and expanded sense of responsibility and is based on the realization that the strength and resourcefulness of the family and the liberation of the people require it; that some of the most acute problems facing the Black community within are posed by Black males who have not stood up: that the caring and responsible father in the home; the responsible and future focused male youth; security in and of the community; the quality of male/female relations, and the family's capacity to avoid poverty and push the lives of its member forward, all depend on Black men's standing up; that in the context of a real and principled brotherhood, those of us who have stood up, must challenge others to stand also; and that unless and until Black men stand up, Black men and women cannot stand together and accomplish the awesome tasks before us. (p. 141)

The previous sentiments and goals can revitalize the Village to embrace and nurture African American men. Community-building efforts must reflect partnerships and collaborations within the African American community at all levels. The most prominent and significant partnership is that between African American men and women. A multilevel approach toward community building in the truest sense can be operationalized within the principles of *Nguzo Saba*. Striving for operational unity (*Umoja*) within the community should be become a driving force behind reconstructing the Village.

Restoring Village Consciousness

The community is viewed as integral to the experiences of African Americans and is consistent with an Africentric worldview. From an Africentric perspective, the individual is an integral part of the collective whole (Mbiti, 1970; Nobles, 1980). The concept of the extended self can be described as "I am, because we are, therefore I am." The "I" is both an individual and a part of the collective whole and cannot be fully grasped apart from the whole. The "We" enfolds the individual subjectivity while being the collective expression of the whole.

In addition to shaping the "self," the community has a temporal dimension. A community includes not only its current members but also its ancestors and the unborn. From an Africentric perspective, the community has an ontological status. It is not merely a free association of individuals but rather it is an inherent part of the structure of reality. To lose connection with one's community violates something very fundamental about the nature of the cosmos. That is, lost connections with the community can result in metaphysical, social, and existential alienation.

In discussions among middle-aged and elderly African Americans, there is concern about the "loss of a sense of community." Proctor (1996) describes a time immediately after World War II when the culture of the African American community was characterized by the existence of a set of tacit but clearly understood values and expected and accepted behaviors. The emergence of the Village concept is an effort to resurrect, reconstruct, and re-create that lost sense of community.

Regarding community practice with African American men, we believe the goal is to enhance their participation and belongingness in the community. Reflecting on Fanon's (1967) analysis of alienation resulting from racism, many African American males, especially those from impoverished communities, move through life with a sense of alienation and a diminished future. To strengthen the Village involves bringing these men back to the Village by creating avenues for participation and belonging. This can be done by providing opportunities in which African American men can invest in the community and the community can invest in them.

RESTORING THE VILLAGE: IMPLICATIONS FOR PRACTICE
Developing a Plan of Action

A comprehensive blueprint for restoring the Village for African American men and boys is contained in a report from the National Task Force on African American Men and Boys. This report, *Repairing the Breach* (Austin, 1996), gives attention to "key ways to support family life, reclaim our streets, and rebuild civil society in America's communities" (p. 2). Funded by the W. K. Kellogg Foundation, this report represents the cumulative efforts of many key institutional representatives, and grassroots and community practitioners. Their prime concern is to develop a comprehensive strategy for addressing the issues facing African American males. This task force is guided by a vision that states (Austin, 1996),

> We will support communities characterized by service and a keen sense
> of ethical behavior and moral responsibility. In these communities, we
> will continue to develop individuals and families who give voice to an
> innovative and entrepreneurial impulse. We will work to create commu-
> nities grounded in cooperation, industry, self-reliance, and prosperity.
> We know this quest to be a cultural mission, as we reexamine and
> strengthen our ancient African sensibilities, and as we grow, develop, and
> inform our American experience. We envision this mission as one of
> reclamation—reclamation of the common good and our common culture,
> as well as reclamation of the neighborhoods and institutions which nur-
> ture our families. We understand that once this internal healing is begun,
> its effect will be the healing of a nation. (p. 14)

The task force generated a 5-year plan of action titled "Project 2000." This plan, which is to be implemented between September 1996 through September 1999, represents an effort to develop a network of civic, social, religious, and cultural organizations as well as inclusion of the Black press to dialogue and support the implementation of the task force plans.

We do not attempt to discuss the task force recommendations in detail. The key ideas or themes are briefly outlined here, however. Project 2000 represents a significant movement toward a broad community-based effort to address issues pertaining to African American men. From this report, specific community practice initiatives can be designed and implemented on the behalf of African American men.

In their deliberations, the task force attempted to formulate their discussions and recommendations around several key ideas: *polis, civic storytelling, grassroots civic leadership, common good, restoring community institutions,* and *civic dialogue.* These ideas or themes are seen as fundamental to any discussion of how to proactively respond to the needs of African American men. We suggest that these ideas be incorporated into any community practice initiative with African American men. Therefore, community practice strategies with African American men should address the following themes:

Polis: understanding and articulating the values, manners, morals, and etiquette needed for structuring the public life in communities on both a social and a political level

Civic storytelling: honoring the lives of ordinary heroes who successfully create public kinship while articulating and defining the African American male's place in society and in the public kinship

Grassroots civic leadership: empowering individuals (parents, teachers, ministers, and young people) to take control of their lives and communities and the development of programs to reinvent civic and economic life

Common good: creating communities that meet common needs through such ideas as economic development, entrepreneurship, and educational reform

Restoring community institutions: defining elements for restructuring and reinventing civic and social life in communities through such means as developing new funding organizations, focusing on housing issues, and developing new apparatus for delivering grassroots multifocused, multipurpose programming to African American males in these communities

Civic dialogue: creating the community's capacity to understand and respond to the needs of African American men through dialogue as opposed to hate and mistrust

These ideas have taken shape through one of the key institutions in the African American community—the church.

The African American Church: The Ontological Community

The African American church is one of the primary structures in the African American community. No other institution claims the loyalty and attention of African Americans as does the Black church (Boyd-Franklin, 1989). The church as a community institution serves multiple functions as it addresses the needs of African Americans. The African American church can be described as an ontological community or a community of meaning in that it provides the spiritual, emotional, and existential meaning and supports for a vast number of African

Americans (Brueggemann, 1996). For many, the African American church symbolizes the heart and soul of the community. In the arena of Village restoration, the church can take the lead and serve in partnerships for community revitalization.

The African American church is one of the largest economic institutions in the African American community. There are more than 75,000 Black churches that receive contributions in excess of $2 billion, with assets of more than $50 million (Malone, 1994). Increasingly, the church has become the center of community and economic development. For example, the Black church has engaged in buying property, developing low-income housing, opening restaurants and other microenterprises, developing strategies for capital acquisition, developing employment ministries, and developing men's ministries. The following is one of the recommendations of the task force (Austin, 1996): "The black church and the black middle class must do more to promote business development within the local community. This includes establishing business partnerships with other community business groups and providing financial and technical support for business development" (p. 91).

One of the authors has served as consultant and adviser to several churches regarding the development of male ministries. These ministries are not focused on shaping a theological message in a masculine framework or on developing a male-centered faith. Rather, these ministries are focused on helping African American adult males become more effective in coping with the tasks of living. African American men with skills and knowledge in career development, financial management, and small business development provide instruction and direction for men who are having difficulties in these areas. Ongoing forums for family life issues are also developed focusing on marital and parental responsibilities. In these forums, there is cross-generational dialogue, providing an opportunity for adult males to dialogue with young males in different ways.

This is but one example of how the African American church can assume a role in restoration of the Village. This example suggests how social work practitioners can assume a role in helping churches engage in these activities. More important, this example demonstrates the critical nature of African American men working with men and boys; this strategy points to developing a community of African American men.

Developing a Community of Men

The notion of an identified *community of men* moves beyond the male bonding retreats indicative of the men's movements of the 1970s and 1980s. The men's movement was highly Eurocentric and called for a returned to some essentialistic notion of masculinity or masculine ideology based on the worldview of White males. The community of men described here is different. It does not have as its prime focus the development of a "Black male identity." Rather, the community of men addresses the role and responsibility of African American men as a part of the polis.

Guidance for the development of a community of men is presented in the Million Man March. This gathering symbolizes African American males coming together to demonstrate caring for their families, communities, and the mentoring of young males. The men who were present heard exhortations to be more aggressive and responsible in maintaining their families, to join faith communities and community-based organizations, to register to vote and become politically and culturally active, and to respect self and women. These exhortations have resulted in some effort on local communities to organize African American men to engage in such activities.

Building the Village: Examples of Community Development

There are many examples of men and community agencies joining together in efforts to engage in community development and social action. For example, a community development organization in Chicago, called *Fishers of Men,* emerged from a Parental Involvement Demonstration project that focused on low-income, noncustodial African American fathers. The goal of this program is to "build a village-like community around the men—to instill a sense of community and personal responsibility in the participants, and to instill a sense of community responsibility in employers and associated human service agencies" (Rasheed, Fitzgerald, & Howard, 1996, p. 15). The Fishers of Men program relies on several service providers to offer all the social services needed by the men. In addition, the program involves local schools, churches, and other institutions to engage the men in the community. This is a clear example of multileveled community partnerships.

Mentoring is also important to this program. The men serve as mentors to each other and to their children. In addition, community members and employers serve as mentors to the men. This strategy is based on the belief that the men will feel empowered when they become contributing members of their community, and the community will likewise be empowered by facilitating the lives of its members.

Another group in Chicago, the *Community of Men,* is an example of a grassroots effort of community organization and social action. As a crime-watch group, it is described as a group of "God-fearing humble and consistent men [who] patrol the streets" (Kunjufu, 1996; p. 160). These men pass out literature and talk to young men about the importance of ridding guns and drugs from the community. With this effort, they offer economic alternatives to selling illegal drugs by providing tutorial support, meals, and cultural and recreational activities.

A grassroots organization called *MAD Dads* is a national organization that was formed in Omaha, Nebraska. This is a group of men who, by virtue of their initiative, have become leaders in the streets of their communities. In these communities, these men act as father figures, mentors, leaders, father confessors, and strict disciplinarians. They maintain a presence on the streets between the hours of midnight and early morning. It is reported that these men have transformed the streets of their communities into "caring sensitive orchestrated workshops" (Austin, 1996, p. 84).

A final example of a community-based effort involving African American men advocating for African American men is a group called *One Hundred Black Men* in Indianapolis, Indiana. This group regularly sits in on the editorial board meetings of local newspapers to ensure more accurate coverage of African American males (Austin, 1996).

The previous examples are a small sample of numerous examples of groups of men and organizations that affect community change. In summary, the previously discussed groups provide examples of African American men involved in restoring the Village. In this fashion, African American men can become mobilized and empowered to influence their own destiny. By helping others, they can help themselves.

CONCLUSION: A CALL FOR ACTION

Jawanza Kunjufu (1996), a noted educational consultant on African American males, outlines the necessary steps for Village restoration. He believes that the first institution in need of restoration is the nuclear and the augmented African American family. Following the family, Kunjufu suggests that attention should be given to the educational institutions within the community. The next area of focus should be the involvement of civic and community organizations. The church, which is one of the key institutions in the African American community, should participate as one of the chief architects in Village restoration.

In addition to this group of stakeholders in the African American community, we suggest another group that should have a vital role in Village restoration— African American men themselves. There is a need for a community of men to participate in partnerships in the task of restoring the Village.

One of the main recommendations in the task force report was the need for dialogue among African American civic, social, religious, and professional organizations to bring about the necessary changes that would support grassroots community leaders (Austin, 1996). These various shareholders in the African American community cannot stand alone. There must be a format for community dialogue to galvanize collaborative and cooperative efforts to build a Village for African American men. This format would include universities, private foundations, research centers, civic groups, religious groups, governmental agencies, Black fraternal orders, local businesses, and chambers of commerce.

The role of a community practitioner in this partnership involves being a community or locality developer, a social planner, and a social activist. In terms of locality development, the community practitioner can be the catalyst, coordinator, and instructor to local community institutions as they move to develop programs for African American men. As a social planner, the practitioner can serve the role of fact gatherer and coordinate the development of partnerships. Finally, as a social activist, the community practitioner can be the advocate and agitator for the concerns of African American men.

Although considered a "macro" social work activity, "micro" practitioners (i.e., counselors and therapists) can clearly engage in these community practice activities. When practitioners are engaged in developing, locating, linking, and managing community resources to help people improve their social functioning and sense of empowerment, they are indeed involved in "community practice" (Hardcastle, Wenocur, & Powers, 1997).

The basic challenge as presented in this chapter is that a renewed and consistent effort is needed to engage in community village restoration. The restoration efforts must be based on a restoration of hope. Hope must be the dominate theme of a new narrative or civic story about the African American male within the polis. It must be a communal and social narrative that speaks of the African American male as a socially committed member of the Village community.

Part IV

CREATING LINKAGES
BETWEEN PRACTICE, POLICY,
AND RESEARCH

Chapter 11

EPISTEMOLOGICAL, CONCEPTUAL, THEORETICAL, AND METHODOLOGICAL ISSUES IN CONDUCTING RESEARCH ON AFRICAN AMERICAN MEN

It is clear that many research projects that pertain to the lives of Black
people are political; therefore, any study of their lives is political.
—Robert L. Williams (1980)

In traditional social science research, epistemological and theoretical questions about methodology are usually divorced from substantive subfield concerns (such as research on African American men) and are typically discussed in a vacuum as philosophy of social science considerations (Stanfield, 1993). These important epistemological, theoretical, conceptual, and methodological questions about research, specific to the study of African American men, are raised in this chapter.

In particular, we address the issue of how the conceptualization of research problems and interpretations of data collected in research on African American men has typically been preceded by a priori ideological and cultural biases that profoundly determine the production of this so-called "objective knowledge." Thus, the gathering and interpretation of research data on African American men has historically served the function of lending a "professional gloss" to what, in reality, is nothing more than cultural and social stereotypes about Black men. In this chapter, we examine these "ideological intrusions" that plague research about African American men.

Although social scientific research has traditionally emphasized males, it has not studied men as men; research has largely been "genderless" (Thompson & Pleck, 1995). During the past 20 years, empirical research on men's problems has lagged far behind theory in the social science literature (O'Neil, Good, & Holmes, 1995). Consequently, little is known about men's gender roles from a scientific perspective. Even less is known (empirically) about men of different ages and from different ethnocultural backgrounds, class levels, and sexual orientations. Hence, theory development on men (especially men of color) is still in its early stages of development because research activities on men of color that are critical to theory development are conspicuously missing from the literature.

Because of this pivotal gap in the literature, research that does not pathologize the behaviors of African American men and that can generate a fuller understanding of the strengths of Black men is sorely needed. To this end, we present emergent theoretical and conceptual frameworks for research that have the potential to generate a more holistic and contextually based examination of the dilemmas and cultural strengths of African American men. In this chapter, we strive to facilitate research on African American men in view of the fact that research is the foundation of and gives guidance to important theory, practice, programming, and policy activities.

HISTORICAL CONTEXT OF AFRICAN AMERICANS, RACE, AND RESEARCH

In his seminal work, Stephen Jay Gould (1981) focused on the reanalysis of classical data sets in craniometry and intelligence testing. Gould was able to locate a priori prejudice that was leading scientists to invalid conclusions from adequate data. Gould was also able to locate prejudices being played out in more subtle roles in what he called "absurd experimental designs ... gross errors in measurement and measurement procedures ... and the distorting of the gathering of the data itself" (pp. 26-27). Unfortunately, the formal challenging of these early *pseudoscientific* studies or rather exercises in *scientific racism* did not occur early enough to subvert future lines of research inquiry. Research on craniometry has culminated in more contemporary scientific racist research efforts.

Hernstein and Murray (1994), in their book *The Bell Curve,* continue this pseudoscientific, scientific racist tradition in their scandalous disregard for scientific objectivity. In their book, they unabashedly assert that scientific evidence demonstrates the existence of genetically based differences in intelligence among social classes and races (Hernstein & Murray, 1994). In *The Bell Curve,* however, these authors repeatedly fail to distinguish between the elementary research concepts of correlation and causation and thus draw many inappropriate conclusions.

These reports are key examples of how, historically, research on African Americans fails to treat racism as a significant variable in the research design, procedures, interpretation of data, or all three. Research on African American men similarly suffers the consequences of this critical conceptual failure. One of the most notorious illustrations of this conceptual failure is the *Moynihan Report* (1965) which was based on the hypothesis that African American men were emasculated by slavery and thus emerged as irresponsible breadwinners. Moynihan attributed the social problems of African American families to Black men's economic dependence on Black women as heads of household. By focusing on Black men's inadequacies in meeting traditional gender role functions, Moynihan sidestepped the societal issues of racism, oppression, and injustice. Fortunately, a more enlightened generation of research scholars have acknowledged the importance of reconciling cultural and male identities with economic and social obstacles in their research on African American men and other men of color (Lazur & Majors, 1995).

In summary, research on African Americans has historically suffered from five essentially racist strategies identified by Howitt and Owusu-Bempah (1994):

1. Stereotyping
2. Marginalizing racism
3. Avoiding the obvious
4. Neo-imperialism
5. Blaming the victim

Consequently, research specific to the study of African American men has suffered a similar plight.

SUBSTANTIVE AREAS OF RESEARCH

Research on African American males spans many disciplines, with no one discipline housing a significant number of studies (Gadsden & Smith, 1994). This trend is a healthy one in that interdisciplinary research efforts have the potential to facilitate diverse foci and value orientations because professional and discipline socialization no doubt serve to influence research efforts in this regard.

The past 20 years have witnessed a tremendous increase in the quantity, quality, and diversity of research on African American men. This recent resurgence of research in the social and behavioral science literature comes after decades of neglect, however. Taylor, Chatters, Tucker, and Lewis (1990), in their decade review on developments in research on Black families, conclude that the role of Black men in families is one of the most conspicuously neglected areas of family research.

Principal Foci and Findings of the Research Literature

We conceptualize the foci and principal findings of the research literature on African American men into three different "waves" of research and three different "generations" of researchers. Hence, we present these three generations of research findings along with critiques of their cultural relevance and sensitivity, methodological adroitness, and the implications and impact for African American men and their communities.

The First Wave or Generation of Research on Black Men

Racial differences in temperament, child-rearing practices, and moral and social development topped the research agendas on African American males from the mid-1920s until the 1950s (Evans & Whitfield, 1988). A significant research focus exclusively on Black men as males, however, as opposed to merely including them as research subjects, did not occur in the social and behavioral science literature until the very late 1970s or early 1980s (the third wave or generation of research).

Research on African American men in this first wave of research seems to be conducted more out of "intellectual curiosity" than any real concern for African American men. The researchers tended to be White, middle-class males who imposed culture and class-bound research questions and hypotheses into their methodologies. Research in this era was typically conducted from an assumption of *cultural deficiency,* devoid of an ecological context and an *emic* (group-specific) view or perspective. By and large, most of the studies in this era posed as genuine pursuits of truth and knowledge but provided no more than "thinly veiled" social, cultural, and racial prejudices. To this end, the cumulative impact of these works served to reinforce and legitimize the inequitable and oppressive environments of African American men, thus rationalizing the maintenance of the status quo in the larger society.

Notable exceptions to the previous critique are the legendary works of E. Franklin Frazier (1932a, 1932b, 1939). Frazier concluded that acculturation to the values and lifestyles of mainstream society was key to the advancement of Black Americans. His thesis and its rationale catalyzed studies in the next wave of research, in which researchers began to explore a new link to pathology and dysfunction for African American families—that is, the primacy accorded the prevailing cultural norms of the dominant core culture (Tidwell, 1990).

The Second Wave or Generation of Research on Black Men

The social concerns of the 1960s and 1970s led to research on a broader range of psychosocial, behavioral, and social status issues that affect African American men (Alejandro-Wright, 1982; Evans & Whitfield, 1988). Three basic themes dominated research on Blacks in this era; intellectual capacity and achievement, self-concept, and family life (Alejandro-Wright, 1982). Hence, research on African American males closely parallels these lines of inquiry during these years. This research focus did not necessarily attempt to uncover explicit male or gender issues unique to Black men, with the exception being research on their roles as fathers and husbands.

This era of research was especially interesting and promising because there was a "changing of the guards" in that a new set of gifted, vastly better informed researchers arrived on the research scene. As a result, recent research efforts on African Americans have demonstrated greater conceptual and methodological rigor. Closer attention began to be paid to underlying epistemological and conceptual biases that profoundly affect problem formulation in that researchers typically employed a *bicultural,* emic (i.e., group-specific) view or perspective to their research. Hence, they began to uncover strengths in African American males that were previously distorted and misrepresented in prior studies of researchers such as Moynihan (1965), Kardiner and Ovesey (1951), and Etzkowitz and Schaflander (1969).

This second generation of researchers conclude that the issue of peripheral-nesss of Black men in their families is vastly overstated; rather, they interpret the familial behaviors of Black men as flexible, adaptive, egalitarian (not emasculat-ed), highly functional, and effective (Billingsley, 1968; Hill, 1972; McAdoo, 1978; Nobles, 1978; Rainwater, 1966, 1970; Scanzoni, 1971; Stack, 1974; Staples, 1971; Willie, 1970).

Despite the vigor of these well-conceptualized lines of research, one cannot help to consider how much of the efforts of these gifted researchers could have been spent engaging in *proactive* research as opposed to *reactive* research. Banks (1980) refers to this type of research as "deconstructive" or "falsification research"—that is, research that demonstrates the fallacy of the inferences and methodological distortions of traditional research. Essentially, this research is a process of undoing the destructive inferences about African American men ema-nating from earlier lines of research. Deconstructive research involves both theo-retical dismantling and empirical rebuttal.

It is highly unfortunate that these reactive or deconstructive lines of research were necessary to counter the deleterious impact of the earlier misguided research efforts. These earlier works, however, were profoundly and swiftly reinforcing negative images of Black men in the mass media and also shaping public policy and important social programming.

Despite this detour, groundbreaking research specifically exploring the expe-riences of African American men emerged in the works of Elliot Liebow (1967) and Grier and Cobbs (1968). These scholarly pieces represent an important widening of the previous family research in that they respectively explore the cop-ing and adaptational experiences of low-income, unemployed Black men and the impact of racism on personality development and masculinity. These works were among the first to examine the internal world of Black men, thus validating its importance; equally significant, they conceptually weaved into their analysis and interpretation the profound influence of environmental variables, such as racism and oppression on psychosocial functioning.

The Third Wave or Generation of Research on Black Men

In the 1980s and 1990s, there was a widening of prior research interests specif-ically targeting the unique dilemmas of African American males (especially young, urban, unmarried fathers). With the alarming decline in social status indices for young African American males and the highest rates of social malad-justment among all subgroups, African American men were aptly labeled an "endangered species" (Gibbs, 1988). Descriptive and exploratory research was conducted on many topics, such as mortality, morbidity, health, education, unem-ployment, crime and imprisonment, family life and paternal role functioning, mental health, and substance abuse. Additional lines of research on Black men were investigated for the first time, namely, male gender role strain, psychosocial adaptation and coping, and personality development.

This third wave or generation of researchers directly benefited from the efforts of the prior wave of researchers in that they were not held hostage by misguided and misinformed research and were free to proactively address the contemporary concerns of African American men. Additionally, this generation of researchers continue to improve on the conceptual, theoretical, and methodological skills gained by the previous generation of researchers. Numerous exciting edited volumes replete with rich, well-executed research studies on African American men, as well as exciting conceptual and theoretical chapters, emerged during this era (Gary, 1981; Gibbs, 1988; Jones, 1989; Majors & Billson, 1992; Majors & Gordon, 1994, Wilkinson & Taylor, 1977).

Future Directions for Research on African American Men

Although the breadth of research on African American males is encouraging and appears to be widening, a major criticism of research in this area is its lack of depth, especially theoretical explanatory depth. Contemporary research on African American males continues to primarily focus on descriptive research of current social problems. More in-depth theoretical understanding of the nature of these well-documented social problems is acutely needed. It is time for researchers to move beyond the descriptive and exploratory focus and begin to examine programmatic solutions to these social problems.

Future lines of research must focus on a better understanding of the impact of racism, sexism, and oppression on the role functioning and behaviors of Black men; understanding the interplay of sociohistorical and politicoeconomic forces and their impact on elderly Black men, Black gay and bisexual men, and biracial (Black) men; the long-term effects of adolescent fatherhood; increasing the understanding of affective roles and functions of Black men in African American families; and the dilemmas and issues of low-income, unmarried, noncustodial fathers and the barriers and incentives to paternal involvement. Finally, a host of phenomenally-based research studies must be performed that explore special issues and circumstances and how these circumstances may differentially affect African American men (i.e., homelessness, substance abuse, depression, suicide, and HIV/AIDS infection).

Epistemological, Theoretical and Conceptual Issues

Here, we present existing and emergent epistemological, theoretical, and conceptual frameworks that are needed to guide research on African American men. Specifically, a proactive or *heuristic,* bicultural, Africentric, emic, ecological, and postmodernist-informed framework or perspective is proposed. (This discussion builds on the theoretical and conceptual frameworks outlined in Chapter 2 and as advanced by Bowman [1989] and Oliver [1989].)

Proactive or Heuristic Research

It is important that research continue its direction of forging innovative, functionally relevant research agendas that respond to the contemporary needs and dilemmas facing African American men. Bowman (1991) defines heuristic research as having the ultimate goal of "articulating culturally adaptive styles and demonstrating benefits which come from adapting that style." (p. 747) This is not to say that conceptual or methodological critiques of shoddy or misleading studies should not be aggressively written and published. Future misguided research attempts that have the potential for deleterious influence on the future of this population, however, may be more efficaciously handled by careful critiques that become similarly widely disseminated. This strategy is proposed in light of the history of research in this area, in which precious progress may have been lost by spending too much time repeating ill-conceived studies (reactive research) rather than forging ahead on important and neglected proactive or heuristic research agendas.

Emic Perspective

One of the most important contributions of cross-cultural psychologists to research methodology in the social and behavioral sciences has been the distinction between phenomena that are considered to be universal (*etic*) versus phenomena that are considered to be group specific (*emic*) (Brislin, 1970). A danger in conducting research on so-called "minority" populations or cross-cultural research (in which the subjects are of a different ethnocultural background from that of the researcher) is to erroneously assume the universality of a concept or construct. Whenever universality is assumed, it is called an *imposed etic* (Berry, 1969) or *pseudoetic* (Triandis, 1972). These are cases in which the researcher imposes a worldview that is culture specific by assuming the *panculturality* (universality) of etic constructs.

It has been the norm in the social sciences to assume that Eurocentric empirical realities can be generalized to explain the realities of people of color. Thus, validity checks are a necessary step in the research process, be it in the construction of questionnaires or the examination of coding schema in qualitative data. Hence, it is important for researchers to consider whether conceptual and operational definitions of key variables are also valid emic ("insider" or group-specific) constructs accepted by African American men as a subgroup.

Africentric Research

Africentrism is a perspective or a cognitive map that reflects one's worldview. Africentrism is a juxtaposing of the African and American ways—an integration of the values derived from the historical experience of African Americans to give us the clearest perspective on the unique group of people called African Americans (Asante, 1988). In essence, Africentrism is reflected in one's philosophical and spiritual acceptance, the intellectual acknowledgment and celebration of the unique hybrid and historical development of the African American ethnocultural heritage. Therefore, researchers who are non-African Americans can similarly adopt an Africentric perspective in their research (Rasheed & Johnson, 1995).

One of the most significant aspects of this perspective is that it takes the ontological position that behavioral observations are, at best, approximates to visualizing the true nature of the human being because spirituality is viewed as endemic to the human makeup (Akbar, 1991). Thus, inherent in this perspective is the notion that researchers can only hope to approach knowing or understanding their subjects, which is a vastly different perspective as that espoused by *logical positivists,* who seek ultimate "truth." Additionally, this perspective encourages a holistic approach to methodology—that is, to study people in a non-fragmented way.

The researcher's conceptual system is grounded in Africentrism by paying unique attention to (culturally based and functional) sex role differences. Hence, research infuses the ontological values of Africentrism in the hypotheses and subsequent problem formulation, the conceptualization and operationalization of constructs, the data collection instruments, and the interpretation of data. (Hence, future research efforts need to focus on establishing levels of validity and reliability with existing standardized instruments specifically for African American males and on developing new instruments with culture-specific or emic Africentic criteria used in their development.)

Bicultural Research

It is important to make a subtle but critical distinction regarding the difference between the Africentric and the bicultural perspectives in research. Research conceptualized within a bicultural perspective (i.e., research that does not impose ethnocentric notions of normality and cultural superiority and does not view ethnocultural differences as pathology) does not necessarily embrace the emic perspective of Africentrism (Rasheed & Johnson, 1995). Africentricity ensures that the *subjective culture* of the research population is captured and reflected throughout the research process. A bicultural perspective (as opposed to a cultural-deficiency perspective), however, is a necessary but not sufficient perspective for culturally sensitive research. The use of an Africentric perspective along with the bicultural perspective is essential to a research process that seeks to understand and explain issues and behaviors of African American communities.

In assuming a bicultural perspective, the researcher is able to be more objective in examining the ecological context and impact of any given behavior, which may be adaptive or dysfunctional depending on the interplay of contextual variables at different points in time; thus the notion that all cultures have "cultural vulnerabilities." That is, any given sociocultural trait or pattern may serve as a strength in one regard but may render a person more vulnerable in another regard; hence the double-edged sword of cultural characteristics. The notion of *cultural vulnerabilities* is not to be construed as implying cultural inadequacies or cultural structural weaknesses or flaws. Rather, this notion serves as a safeguard against ethnocentric assumptions that any given cultural characteristic is somehow inherently pathological or flawed, and it also operates to challenge the "romanticization" of culture characteristics (i.e., the unwillingness to admit to the dysfunctionality of a characteristic for fear of being viewed as racist or ethnocentric).

Ecological and Developmental Framework

The community context is intricately linked to the life status and experiences of African American men. Often, the social vitality and the physical resources of poor, urban African American communities are not examined or linked in a systematic method to explore the synchrony between the socioeconomic structure and the life expectations and opportunities for African American males. This missing component represents a conceptual failure in understanding the life cycle development and behaviors of African American males.

The collective and interdependent nature of the African American community, however, provides a legitimate basis for the development of an ecological research approach for studies on Black men. Thus, research studies attempting to comprehensively understand the experiences and dilemmas facing African American men must systematically build in methodologies that seek to understand the complex interplay of micro and macro systems factors that serve to dynamically interact with each other and profoundly shape the life space of African American men. Hence, there is a need for future research to be more holistic in examining the dilemmas of African American men and not to continue to isolate the study of potentially interrelated issues, such as education, employment, crime, violence, gang behavior, and family relationships.

Postmodern Perspective

Lincoln and Guba (1985) lay the blame for research failure to meet the needs of its subjects at the feet of the unquestioned reliance on the *scientific* or positivistic paradigm of research. On the basis of *relativism,* these authors espouse a unity between the "knower" and the "known." The postmodern paradigm of research with its emphasis on a *subjective epistemology* has the potential to unite the researcher and the "stakeholder" in a research process that emphasizes empowerment, the enfranchisement of the stakeholder, and an action orientation.

The postmodernist perspective as a framework for conceptualizing research on African American men can also be an important tool in countering the fallacy of homogeneity and the fallacy of the monolithic racial identity. The positivists' search for "grand theory" has marginalized and discouraged the exploration and expression of multiple voices and multiple ethnocultural realities. In their journey to establish the truth, positivists have designed methodologies to further more rational forms of knowing (Graff, 1979). These methodologies, however, may hinder knowledge building by marginalizing and devaluing questions and methodologies that emphasize personal experiences and embrace the narrative as a method of inquiry.

The postmodernist perspective, however, is not meant to replace the search for the grand theory with the search for the "grand narrative." Rather, it is an attempt to legitimize the role that personal experiences play in theory building as opposed to an exclusive reliance on community experiences or the "collective story of the disempowered" (Richardson, 1988, p. 204). Postmodernists also seek to legitimize the role of folklore, folk wisdom, folk legends, and popular stories that can emerge in the personal narratives of their subjects (Graff, 1979). This indigenous knowledge or subjugated knowledge calls into question the politicized knowledge of gender studies (or stories) on Black men as the dominant discourse. Thus, Black men's cultural narratives of their own lives are viewed as ways to liberate truly indigenous ways of knowing that may have been obscured by positivists' narrow range of research methodologies.

METHODOLOGICAL ISSUES

As rigorous methodological critiques of research on African American men emerged in the literature (Bowman, 1991; Gary, 1981), researchers began to exact more methodological rigor in research with this population. Contemporary research appears to take more care in the selection of sampling frames, or avoiding distorted (over)generalizations of data based on skewed (dysfunctional or deviant) sampling frames, in selecting and refining data collection instruments to minimize cultural bias and distortions, and in executing a wider array of data collection methods and research designs to facilitate the examination of previously "suppressed" data. The cumulative result is research on African American men that is more methodologically sound and more culturally sensitive.

The nature of research, however, is that "there is always a better 'mousetrap' to be built." The kinds of methodological issues that plague today's generation of researchers on African American men are more sophisticated and complex in nature compared to earlier violations of elementary research principles. Thus, there is a need for:

more attention to be paid to the pretesting of actual survey research questions to determine their cognitive (construct) validity—that is, whether these questions are meaningful to African American men;

longitudinal research to examine the unique developmental issues of African American males;

less reliance on self-report measures as data collection instruments;

a wider array of data collection instruments;

the use of more varied (typically underutilized) sources of data (i.e., ethnographic interviews, key informants, documents, artifacts, direct observation, and participant observation) as important potential sources of data (Yin, 1994);

the use of more complex designs, with emphasis on including comparison or cohort groups to facilitate analysis of independent and intervening variables and the analysis of intragroup differences between important structural variables (i.e., social class, sexual orientation, family structure, and differences in acculturation);

a wider array of research designs that promote mixed-method designs (i.e., use of both qualitative and quantitative approaches)—for example, the case study research method (Yin, 1994); and a wider array of ideographic (vs. nomothetic) research designs (i.e., ethnographic and phenomenological research and focus groups) that have the ability to identify strengths and self-affirming patterns in African American men rather than to merely catalog deficiencies.

APPLICATION OF SPECIFIC METHODOLOGY TO RESEARCH ON AFRICAN AMERICAN MEN

A Case Study Research Approach

The case study research approach is a quintessential form of postpositivistic research methodology. Yin (1994) conceptualized this method of research as encompassing both qualitative and quantitative methods of research. The case study research method has the ability to capture the complexity of the African American male experience without engaging in context stripping. The inability to maintain the holistic meaning of real-life events in research on the lives of Black men is a major conceptual failure of earlier studies.

The case study research method embraces the use of multiple sources of evidence in data collection efforts. These underutilized sources of evidence (data), such as the use of key informants, documents, artifacts, open-ended and ethnographic interviews, focus groups, direct observation, and participant observation, are important potential sources of data. Varied sources of data can be especially helpful in developing vastly underdeveloped theory on African American males, notwithstanding the ability to conduct initial research on "hard to reach" and underresearched subpopulations, such as poor, never-married, noncustodial fathers and adolescent fathers.

The design choices available within this research approach (i.e., single vs. multiple case studies [the study of several individuals, families, or sites] and *embedded* vs. *holistic* case studies [the study of several subunits of analyses, such as a whole family constellation, the father-child dyad, and the parental dyad]) can play a significant part in the ability to capture and understand cultural variation within a group or a family and between individuals or different communities. These design choices facilitate a richer cultural gestalt to be pieced together and can serve to challenge the homogenization and oversimplification of "the Black male experience" in research studies.

A Hermeneutic Phenomenological Approach

The hermeneutic phenomenological approach is a qualitative, descriptive research methodology that attends to examining the *meaning structures* of the *lived world* ("lifeworld") as experienced in everyday situations and relations (van Manen, 1990). As understood from a hermeneutic phenomenological perspective, lived meaning structures are the ways a person experiences life as real and meaningful. Lived meaning structures further describe aspects of a situation as experienced by the person in that situation.

The hermeneutic phenomenological methodology examines lived meaning structures from the perspective of four *existential lifeworld themes*: *spatiality* (lived space—space in which we existentially experience the affairs of day-to-day existence), *temporality* (lived time—the time we are in, past, present, or future), *corporeality* (lived body—the body, including race and gender, through which we are present or embodied in the world), and *relationality* (lived human relationships—where and when we are interpersonally connected). These fundamental existential themes are believed to pervade the lifeworld of all human beings regardless of their historical, cultural, or social situatedness (van Manen, 1990). These themes reflect the dimensions through which all human beings experience the world. The phenomenological interview, however, elicits a description of the existential themes or experience(s) of African American men without reliance on a priori hypotheses or theories, which may be biased, skewed, or based on erroneous or overgeneralized data.

Key to the hermeneutic phenomenological method is the open-ended, unstructured research interview, which allows the researcher to elicit an in-depth description of the experience with a particular African American male being investigated. In contrast to other research methodologies, the hermeneutic phenomenological approach allows the researcher to grasp the emic dimension of the Black male experience. For example, through a rigorous thematic and existential analysis of multiple interviews (narratives) with several African American male subjects, the nature of that experience for that particular Black male (research participant) emerges. Thus, the researcher is able to gather a rich contextualized description of an African American male's experience in the domain of his lifeworlds.

This research approach, however, permits the researcher to discover common themes across the experiences of African American men because this method also illuminates the shared lived meanings for Black men who share specific contexts, situations, or roles. Thus, this research method, as does the case study research method, allows the researcher to capture the within-group variability among African American men.

The hermeneutic phenomenological approach has significant potential in researching the African American male experience because it allows the researcher to uncover what constitutes the structure of lived experiences, specifically for African Americans males. By providing an in-depth examination of the complex dynamics of the African American male experience, this methodology can capture what it is like to be an African American male in the concreteness of his day-to-day experiences within (a) the domain of his social location, (b) his personal and collective history, (c) his bodily presence in the world, and (d) his social and personal relationship network (Rasheed, 1997).

FUTURE GOALS, OBJECTIVES, AND STRATEGIES FOR RESEARCH DEVELOPMENT AND DISSEMINATION

Stakeholder Involvement in Research

A review of the literature suggests the following main strategies for increasing the functional relevance and thus stakeholder (community) involvement in the research process (Bowman, 1993):

1. Explicitly target the needs of the community.
2. Seek assistance from indigenous consultants or an advisory board with residents from the community or both.
3. Use indigenous interviewers in the collection of data.
4. Arrange for exchanges and "trade-offs"—that is, provide technical assistance to community-based organizations at the conclusion of the research project.

Research Development and Dissemination Strategies

It is no coincidence that the vast improvement of research generated in this area is a direct result of an increase in the number of well-trained researchers with a genuine altruistic commitment to research on African American men. Graduate assistantships, research fellowships, and doctoral and postdoctoral trainee and apprenticeships are critical components if this area of research is to flourish. Additionally, training seminars and conferences that specifically target and thus promote research on Black men are important activities that can promote networking and mentoring among researchers and scholars. It is incumbent on colleges, universities, research institutes, professional organizations, and human service agencies to be active (sponsoring) participants in this regard.

These institutions and organizations can also play critical roles in establishing research institutes that can serve a crucial role of nurturing future researchers and research development and dissemination on African American men. These research institutes can serve important "clearinghouse" functions of research development and dissemination and act as general "think tanks" that coordinate systematic research agenda (i.e., sponsor the coordination of periodic annotated-interdisciplinary bibliographies of research). Research centers or institutes can also function as consultants in all aspects of the research process or in assisting communities in identifying problems important to African American men and enabling them to design their own solutions.

Finally, these research centers or institutes can perform important advocacy roles in seeking to develop funding for new and innovative lines of research for scholars. Also, these centers can play pivotal roles in influencing micro and macro systemswide changes by helping to disseminate important research developments to key political groups, organizations, the mass media, and policymakers.

CONCLUSION

Research models on African American men must be action oriented, problem solving, and not only contribute to the study of complex social issues but also facilitate the development of innovative solutions that empower Black men. In designing research programs for African American men, research strategies should promote community organizing, consumer involvement, and leadership development by using the principles of empowerment, advocacy, self-help, mentoring, and social support.

REFERENCES

Achatz, M., & MacAllum, C.A. (1994). *Young unwed fathers pilot project: Report from the field.* Philadelphia, PA: Public/Private Ventures.

Ahmad, B. (1990). *Black perspectives in social work.* Birmingham: Venture Press.

Akbar, N. (1979). African roots of black personality. In W.D. Smith, H. Kathleen, M.H. Burlew, & W.M. Whitney (Eds.), *Reflections on black psychology* (pp. 79-87). Washington, DC: University Press of America.

Akbar, N. (1984). Africentric social sciences for human liberation. *Journal of Black Studies,* 14, 395-414.

Akbar, N. (1991). Paradigms of African American research. In R.L. Jones (Ed.), *Black Psychology* (3rd ed., pp. 709-726). Berkeley, CA: Cobb & Henry.

Aldridge, D.P. (1991). *Focusing: Black male and female relationships.* Chicago: Third World Press.

Alejandro-Wright, M. (1982). An intracultural perspective on research. *Child Care Quarterly, 11*(1), 67-77.

Allen-Meares, P., & Burman, S. (1995). The endangerment of African American men: An appeal for social work action. *Social Work, 40*(2), 268-274.

Archer, D., & Gartner, R. (1983). *Violence and crime in cross national perspective.* New Haven, CT: Yale University Press.

Asante, M.K. (1980). *Afrocentricity: Theory of social change.* Buffalo, NY: Amulefi.

Asante, M.K. (1981). Black male and black female relationships: An Afrocentric context. In L. Gary (Ed.), *Black men* (pp. 75-82). Beverly Hills, CA: Sage.

Asante, M.K. (1988). *Afrocentricity.* Trenton, NJ: African World Press.

Austin, B.W. (1996). *National task force on African American men and boys: Repairing the breach.* Dillon, CO: Alpine Press.

Baldwin, J.A. (1981). Notes on an Afrocentric theory on black personality. *Western Journal of Black Studies, 12,* 172-179.

Baldwin, J.A. (1985). Psychological aspects of European cosmology in American society and European culture. *Western Journal of Black Studies, 9*(4), 216-222.

Baldwin, J. (1993). *Nobody knows my name.* New York: Dial. (Original work published 1963)

Banfield, E.C. (1970). *The unheavenly city: The nature and future of our urban crisis.* Boston, MA: Little, Brown.

Banks, W.M. (1980). *Theory in black psychology.* Paper presented at the 13th annual National Convention of the Association of Black Psychologists, Cherry Hill, NJ.

Bell, Y.R., Bouie, C.L., & Baldwin, J. (1990). Afrocentric cultural consciousness and African American male-female relationships. *Journal of Black Studies, 21,* 162-189.

Berry, J.W. (1969). On cross-cultural comparability. *International Journal of Psychology, 4,* 119-128.

180 Social Work Practice with African American Men

Billingsley, A. (1968). *Black families in white America.* Englewood Cliffs, NJ: Prentice Hall.

Billingsley, A. (1992). *Climbing Jacob's ladder.* New York: Simon & Schuster.

Blackwell, J.E. (1975). *The black community: Diversity and unity.* New York: Harper & Row.

Bordin, E.S. (1979). The generalizibility of the psychoanalytic concepts of the working alliance. *Psychotherapy: Theory and Research, 12,* 252-260.

Boszoremenyi-Nagy, I. (1987). *Foundations of contextual therapy.* New York: Brunner/Mazel.

Bowen, M. (1978). *Family therapy in clinical practice.* New York: Jason Aronson.

Bowman, P.J. (1983). Significant involvement and functional relevance: Challenges to survey research. *Social Work Research and Abstract, 19*(4), 21-26.

Bowman, P.J. (1985). Black fathers and the provider role: Role strain, informal coping resources in life happiness. In A. W. Boykin (Ed.), *Empirical research in black psychology* (pp. 9-19). Washington, DC: National Institute for Mental Health.

Bowman, P.J. (1989). Research perspective on black men: Role strain and adaptation across the adult life cycle. In R.L. Jones (Ed.), *Black adult development and aging* (pp. 117-150). Berkeley, CA: Cobb & Henry.

Bowman, P.J. (1991). Race, class and ethics in research: Belmont principles to functional relevance. In R.L. Jones (Ed.), *Black psychology* (3rd ed., pp. 747-768). Berkeley, CA: Cobb & Henry.

Boyd-Franklin, N. (1989). *Black families in therapy: A multisystems approach.* New York: Guilford.

Bradshaw, W.H. (1978). Training psychiatrists for working with blacks in residency programs. *American Journal of Psychiatry, 135,* 1520-1524.

Braithwaite, R.R. (1981). Interpersonal relations between black males and black females. In L. Gary (Ed.), *Black men* (pp. 83-98). Beverly Hills, CA: Sage.

Brayboy, T. (1971). The black patient in group therapy. *International Journal of Group Psychotherapy, 21,* 259-264.

Brislin, R.W. (1970). Black translation for cross-cultural research. *Journal of Cross-Cultural Psychology, 1,* 185-216.

Bronfenbrenner, U. (1979). *The ecology of human development.* Cambridge, MA: Harvard University Press.

Brueggemann, W.G. (1996). *The practice of macro social work.* Chicago: Nelson-Hall.

Brunner, J. (1986). *Actual minds, possible worlds.* Cambridge, MA: Harvard University Press.

Bulhan, H.A. (1985). *Frantz Fanon and the psychology of oppression.* New York: Plenum.

Cazenave, N. (1979). Middle income black fathers: An analysis of the provider role. *Family Coordinator, 28*(4), 583-593.

Cazenave, N. (1981). Black men in America: The quest of "manhood." In H.P. McAdoo (Ed.), *Black families* (pp. 176-186). Beverly Hills, CA: Sage.

Cazenave, N., & Leon, G. (1978). Men's work and family roles and characteristics. In M. Kimmel (Ed.), *Changing men: New directions in research on men and masculinity* (pp. 244-264). Newbury Park, CA: Sage.

Ceechin, G. (1987). Hypothesizing, circularity and neutrality revisited: An invitation to curiosity. *Family Process, 26*(4), 405-413.

Chicago Institute on Urban Poverty. (1993). No work no welfare: Able-bodied men on the streets of Chicago. In *Travelers and Immigrants Aid.* Chicago: August.

Chinula, D.M. (1997). *Building King's beloved community.* Cleveland, OH: United Church Press.

Clark, K.B. (1965). *Dark ghetto.* New York: Harper & Row.

Cloward, R.A., & Ohlin, L.E. (1990). *Delinquency and opportunity.* New York: Free Press.

Cohen, A.P. (1985). *The symbolic construction of community.* New York: Tavistock/E. Horwood.

Comas-Diaz, L. (1994). An integrative approach. In L. Comas-Diaz & B. Greene (Eds.), *Woman of color* (pp. 287-318). New York: Guilford.

Comer, J.P. (1997). *Waiting for a miracle.* New York: Penguin.

Cose, E. (1993). *The rage of a privileged class.* San Francisco: HarperCollins.

Cose, E. (1995). *A man's world.* New York: HarperCollins.

Crawley, B.H. (1996). Effective programs and services for African American families: An African-centered perspective. In S. Logan (Ed.), *The black family* (pp. 112-130). Boulder, CO: Westview.

Crawley, B.H., & Freeman, E.M. (1993). Themes in the life views of older and younger African American males. *Journal of African American Male Studies, 1*(1), 15-29.

Cromwell, N.A. & Leeper, E.M. (1994). *America's Fathers and Public Policy.* Washington, DC: National Academy Press.

Cross, W.E. (1995). In search of blackness and afrocentricity: The psychology of black identity change. In H.W. Harris, H.C. Blue, & E.E.H. Griffith (Eds.), *Racial and ethnic identity* (pp. 53-72) New York: Routledge.

Danealk, J. (1975). *A definition of fatherhood as expressed by black fathers.* Unpublished doctoral dissertation, University of Pittsburgh, Pittsburgh, PA.

Davis, L. (1984). Essential components of group work with black Americans. *Social Work With Groups, 7,* 97-109.

Davis, L., Galinsky, M.J., & Schopler, J.H. (1995). RAP: A framework for leadership of multiracial groups. *Social Work, 40*(2), 155-165.

Davis, L., Cheng, L.C., & Strube, M.J. (1996). Differential effects of racial composition on male and female groups: Implications for group work practice. *Social Work Research 20*(3), 157-166.

Devore, W. (1992). The African American community in the 1990's: The search for a practice method. In F.G. Rivera & J.L. Erlich (Eds.), *Community organizing in a diverse society* (pp. 67-91). Boston: Allyn & Bacon.

Dickson, L. (1993). The future of marriage and family in black America. *Journal of Black Studies, 23*(4), 472-491.

Dubois, W.E.B. (1961). *The souls of black folk.* New York: Anchor.

Edwards, H.E. (1988). Dynamic psychotherapy when both patient and therapist are black. In A. Coner-Edward & J. Spurlock (Eds.), *Black families in crisis: The middle class* (pp. 239-254). New York: Brunner/Mazel.

Ellison, R. (1989). *Invisible man.* New York: Vintage. (Original work published 1952)

Erickson, E.H. (1980). *Identity and the life cycle.* New York: Norton.

Etzkowitz, H., & Schaflander, G. (1969). *Ghetto crisis.* Boston: Little, Brown.

Evans, B.J., & Whitfield, J.R. (Eds.). (1988). *Black males in the United States: An annotated bibliography from 1967 to 1987.* Washington, DC: American Psychological Association.

Fagan, J., & Stevenson, H. (1995). Men as teachers: A self-help program on parenting for African American men. *Social Work With Groups, 17*(4), 29-42.

Fanon, F. (1967). *Black skin, white masks.* New York: Grover.

Federal Bureau of Investigation. (1986). Crime in the United States, 1985. In *Uniform Crime Report.* Washington, DC: U.S. Government Printing Office.

Fish, V. (1993). Poststructuralism in family therapy: Interrogating the narrative/conversational mode. *Journal of Marital and Family Therapy, 19*(3), 221-232.

Fitzgerald, J., & Rasheed, J.M. (1998). Salvaging an evaluation from the swampy lowland. *Journal of Evaluation and Program Planning, 21*(2), 119-209.

Framo, J.L. (1981). The integration of marital therapy with sessions with family of origin. In A.S. Gurman & D.P. Kniskern (Eds.), *Handbook of family therapy* (pp. 133-158). New York: Brunner/Mazel.

Franklin, A.J. (1992). Therapy with African American men. *Families in Society, 73,* 350-355.

Franklin, C.W., II. (1994). Ain't I a man?: The efficacy of black masculinities of men's studies in the 1990s. In R.G. Majors & J.U. Gordon (Eds.), *The American black males* (pp. 285-299). Chicago: Nelson Hall.

Frazier, E.F. (1932a). *The free negro family.* Nashville, TN: Fisk University Press.

Frazier, E.F. (1932b). *The negro family in Chicago.* Chicago: University of Chicago Press.

Frazier, E.F. (1939). *The negro family in the United States.* Chicago: University of Chicago Press.

Freeman, J., & Combs, G. (1996). *Narrative therapy.* New York: Norton.

Freire, P. (1973). *Education for critical consciousness.* New York: Beacon.

Freire, P. (1983). *Pedagogy of the oppressed.* New York: Continuum.

Furstenberg, F.F., Jr., Sherwood, K.E., & Sullivan, M.L. (1992). *Parents' fair share demonstration caring and paying: What fathers and mothers say about child support.* New York: Manpower Demonstration Research Corporation.

Gadsden, V.L., & Smith, R.R. (1994). African American males and fatherhood: Issues in research and practice. *Journal of Negro Education, 63*(4), 634-648.

Garrett, H. (1961, August 14). One psychologist's view of equality of the races. *U.S. News and World Report, 51,* 72-74.

Garvin, C.D., & Reed, B.G. (1994). Small group theory and social work practice: Promoting diversity and social justice or recreating inequities. In R. Green (Ed.), *Human behavior theory* (pp. 173-201). New York: Aldine.

Garvin, C.D., & Seabury, B.A. (1997). *Interpersonal practice in social work.* Boston: Allyn & Bacon.

Gary, L.E. (1981). *Black men.* Beverly Hills, CA: Sage.

Gee, K.L., Walker, J., & Younger, A.C. (1997). The Raamus Academy: Evaluation of an edu-cultural intervention for young African American males. In R.J. Watts & R.J. Jagers (Eds.), *Manhood development in urban African American communities* (pp.87-102). New York: Haworth.

Germain, C.B. (1985). The place of community work within an ecological approach to social work practice. In S.H. Taylor & R.W. Roberts (Eds.), *Theory and practice of community social work* (pp. 30-55). New York: Columbia University Press.

Germain, C.B., & Gitterman, A. (1996). *The life model of social work practice.* New York: Columbia University Press.

Gibbs, J. (Ed.). (1988). *Young, black and male in America: An endangered species.* Over, MA: Auburn.

Gillette, T. (1960). *Maternal employment and family structure as influenced by social class and role.* Unpublished doctoral dissertation, University of Texas, Austin.

Glasgow, D.G. (1980). *The black underclass.* San Francisco: Jossey-Bass.

Goffman, E. (1989). *Stigma: Notes on the management of spoiled identity.* Englewood Cliffs, NJ: Prentice Hall.

Gooden, W.E. (1989). Development of black men in early adulthood. In R. Jones (Ed.), *Black adult development and aging* (pp. 63-89). Berkeley, CA: Cobb & Henry.

Gould, S.J. (1981). *The mismeasure of man.* New York: Norton.

Graff, G. (1979). *Literature against itself.* Chicago: University of Chicago Press.

Green, R.R., & Ephross, P.H. (1991). *Human behavior theory and social work practice.* New York: Aldine.

Grier, W.H., & Cobbs, P.M. (1968). *Black rage.* New York: Bantam.

Gutierrez, L.M., Parsons, R.J., & Cox, E.O. (1998). *Empowerment in social work practice.* Pacific Grove, CA: Brooks/Cole.

Habermas, J. (1971). *Knowledge and human interest.* Boston: Beacon.

Hardcastle, D.A., Wenocur, S., & Powers, P.R. (1997). *Community practice: Theories and skills for social workers.* New York: Oxford University Press.

Harris, S. (1995). Psychosocial development and black masculinity: Implications for counseling economically disadvantaged African American male adolescents. *Journal of Counseling and Development, 73,* 279-284.

Hartman, A., & Laird, J. (1983). *Family-centered social work practice.* New York: Free Press.

Hartmann, H. (1958). *Ego psychology and the problem of adaptation.* New York: International Universities Press.

Harvey, A.R., & Coleman, A.A. (1997). An Afrocentric program for African American males in the juvenile justice system. *Child Welfare League, 76*(1), 197-209.

Herbert, J.L. (1990). Integrating race and adult psychosocial development. *Journal of Organizational Behavior, 11,* 433-446.

Hernstein, R.J., & Murray, C. (1994). *The bell curve: Intelligence and class structure in American life.* New York: Free Press.

Hill, R. (1972). *The strengths of black families.* New York: Emerson-Hall.

Ho, M.K. (1987). *Family therapy with ethnic minorities.* Newbury Park, CA: Sage.

Hoberman, J. (1997). *Darwin's athletes.* Boston: Houghton Mifflin.

Hopkins, T. (1973). The role of agency in supporting black manhood. *Social Work, 18,* 53-58.

Hopson, D.S., & Hopson, D.P. (1998). *The power of soul.* New York: William Morrow.

Howitt, D., & Owusu-Bempah, J. (1994). *The racism of psychology: Time for change.* New York: Harvester Wheatsheaf.

Hudson-Weem, C. (1993). *Africana womanism: Reclaiming ourselves.* Troy, MI: Bedford.

Hunter, A.C., & Davis, J. (1992). Constructing gender: An exploration of Afro-American men's conceptualization of manhood. *Gender and Society, 6*(2), 464-479.

Hutchinson, E.O. (1994). *The assassination of the black male image.* Los Angeles: Middle Passage Press.

Ivey, A.E. (1995). Psychotherapy as liberation. In J.G. Ponterotto, J.M. Casas, L. A. Suzuki, & C.M. Alexander (Eds.), *Handbook of multicultural counseling* (pp. 53-72). Thousand Oaks, CA: Sage.

Jagers, R.J., & Watts, R.J. (1997). Prospect and challenges for African-American manhood. In R.J. Jagers & R.J. Watts (Eds.), *Manhood development in African American communities* (pp. 147-155). New York: Haworth.

Jansson, B.S. (1994). *Social policy: From theory to policy practice* (2nd ed.). Pacific Grove, CA: Brooks/Cole.

Jensen, A. (1973). *The differences are real.* Psychology Today, 7, 80-86.

Johnson, E.H. (1998). *Brothers on the mend.* New York: Pocket Books.

Jones, A.C. (1989). Psychological functioning in African-American adults: Some elaborations on a model, with clinical implications. In R. Jones (Ed.), *Black adult development and aging* (pp. 297-310). Berkeley, CA: Cobb & Henry.

Jones, B.E., & Gray, B.A. (1983). Black males and psychotherapy: Theoretical issues. *American Journal of Psychotherapy, 37*(1), 77-85.

Kambon, K.K. (1992). *The African personality in America: An African-centered framework.* Tallahassee, FL: Nubia Nations.

Kardiner, A., & Ovesey, L. (1951). *The mark of oppression.* New York: Norton.

Karenga, M. (1996). The nguzo saba (the seven principles): Their meaning and message. In M.K. Asante & A.S. Abarry (Eds.), *African intellectual heritage* (pp. 543-554). Philadelphia: Temple University Press.

Kasarda, J. (1989). Urban industrial transition and the underclass. *Annals of the American Academy of Political Science, 501,* 26-47.

Katz, A., & Bender, E.I. (1976). *The strength in us: Self-help in the modern world.* New York: Franklin Watts.

Kilpatrick, A.C., & Holland, T.P. (1995). *Working with families.* Boston: Allyn & Bacon.

Kimmel, M.S., & Messner, M.A. (1995). *Men's lives.* Boston: Allyn & Bacon.

King, M.L. (1963). *Strength to love.* New York: Harper & Row.

Korin, E.C. (1992). Social inequalities and therapeutic relationships: Applying Friere's ideas to clinical practice. *Journal of Feminist Family Therapy, 5,* 75-98.

Kunjufu, J. (1982). *The conspiracy to destroy black boys.* Chicago: African-American Images.

Kunjufu, J. (1996). *Restoring the village, values and commitment.* Chicago: African American Images.

Laird, J. (1989). Women and stories: Restorying women's self construction. In M. McGoldrick, C.H. Anderson, & F. Walsh (Eds.), *Women in families* (pp. 427-450). New York: Norton.

Laird, J. (Ed.). (1993). *Revisioning social work education: A social constructionist approach.* New York: Haworth.

Lamb, M.E., & Sagi, A. (1983). *Fatherhood and family policy.* Hillsdale, NJ: Lawrence Erlbaum.

Langley, M.R. (1994). The cool pose: An Africentric analysis. In R.G. Majors & J.U. Gordon (Eds.), *The American black male* (pp. 231-244). Chicago: Nelson-Hall.

Laseter, R.L. (1997). The labor force participation of young Black men: A qualitative examination. *Social Service Review,* March.

Lazur, R.F., & Majors, R. (1995). Men of color: Ethnocultural variations of male gender role strain. In R.F. Levant & W.S. Pollack (Eds.), *A new psychology of men* (pp. 337-358). New York: Basic Books.

Leashore, B.R. (1981). Social services and black men. In L. Gary (Ed.), *Black men* (pp. 257-267). Beverly Hills, CA: Sage.

Leashore, B.R. (1997). African American men, child welfare and permanency planning. *Journal of Multicultural Social Work, 5*(1), 39-48.

Lee, C.C. (1990). Black male development: Counseling the "native son." In D. Moore & F. Leafgren (Eds.), *Problem solving strategies for men in conflict* (pp. 125-137). Alexandria, VA: American Association for Counseling and Development.

Lee, J.A.B. (1994). *The empowerment approach.* New York: Columbia University Press.

Lefkowitz, M. (1996). *Not out of Africa.* New York: Basic Books.

Leong, F.T.L. (1992). Guidelines for minimizing premature termination among Asian-American clients in group counseling. *Journal for Specialists in Group Work, 17*(4), 218-228.

Levant, R.F., & Brooks, G.R. (Eds.). (1997) *Men and sex: New psychological perspectives.* New York: John Wiley.

Levine, J.A. (1993). Involving fathers in head start: A framework for public policy and program development. *Families in Society, 74,* 4-20.

Levinson, D.J. (1980). Toward a conception of the adult life cruise. In N.J. Smelser & E.H. Erickson Eds.), *Themes of work and love in adulthood* (pp. 265-290). Cambridge, MA: Harvard University Press.

Levinson, D.J., Darrow, C.N., Klein, E.B., Levinson, M.H., & McKee, B. (1978). *The seasons of a man's life.* New York: Kropf.

Lewis, E. (1992). Regaining promise: Feminist perspectives for social group work practice. In J. Garland (Ed.), *Reaching out: People, places, and power* (pp. 271-284). New York: Haworth.

Liebow, E. (1967). *Tally's corner: A study of negro street corner men.* Boston: Little, Brown.

Lincoln, E., & Guba, E. (1985). *Naturalistic inquiry.* Beverly Hills, CA: Sage.

Long, L.C. (1993). An Afrocentric intervention strategy. In L.L. Goddard (Ed.), *An African-centered model of prevention for African American youth at high risk* (CSAP Technical Report No. 6, pp. 87-92). Rockville, MD: U.S. Department of Health and Human Services.

Louw, L. (1995). Ubuntu: Applying African philosophy to diversity training. In L.B. Griggs & L. Louw (Eds.), *Valuing diversity: New tools of a new reality.* New York: McGraw-Hill.

Madhubuti, H.R. (1990). *Black men: Obsolete, single, dangerous.* Chicago: Third World Press.

Madhubuti, H.R., & Karenga, R. (1996). *Million man march/day of absence.* Chicago: Third World Press.

Majors, R., & Billson, J. (1992). *Cool pose: The dilemmas of black manhood in America.* New York: Touchstone Books.

Majors, R., & Gordon, J.V. (Eds.). (1994). *The American black male: His present status and his future.* Chicago: Nelson-Hall.

Malone, W. (1994). *From holy power to holy profit.* Chicago: African American Images.

Marsiglio, W. (1989). Adolescent males' pregnancy resolution preferences and family formation intentions: Does family background make a difference for Black and Whites? *Journal of Adolescent Research, 4*(2), 214-237.

Martin, E.P., & Martin, J.M. (1995). *Social work and the black experience.* Washington, DC: National Association of Social Workers.

Martin, J.M., & Martin, E.P. (1985). *Helping traditions in the black family and community.* Silver Springs, MD: NASW Press.

Mbiti, J. (1970). *African religions and philosophy.* New York: Doubleday.

McAdoo, H.P. (1978). Factors related to stability in upwardly mobile black families. *Journal of Marriage and the Family, 40*(4), 761-776.

McAdoo, J.L. (1981). Involvement of fathers in the socialization of black children. In H.P. McAdoo (Ed.), *Black families* (pp. 225-238). Beverly Hills, CA: Sage.

McAdoo, J.L. (1988). Changing perspective on the role of the black father. In P. Bronstein & C.P. Cowan (Eds.), *Fatherhood today: Men's changing role in the family* (pp. 79-92). New York: John Wiley

McAdoo, J.L. (1993). The roles of African American fathers: An ecological perspective. *Journal of Contemporary Human Services, 74*(1), 28-35.

McClean, V. (1997). African American men and nonrelational sex. In R.F. Levant & G.R. Brooks (Eds.), *Men and sex: New psychological perspectives* (pp. 205-228). New York: John Wiley.

Miller, D.B. (1994). Influences on paternal involvement of African American adolescent fathers. *Child and Adolescent Social Work Journal, 11,* 363-376.

Minuchin, S. (1974). *Families and family therapy.* Cambridge, MA: Guilford.

Montagu, A. (1941). The biologist looks at crime. *Annals of the American Academy of Political and Social Science, 217,* 46-57.

Moore, T.S. & Laramore, A. (1990). Industrial change and urban joblessness: An assessment of the mismatch hypothesis. *Urban Affairs Quarterly, 25,* 640-58.

Moreno, J.L. (1934). *Who shall survive?* (Publication No. 58) Washington, DC: Nerrow & Mental.

Moynihan, D. (1965). *The negro family: The case for national action.* Washington, DC: U.S. Government Printing Office.

Myers, L.J. (1985). Transpersonal psychology: The role of the Afrocentric paradigm. *Journal of Black Psychology, 12,* 31-42.

Nobles, W.W. (1978). Toward an empirical and theoretical framework for defining black families. *Journal of Marriage and the Family, 40,* 679-687.

Nobles, W.W. (1980). African philosophy: Foundations for black psychology. In R. Jones (Ed.), *Black psychology* (3rd ed., pp. 23-35). New York: Harper & Row.

Nobles, W.W., & Goddard, L.L. (1992). An African centered model for African American youth of high risk. In *An African centered model of prevention for African American youth of high risk* (DHHS Publication No. ADM 92-1925). Washington, DC: Department of Public Health.

Okonji, J.M.A., Ososkie, J.R., & Pulos, S. (1996). Preferred style and ethnicity of counselors by African American males. *Journal of Black Psychology, 22*(3), 329-339.

Oliver, W. (1989). Black males and social problems: Prevention through Afrocentric socialization. *Journal of Black Studies, 20*(1), 15-39.

O'Neil, J., Good, G.E., & Holmes, S. (1995). Fifty years of theory and research on men's gender role conflict: New paradigms for empirical research. In R.F. Levant & W.S. Pollack (Eds.), *A new psychology of men* (pp. 164-206). New York: Basic Books.

Osherson, S. (1986). *Finding our fathers.* New York: Fawcett Columbine.

Pack-Brown, S.P., Whittington-Clark, L.E., & Parker, W.M. (1998). *Images of me.* Boston: Allyn & Bacon.

Parham, T.A., & McDavis, R.J. (1987). Black men, an endangered species: Who's really pulling the trigger? *Journal of Counseling and Development, 66,* 220-228.

Perkins, U.E. (1986). *Harvesting new generations: The positive development of black youth.* Chicago: Third World Press.

Pierce, C.M. (1970). Offense mechanism. In F. Barbour (Ed.), *The black 70's* (pp. 265-282). Boston: Porter Sargent.

Piven, F.F., & Cloward, R.A. (1971). The relief of welfare. *Transaction, 8,* 31-39.

Pleck, J.H. (1981). *The myth of masculinity.* Cambridge: MIT Press.

Pleck, J.H. (1995). The gender role strain paradigm: An update. In R.F. Levant & W.S. Pollack (Eds.), *A new psychology of men* (pp. 11-32). New York: Basic Books.

Polkinghorne, D.E. (1988). *Narrative knowing and the human sciences.* Albany: State University of New York Press.

Proctor, S.D. (1996). The context for communities and youth development: Community or chaos. In J. Austin (Ed.), *Repairing the breach* (pp. 47-50). Chicago: Noble Press.

Rainwater, L. (1966). Be*yond ghetto walls: Black families in a federal slum.* Chicago: Aldine.

Rainwater, L. (1970). Crucible of identity: The lower-class negro family. *Daedalus, 95,* 172-216.

Randolph, S.M., & Banks, D. (1993). Making a way out of no way: The promise of Africentric approaches to HIV prevention. *Journal of Black Psychology, 19*(2), 215-222.

Raphael, R. (1988). *The men from the boys.* Lincoln: University of Nebraska Press.

Rasheed, J.M. (1998a). Obstacles to the paternal role functions of inner-city, low-income, non-custodial African American fathers. *Journal of African American Men, 3*(3) (in press).

Rasheed, J.M. (1998b). The adult life cycle of poor African American fathers. *Journal of Human Behavior and the Social Environment, 1*(2/3), 125-140.

Rasheed, J.M., Fitzgerald, J., & Howard, W.D. (1996). *Final Technical Report on the Research and Evaluation Project* (Project No. 360). Chicago: The Paternal Involvement Demonstration Project.

Rasheed, J.M., & Johnson, W.E. (1995). Non-custodial, African-American fatherhood: A case study research approach. *Journal of Community Practice, 2*(2), 99-116.

Rasheed, M.N. (1997). *The experiences of African American male clinical social work supervisors in cross-racial supervision: A hermeneutic phenomenological analysis.* Unpublished Doctoral Dissertation, Loyola University Chicago.

Reichardt, C., & Cook, T. (1979). Beyond qualitative versus quantitative methods. In T. Cook & C. Reichardt (Eds.), *Qualitative and quantitative research methods in evaluation research* (pp. 10-29). Beverly Hills, CA: Sage.

Richardson, L. (1988). The collective story: Postmodernism and the writing of sociology. *Sociological Focus, 21,* 199-207.

Riessman, F. (1965). The "helper" therapy principle. *Social Work, 10,* 27-32.

Roberts, G.W. (1994). Brother to brother: African American modes of relating among men. *Journal of Black Studies, 24*(4), 390-397.

Robinson, L. (1995). *Psychology for social workers.* London: Routledge.

Rothman, J. (1987). Models of community organization and macro practice perspective: Their mixing and phasing. In F.M. Cox, J.L. Erlich, J. Rothman, and J. E. Trapman (Eds.), *Strategies of community intervention* (pp.26-63). Itasca, IL: F. E. Peacock.

Rothman, J., & Sager, J.S. (1998). *Case management.* Boston: Allyn & Bacon.

Saleebey, D. (Ed.) (1997). *The strengths perspective in social work practice* (2nd ed.). White Plains, NY: Longman.

Satir, M.P. (1986). A partial portrait of a family therapist in process. In H.C. Kishman & B.L. Rosman (Eds.), *Evolving models for family change: A volume in honor of Salvador Minuchin.* New York: Guilford Press.

Scanzoni, J.H. (1971). *The black family in modern society.* Boston: Allyn & Bacon.

Schiele, J. (1996). Afrocentricity: An emerging paradigm in social work practice. *Journal of Social Work, 41*(3), 284-294.

Schiele, J.H. (1994). Afrocentricity as an alternative world view for equality. *Journal of Progressive Human Services, 5*(1), 5-25.

Schön, D. (1983). *The reflective practitioner.* New York: Basic Books.

Sechrest, L., & Sidanl, S. (1995). Quantitative and qualitative methods: Is there an alternative? *Evaluation and Program Planning, 18,* 77-87.

Shadish, W.R. (1995). Philosophy of science and quantitative-qualitative debates: Thirteen common errors. *Evaluation and Program Planning, 18,* 63-75.

Solomon, B.B. (1976). *Black empowerment.* New York: Columbia University Press.

Speck, R.V., & Attneave, C.A. (1973) *Family networks: Rehabilitation and healing.* New York: Pantheon.

Stack, C.B. (1974). *All our kin: Strategies for survival in a black community.* New York: Harper & Row.

Stanfield, J.H., II. (1993). Epistemological considerations. In J.H. Stanfield II & D.M. Rutledge (Eds.), *Race and ethnicity in research methods* (pp. 16-38). Newbury Park, CA: Sage.

Staples, R. (1971). Toward a sociology of the black family: A theoretical and method-ological assessment. *Journal of Marriage and the Family, 33,* 119-138.

Staples, R. (1995). Stereotypes of black male sexuality: The facts behind the myths. In M.S. Kimmel & M.A. Messner (Eds.), *Men's lives* (pp. 375-380). Boston: Allyn & Bacon.

Stevens, P.E. (1989). A critical social reconceptualization of environment in nursing: Implications for methodology. *Advances in Nursing Science, 11*(4), 56-68.

Stier, H., & Tienda, M. (1993). Are men marginal to the family? Insights from Chicago's inner city. In J. Hood (Ed.), *Men, work, and family* (pp. 23-24). Newbury Park, CA: Sage.

Sudarkasa, N. (1981). Interpreting the African heritage in Afro-American family orga-nization. In H.P. McAdoo (Ed.), *Black families* (pp. 37-53). Beverly Hills, CA: Sage.

Sutton, A. (1996). African American men in group therapy. In M.P. Andronico (Ed.), *Men in groups: Insights, interventions and psychoeducational work* (pp. 131-149). Washington, DC: American Psychological Association.

Swigonski, M.E. (1996). Challenging privilege through Africentric social work prac-tice. *Social Work, 41,* 153-161.

Taylor, J. (1992). Relationship between internalized racism and marital satisfaction. In A.K.H. Burlew, S.C. Banks, H.P. McAdoo, & D.A. Azibo (Eds.), *African American psychology* (pp. 127-134). Newbury Park, CA: Sage.

Taylor, J.B. (1997). Niches practice: Extending the ecological perspective. In D. Saleeby (Ed.), *The strengths perspectives in social work practice* (pp. 217-227). New York: Longman.

Taylor, R.J., Chatters, L.M., Tucker, M.B., & Lewis, E. (1990). Developments in research on black families: A decade review. *Journal of Marriage and the Family, 52,* 993-1014.

Taylor, R.L. (1995). The plight of Black men: Black males and social policy. In P.H. Collins & M.L. Anderson (Eds.), *Race, class, gender: An anthology.* Belmont: Wadsworth.

Taylor, R.L. (1987). Black youth in crisis. *Humboldt Journal of Social Relations, 14,* 106-133.

Taylor, R.L., & Wilkinson, D.Y. (1977). *The black male in America.* Chicago: Nelson-Hall.

Testa, M. (1989). Employment and marriage among inner-city fathers. *The Annuals, 501,* 79-91.

Thompson, E.H., Jr., & Pleck, J.H. (1995). Masculinity ideologies: A review of research instrumentation on men and masculinities. In R.F. Levant & W.S. Pollack (Eds.), *A new psychology of men* (pp. 129-163). New York: Basic Books.

Tidwell, B.J. (1990). Research and practice issues with black families. In S.M. Logan, E.M. Freeman, & R.G. McRoy (Eds.), *Social work practice with black families* (pp. 259-272). New York: Longman.

Triandis, M.C. (1972). *The analysis of subjective culture.* New York: John Wiley.

Valliant, G. (1977). *Adaptation to life.* Boston: Little, Brown.

van Manen, M. (1990). *Researching lived experience: Human science for an action sensitive pedagogy.* Albany: State University of New York Press.

Warfield-Coppock, N. (1995). Toward a theory of Afrocentric organizations. *Journal of Black Psychology, 21*(1), 30-48.

Washington, C.S. (1987). Counseling black men. In M. Scher, M. Stevens, G. Good, & G.A. Eichenfield (Eds.), *Handbook of counseling and psychotherapy with men* (pp. 192-202). Newbury Park, CA: Sage.

Watts, R.J. (1993). Community action through manhood development: A look at concepts and concerns from the front line. *American Journal of Community Psychology, 21*(3), 333-359.

Watts, R.J., & Abdul-Adil, J.K. (1997). Promoting critical consciousness in young African-American men. In R.J. Watts & R.J. Jagers (Eds.), *Manhood development in urban African-American communities* (pp. 63-86). New York: Harper.

White, M., & Epston, D. (1990). *Narrative means to therapeutic ends.* New York: Norton.

Wilkinson, D., & Taylor, R. (1977). *The black male in America.* Chicago: Nelson-Hall.

Williams, O.J. (1994). Groupwork with African American men who batter: Toward more ethnically sensitive practice. *Journal of Comparative Family Studies, 25,* 91-103.

Williams, R.L. (1980). The death of white research in the black community. In R.L. Jones (Ed.), *Black psychology* (2nd ed., pp. 403-417). New York: Harper & Row.

Willie, C.V. (1970). *The family life of black people.* Columbus, OH: Merrill.

Wilson, A. (1990). *Black on black violence: The psychological dynamics of black self-annihilation in the service of white domination.* New York: Afrikan World Infosystems.

Wilson, W.J. (1987). *The truly disadvantaged: The inner city, the underclass and public policy.* Chicago: University of Chicago Press.

Wimberly, E. (1997a). The men's movement and pastoral care of African American men. In C.C. Neuger & J. N. Poling (Eds.), *The care of men* (pp. 104-121). Nashville, TN: Abindon.

Wimberly, E. (1997b). *Counseling African American marriages and families.* Louisville, KY: Westminster John Knox Press.

Witkin, S.L. (1995). Family social work: A critical constructionist perspective. *Journal of Family Social Work, 1,* 33-45.

Wright, R. (1940). *Native son.* New York: Harper & Row.

Yin, R.K. (1994). *Case study research.* Thousand Oaks, CA: Sage.

SUBJECT INDEX

Headnote: Author names appearing in this index are limited to those for whom there is substantial text discussion, and those whose materials are directly quoted. Endnote references are denoted with n's included in the page references.

ABOUT THE AUTHORS

Janice Matthews Rasheed is a faculty member at Loyola University Chicago, School of Social Work. She received a masters degree in social work from the University of Michigan (Ann Arbor) and a doctorate degree in social welfare from Columbia University. She was coprincipal investigator for a multiyear grant funded by the John D. and Catherine T. MacArthur Foundation for the study of poor, noncustodial African American fathers. She has published articles in the *Journal of Community Practice, Journal of Human Behavior and the Social Environment, Journal of African American Men,* and *Journal of Evaluation and Program Planning.* She teaches research in the masters and doctoral programs and clinical practice courses (e.g., couple therapy, family theory and therapy, and cross-cultural practice) in the masters program and conducts workshops in these areas. She is a licensed clinical social worker in the state of Illinois and has maintained a part-time private practice since 1978 that specializes in practice with people of color and with couples and families.

Mikal N. Rasheed is a faculty member at the George Williams College at Aurora University. He received a masters degree from the University of Chicago, School of Social Service Administration, and a doctorate degree in social work from Loyola University Chicago. He has conducted research on the experiences of African American men in cross-racial clinical social work supervision and is currently publishing articles from this research. He teaches clinical practice courses (e.g., family theory and family therapy, couple therapy, cross-cultural practice, and clinical practice with men) and courses in generalist social work practice, social work supervision, and child welfare practice in the undergraduate and graduate programs. Prior to joining the faculty at Aurora University, he was director of the Undergraduate Social Work Program at Texas Southern University in Houston. There, he developed and directed the *Texas Southern University's Black Male Initiative Program,* which developed Black male leadership and promoted academic retention and academic success among the African American male student population. As a featured columnist in a national popular magazine for Black men, he wrote articles on Black male sexuality. He provides consultation and conducts training in the areas of male development and male issues and on issues concerning Black men. He has worked with various churches both in the Houston and Chicago areas in developing programs for men. He has more than 20 years of experience in the family service field as both a social work practitioner and an administrator. He is a licensed clinical social worker in the state of Illinois and currently maintains a part-time private practice in individual, family, and couple therapy and specializes in men's issues.